THE MEANING OF REMINISCENCE AND LIFE REVIEW

Edited by

Jon Hendricks

Oregon State University

Perspectives on Aging and Human Development Series
Jon Hendricks: Series Editor

BAYWOOD PUBLISHING COMPANY, INC.
Amityville, New York

Library of Congress Catalog Number: 94-16680
ISBN: 0-89503-170-1

Library of Congress Cataloging-in-Publication Data

The Meaning of reminiscence and life review / edited by Jon Hendricks.
    p.   cm. - - (Perspectives on aging and human development series)
    Includes bibliographical references.
    ISBN 0-89503-170-1
    1. Social work with the aged. 2. Reminiscing in old age.
3. Gerontology- -Biographical methods.   I. Hendricks, Jon, 1943- .
II. Series.
HV1451.M36 1995
362.6- -dc20
                                      94-16680
                                         CIP

Table of Contents

Introduction
LOOKING BACK ON MY SELF:
THE MEANING OF THE PAST

Jon Hendricks

THE CONTOURS OF MEMORY

The contours of our memories are much like the features of a distant landscape: we cannot be sure if what we think we see is what is really there. Nonetheless, memories, however ephemeral they may be, are essential to our sense of self. Imagine the amnesiac, bereft of memory, without a past and therefore without essential anchorages the rest of us rely on to create the continuities that provide meaning in our lives. Memory, real or imagined, functions as a valuable mechanism for maintaining a sense of integration, reconciling past identities and self-concepts with present situations. Inevitably, looking back is a perspective affected by the vantage point of current concerns and priorities. That is to say, the way we write the scripts of our lives reflects the roles we are in at the time the writing or the rewriting occurs. In other words, what we see, what we think we see, is relativity personified. It is a misconception to think of memory as something akin to an exact photographic reproduction of bygones. Like time in general, memory is a tricky business. These time journeys, like most journeys, cannot be charted to bypass things we would rather not encounter. Whatever is in one's past is undoubtedly a mixture of the enjoyable, the not so enjoyable, the pleasant and the painful. Still, it is within our power to accentuate the positive and rewrite the rest.

As we look back on our selves, it is likely that part of what we do when we contemplate our pasts is to reconfigure those things we might wish had never happened; giving them a different slant depending on where we are now. Memory's role in shaping one's self concept and sense of interconnectedness is more complex that most of us recognize. As we look back on our lives, or ahead to the future, there seems to be a sense of direction. As we try to integrate our experiences, our situation and our aspirations we engage in a form of first order temporizing.

In the years since Butler [1] began to focus attention on the positive consequences of life review, a great deal has been written about how reviewing the past, reminiscing about unresolved issues and events of earlier years can promote a sense of well-being. Following Butler, some have asserted that life review is actually a developmental process in itself and therefore universal [2]. In her chapter, Merriam reviews much of the available research and calls that proposition into question. Yet, as she points out, the notion that life reviews are universal and salutatory is ingrained in the field. So ingrained in fact that in 1988 a special issue of *Journal of Gerontological Social Work* was devoted to a discussion of the therapeutic role and ramifications of life review and reminiscing.

As Butler has explained it, life reviews can take many forms: from story telling, to reminiscing, to nostalgia and regret [3]. It may help to have a listener but having one may not be a prerequisite to being able to conduct a review. In the actual process of life reviewing, many emotions roil to the surface. Needless to say, these can be troublesome or tumultuous. Butler readily notes that not all outcomes are positive, there can be a sense of dismay and suicidal thoughts that may occur. Yet, as will be seen below, Haight reports that only about seven percent of the nearly one hundred reports she reviewed describe negative outcomes; the rest are either positive or nonevaluative. When life reviews are positive, a sense of serenity and pride can result. Butler maintains that positive results help reminiscers prepare for their own demise by helping them "put their houses in order."

GLANCING IN THE MIRROR

As the literature makes clear, the process of reminiscing is prompted when subjective perceptions of either external occurrences or inner turmoil prompt an introspective examination of the contents of our memories. Butler has contended that the whole process has profoundly useful therapeutic potential. Working as a team, Butler and Lewis [4,5] have used reminiscence as a therapeutic group counseling technique, even though they have felt compelled to offer caveats about its usefulness after people passed beyond the so-called young-old years. Merriam wonders whether or not there may be particular skills involved, skills not found among typical older persons.

Elsewhere, Haight has summarized the literature that has reported positive outcomes from the experience of life review counseling [2]. She noted there that not all research has supported the presumption of efficacious outcomes. Not yet ready to throw the baby out with the bathwater, she suggests here that the resulting ambiguity mandates a thorough review and further analysis before any conclusions can be formulated. Part of her concern derives from her belief that life reviews and reminiscing are not identical modalities. For one thing, life reviews are thought to be more complex than the process of skimming through old memories. Further, the life review is valuative, leading to a reframing of certain occurrences past or present [2]. Haight provides an exhaustive review of the available literature over a thirty year period and examines its contradictions and applicability for various forms of therapy.

Merriam's chapter picks up where an earlier piece by Hughston and Merriam [6] left off. In the decade or more that has passed since the original publication, Merriam has reexamined her position. For one thing, she is more insistent on keeping life review distinct from other forms of therapy that also incorporate emotional recall. Reporting empirical data from a sample which ranged in age from their 60s to over 100, Merriam reports that little more than half of her three age groups reported engaging in life reviews. In light of the advancing age of some of her respondents, the nearness of death, at least as indicated by chronology, is not predictive of the need to reminisce. It is somewhat paradoxical how the shades of disengagement theory show-up in many aspects of gerontology.

Whether or not one agrees with the type of distinction Haight calls for, the point remains that reminiscing and life reviews find many distinct applications. Section II brings together five different applications that reflect differing styles and types. Martin looks specifically at biographies as a way to discover life themes. He utilizes a somewhat distinctive methodology not always associated with life reviews. He asked respondents to perform a card sort and conducted interviews to identify what people regard as life themes or patterns. His assertion that there are "life markers" that relate to individual life themes sheds an interesting light on how "life reviews" are created. Fry also broadens the focus in her analysis of the frequency of self-reported reminiscence, how it relates to personality traits, psychological well-being and sense of purpose among a sample of seventy respondents between the ages of sixty-seven and eighty-two. She goes on to outline the most beneficial use of reminiscence as a therapeutic tool and what types of personality are most likely to attain maximum benefit.

DeGenova's chapter also takes a unique approach. She asked 122 retired persons what they would do differently if they could live their lives over again. Among her other findings are some interesting gender differences; with males focusing more on instrumental activities and females more concerned with developing their intellect and their minds. The implications these differences have for the content of self-reported life reviews provide an important alloy in therapeutic applications. Not too surprisingly, depressed and non-depressed individuals also reveal distinctive affective dimensions to what they remembered. Yang and Rehm point out that these differences are congruent with what is termed a "mood congruence" hypothesis. In other words, present status and context color the way the past is perceived. Lamme and Baars take up the cudgel next, but make their argument in terms of paying greater heed to the role social factors play in the analysis of reminiscence and the importance of incorporating environmental factors. They call for the melding of sociological perspectives on the life course with psychological attention to developmental processes, especially as they focus on the meaning of life review. Reading through the five chapters is enough to convince all but the most skeptical that there really is something to reminiscence if only because the research findings identify markedly different patterns of meaning.

Whatever the research suggests, reminiscence and life reviews will undoubtedly be used by mental health professionals as they attempt to help their elderly patients deal with their sources of stress. As a well-known sociologist once said, sometimes it is more important to be fruitful than to be right. In the six selections reprinted in Section III, a variety of intervention applications is apparent. There can be little doubt about how the authors perceive the potential for beneficial application. Let the reader beware: each of these contexts is unique. But then is that not the plaint frequently heard when survey research data is challenged by those who prefer a richer, context specific focus?

REFERENCES

1. R. N. Butler, The Life-review: An Interpretation of Reminiscence in the Aged, *Psychiatry, 26,* pp. 65-76, 1963.
2. B. K. Haight, Reminiscence and Life Review, in *Encyclopedia of Adult Development,* R. Kastenbaum (ed.), Oryx Press, Phoenix, 1993
3. R. N. Butler, Life Review, in *The Encyclopedia of Aging,* G.L. Maddox (ed.) Springer, New York, 1987.
4. R. N. Butler and M.I. Lewis, *Aging and Mental Health* (2nd Edition), Mosby, St. Louis, 1974.
5. M.I. Lewis and R.N. Butler, Life Review Therapy: Putting Memories to Work in Individual and Group Psychotherapy, *Geriatrics, 29,* pp. 161-173, 1974.
6. G.A. Hughston and S. B. Merriam, Reminiscence: A Non-formal Technique for Improving Cognitive Functioning in the Aged, *International Journal of Aging and Human Development, 15,* pp. 139-149, 1982.

Section I

Life Review as Conceptual Integration

Chapter 1

BUTLER'S LIFE REVIEW:
HOW UNIVERSAL IS IT?

Sharan B. Merriam

It has been almost thirty years since Butler published his first article on the life review [1]. Since then the idea that nearly all people, especially older persons, review their lives in the face of death has become firmly entrenched in both the literature and the practice of gerontology. Numerous articles (including subsequent ones by Butler himself) present expanded discussions of the nature of the life review, its various reforms, its therapeutic value, and so on. The literature also consists of research reports wherein life review is a structured intervention that seeks to bring about changes on various dependent measures such as life satisfaction, ego integrity, and self-concept. That this concept/theory has achieved a certain status in the field is further underscored by an entire issue of *Journal of Gerontological Social Work* being devoted to the life review (1988).

A sense of ready acceptance of the occurrence and value of the life review pervades most of this literature. Near universality is assumed; lack of significant findings as to its value in some studies has not seemed to dampen practitioners' enthusiasm for its use as a therapeutic intervention; potentially negative outcomes while acknowledged, are rarely dealt with in any substantive way; finally, there is a blurring of life review with other forms of recall such as simple reminiscence and storytelling. The purposes of this chapter are: 1) to examine the commonly-held assumptions underlying the life review and what previous studies have found with regard to these assumptions; and 2) to present data from a recent study of centenarians that further calls into question some aspects of the life review.

7

BUTLER'S LIFE REVIEW

Concepts or theories that capture the imagination often go through a number of interpretations and iterations such that one is no longer sure what the major tenants of the original theory are. Going back to original sources for a clear understanding of what was actually proposed makes it easier to assess the permutations and applications over the years. Five articles by Butler [1-3] including two coauthored with Lewis [4, 5], are the sources of this review of Butler's theory. Addressed by Butler, and Butler and Lewis, are descriptions of the life review, what precipitates it, modes of doing it, and the goals or consequences of the review.

Butler's often-quoted description comes from his original article on the life review. He writes:

> I conceive of the life review as a naturally occurring, universal mental process characterized by the progressive return to consciousness of past experiences, and, particularly, the resurgence of unresolved conflicts; simultaneously, and normally, these revived experiences and conflicts can be surveyed and reintegrated [1, p. 66].

The life review is a "reorganization of past experiences" wherein the past as it "marches in review, is surveyed, observed, and reflected upon by the ego" [1, p. 68]. The life review is not a particularly neat and orderly process. It may consist of "stray and seemingly insignificant thoughts about oneself and one's life history," dreams and highly visual thoughts, and/or "mirror-gazing" [1, p. 68]. It may take place silently [1, p. 67] and some may not even be aware that they are involved in the process [4]. Reminiscing is part of the life review, but "not synonymous" with it [1, p. 67]. In other places Butler notes that the life review "includes the taking of an extensive autobiography" [5, p. 326], and uses life review interchangeably with oral history [3].

With regard to what precipitates the life review, Butler is usually quoted as saying that it is "prompted by the realization of approaching dissolution and death," that it is a response to the "biological and psychological fact of death" [1, p. 66]. It is more likely to be engaged in by elderly individuals since they are, by the mere fact of their age, nearer to death than a young person. Approaching death is a stronger factor than age, however, as Butler points out: "it occurs not only in the elderly but also in younger persons who expect death—for example, the fatally ill or the condemned . . . or those preoccupied by death" [1, p. 67]. Butler does say that the life review may be a response to "crises of various types," [1, p. 67] or "current problems and crises" [1, p. 73]; however, much more attention is given to why approaching death triggers the life review.

While he acknowledges that the life review can be precipitated by a crises other than impending death, and that it can occur in younger persons, Butler clearly focuses on its occurrence in old age. "Only in old age," he writes, "can one experience a personal sense of the entire life cycle. This comes to its fullness with the awareness of death" and "old age inaugurated the process of the life review, promoted by the realization of approaching dissolution and death" [2, p. 534]. It is more likely to occur in the aged, he feels, because of an older person's actual nearness to death, because an older person is retired and thus has more time for self-reflection, and because "the customary defensive operation provided by work has been removed" [1, p. 67]. While it may occur earlier, "it takes on a striking intensity in early old age" [4, p. 165]. Lewis and Butler also speculate that "the most introspective part of the life review seems to occur in the 60s and then begins to abate in the 70s and 80s" [4, p. 169].

Although Butler characterizes the life review as an "inner experience or mental process" that often takes place "silently" [1, pp. 65, 67], he also writes that it can "be conducted as part of a group activity. Groups of all kinds—nursing home residents, senior center participants, social groups, therapy groups—can use the life review to help older persons reconstruct and reevaluate their lives" [5, p. 326]. Also suggested is the use of family albums, scrapbooks, genealogies, pilgrimages, and so on to "evoke crucial memories" [5, p. 326].

In a number of places Butler spells out the potential outcomes—good and bad—of the life review. Hopefully, the life review results in "candor, serenity, and wisdom" [1, p. 65] and/or "expiation of guilt, the resolution of intrapsychic conflicts, the reconciliation of family relationships" [5, p. 326]. On the other hand, Butler notes, the process can contribute "to the occurrence of certain late-life disorders, particularly depression" [1, p. 65]. In addition to depression, the life review can result in "states of panic, intense guilt, and constant obsessional rumination; instead of increasing self-awareness and flexibility, one may find increasing rigidity" [1, p. 69]. He suggests that an extreme reaction might be a state of terror resulting in suicide [1].

Because of the data to be presented in the second half of this chapter, of particular interest is Butler's position on the universality of the life review. In all five sources reviewed here, Butler describes the life review as a "universal" process. In his earliest and most comprehensive discussion of the life review, Butler states flatly, "I consider it to be a universal and normative process" [1, p. 68]. In a later writing he notes that "it marks the lives of all older persons in some manner" [4, p. 165]. In only one place—in a very brief discussion of listening as a form of therapy—does Butler imply that the life review might be less than universal. He writes that listening to older persons reminisce is important because reminiscence is part of the life review "that occurs in nearly all people" [5, p. 193]. It might be noted that while he feels it is *nearly* if not wholly a universal process, some persons are "fully aware of the process," others are "only dimly conscious of something compelling them to muse about the past," and some are "totally unaware" [4, p. 166].

In summary, the life review as proposed by Butler is a process engaged in primarily by older persons who become aware that the end of their life is near. It is an attempt to integrate past life experiences such that one feels his or her life has meaning, that in turn can "prepare one for death, mitigating one's fears" [1, p. 68]. His delineation of possible outcomes of the life review and his suggestion that this can be done as a group exercise has led to numerous research studies designed to test the effects of life review interventions. Empirical research on the life review will be reviewed in the next section.

RESEARCH STUDIES ON THE LIFE REVIEW

Several assumptions derived from Butler's writings seem to underlie the research on the life review. First, it is assumed that the life review is indeed a universal process precipitated by an awareness of death; therefore, all older adults can be potential participants in research on the phenomenon. It is also assumed that it need not be a private undertaking, that it can be done in the presence of a single listener or in a group. In fact, "even nonprofessionals can function as therapists by becoming trained listeners as older persons recount their lives" [2, p. 534]. It is also assumed that the life review is a good thing to do having positive outcomes. Finally, while not an assumption, there is some confusion in the research as to terminology. Perhaps because Butler speaks of reminiscence, autobiography, memory, oral history, and the "transmission of knowledge and values to those who follow" [5, p. 326] in discussions of the life review, it is not clear in the design of some studies whether life review is actually what is being investigated. Selected studies of the life review will be discussed to underscore these observations.

As noted above, the universality of the life review is generally assumed; in only a couple of studies has this assumption even been addressed and then only cursorily. Romaniuk and Romaniuk [6] as part of a larger study of reminiscence functions and triggers asked their ninety-one respondents (average age, 78.5 years) whether they had engaged in the life review process. Eighty-one percent reported having reviewed, or were currently reviewing their lives. Lieberman and Tobin found only 49 percent of their participants (85 community-dwelling older people who voluntarily entered homes for the aged) had or were currently reviewing their lives [7]. Finally, in a recent study by Taft and Nehrke of dimensions of reminiscence and their relationship to ego integrity, they found that 67 percent of their sample reported engaging in the life review form of reminiscence [8]. Their sample consisted of thirty skilled-care nursing home residents having an average age of 84.13 years. Thornton and Brotchie, in a review of empirical research on reminiscence and life review, conclude that "the evidence for the universal occurrence of the life review in old age is at best equivocal" [9, p. 96].

Marshall makes the interesting observation that the life review may be specific to our society which focuses on individualism, and which has certain views of aging not found in other cultures; there may even be cohort differences "differentiating people living in our century from all previous cohorts" [10, p. 121]. He thus maintains that the life review cannot claim to be "universal." Moody [11] and Tarman [12] suggest that life review can be interpreted in ways that support Marshall's historical and cultural-bound perspective. That is, life review may function to counter our society's negative perception of elderly individuals. Moody notes, for example, that life review can be seen as a proactive/political endeavor that helps "marginalized" elderly persons to acquire a voice that can lead to change. Tarman argues that life review can be employed to "boost[s] the individual's status in a social interaction" [12, p. 187].

It is implicitly assumed in most studies that the life review is precipitated by an awareness of the finitude of one's life and approaching death. This may explain why no studies were found that used samples who were middle-aged or younger; the older one is, the closer to death one is presumed to be, therefore the more likely to have conducted a life review. The findings of one study support this assumption. Taft and Nehrke found a relationship between the life review form of reminiscence, a measure of ego integrity, and age [8]. This was not unexpected, they write, "since the likelihood of achieving ego integrity increases as one has more time to resolve issues, distance one's self from the impact of events, and approach the reality of death" [8, pp. 193-194]. By contrast, Lieberman and Tobin found no evidence "to suggest that those approaching death were more likely to be engaged in a life review process" [7, p. 290]. In fact, they found that "those closest to death showed significantly less reminiscence activity and significantly less introspection when compared with matched controls."

Marshall reviews numerous research studies concerning the relationship between awareness and nearness of death and the life review [10]. He concludes that Butler's claim can be generally supported. However, there is little to support the notion that the process of the life review is age-dependent. Rather, his own studies and other well-known studies [13, 14] suggest that "the process is transitory; that is, in response to awareness of finitude, reminiscence is heightened" [10, p. 116] and that "willingness to introspect on the past is a transitional phase in relation to anticipated life expectancy" [10, p. 117]. Tarman who also tried to understand contradictory findings across numerous studies, comes to much the same conclusion as Marshall about the ebb and flow of this process [12]. She writes that "it is a process which occurs more intensely for some" and that "once these individuals have made meaningful sense of their life in such a way that death and further interaction can be confronted with ease, reminiscence may be expected to diminish to levels concurrent with the integrated personality" [12, pp. 187-188]. It is important to note that all of the studies reviewed by these authors are with older adults. Since there are no studies with younger adults it cannot be determined if younger adults engage in life reviews, and if they do, if such reviews are precipitated by an awareness of death. Two writers have made a connection between life review and near-death experiences [15, 16] and others have suggested the use of life review with people with AIDS [17] and the terminally-ill [18].

That the life review is assumed to be therapeutic underlies much of the empirical research. Typically in these studies elderly persons, individually with interviewers, or in groups, are asked to review their lives. The amount of structure imposed by the researcher varies as does the length of treatment. The dependent variables include, for example, measures of self-concept [19], ego integrity [8], life satisfaction [20], self-actualization [21], adaptation [22], morale [23], death anxiety [24], and loneliness [25]. Taken as a whole, studies of the effect of the life review on dependent measures are inconclusive; some studies show significant results, some find no significance, and others have mixed results. Nevertheless, life review continues to be viewed optimistically, even by those who find no significant results. Malde, for example, writes that "despite a lack of significant results on the dependent measures, informal evaluations and a follow-up study indicated that the course had resulted in some positive changes" [19, p. 290]. This optimistic view is shored up by numerous personal testimonials as to its value, articles that promote its use in various settings, and articles that suggest particular formats, tools, strategies, and variations in the use of the life review. Only rarely are the potential negative outcomes acknowledged. Shute, in a brief article, presents the case report of an eighty-five-year-old woman who became depressed as a result of engaging in a life review [26]. Malde, in an informal follow-up of those who had participated in a study of the effects of conducting a life review, noted that "there were a few responses indicating negative changes" and that "one of the participants indicated significant negative change" [19, p. 293]. Both Shute and Malde advocate caution in using the life review.

It should be noted that there is a fair amount of confusion in the literature with regard to terminology. It is not always clear whether what is being studied is the life review as proposed by Butler, or simple reminiscence, or reminiscence that has more of a storytelling or historically-informative orientation. Further, when related terms or concepts are used such as reminiscence group therapy [27], retrospective lifespan analysis [28], personal narrative [29], daydreaming [30], life history [31], oral history [32], it is not always readily evident whether they are or are not synonymous with life review.

In summary, research that focuses on the life review as proposed by Butler (rather than other forms of reminiscence), is supportive of some aspects of his theory, and inconclusive regarding other aspects. While it is generally assumed to be a universal process, a few instances were found where not all older persons had engaged in it. Also generally assumed *and* generally supported is the notion that awareness of death precipitates the life review. However, the timing of such an awareness, and hence life review, was found to vary and not be linearly related to age. This would seem to call into question Butler's statement about the review being most intense in early old age (the 60s) and "then begins to abate in the 70s and 80s" [4, p. 169]. Finally, with regard to the benefits of conducting a life review, findings from dozens of studies are inconclusive. Of course, as with any research, the methodological limitations may explain some of the inconsistencies. All of the research on life review, for example, is cross-sectional; thus the wax and wane of the process of life review over time would not be captured. Study samples are generally small and selective, and finally, measures of dependent variables are limited by the validity and reliability of the instruments used. Presented next are findings from a study of centenarians designed to test some of the assumptions of Butler's theory.

HOW UNIVERSAL IS THE LIFE REVIEW?

The Georgia Centenarian Study was undertaken for the purpose of determining how biological, psychological, and social factors combine to contribute to successful adaptation in the oldest-old [33]. This study presented an opportunity to collect data on the life review and it is these findings that are presented here.

Sample and Instrumentation

Begun in 1988 with a grant from the National Institute of Mental Health, the study sample for the data reported herein consists of 105 centenarians, ninety-four eighty-year-olds, and ninety sixty-year-olds. Eighty-year-olds and sixty-year olds were included because it was thought that different patterns of adaptation might emerge for different cohorts. The centenarians in the sample were identified and recruited by referrals from state and local agencies, community organizations, and the media. Eighty and sixty-year-olds were recruited from probability samples representing the gender and racial characteristics of Georgians for those cohorts.

Because this study examined successful adaptation, each participant had to be community-dwelling and cognitively intact. A community-dwelling person was defined as anyone who was self-sufficient or partially self-sufficient and who was living in the community and not in custodial institutions. Persons who lived in their own or relatives' homes, group or old-age homes, and life care communities were defined as community-dwelling. Cognitively intact was defined as not being demented or disoriented; the Mini-Mental Status Examination was used as a screening tool at the time of recruitment.

A questionnaire on reminiscence and life review was included as part of the test battery given to all participants. Centenarians were tested on a one-to-one basis in their homes; individual items were read to the participants and responses were recorded by the tester. The eighty- and sixty-year-old cohorts were, for the most part, tested in centralized locations around the state; where eyesight or illiteracy was a problem respondents were tested like the centenarians.

The life review component of the reminiscence/life review instrument consists of several questions designed to test several aspects of Butler's theory. Of particular interest was whether the life review is a universal process, whether the occurrence is related to age, whether it is precipitated by an awareness of death, and whether there is a relationship between having reviewed one's life and being satisfied with one's past life. The first question is stated as follows: "Some people review and *evaluate* their past in order to get an overall picture of their life. This is called the life review. Have you reviewed, or are you currently reviewing your life?" Respondents could answer yes, no, or currently reviewing. For those who indicated they had reviewed their lives they were asked to recall what caused them to begin reviewing their lives. Finally, all respondents were asked if they were satisfied with their past life. A chi-square test was used to determine age-group differences on conducting a life review, and on the relationship between life review and satisfaction with past life.

FINDINGS

The first question that defines the life review and then asks respondents if they have reviewed, or are currently reviewing their lives, was designed to test the universality of the life review as well as Lewis and Butler's speculation that it is more intense in "early old age," and "then begins to abate in the 70s and 80s" [4, pp. 165, 169]. As can be seen in Table 1, 134 or 46.4 percent of the total sample say they have not reviewed their lives. When looked at by cohort, a surprising 43.8 percent of the centenarians, 44.7 percent of eighty-year-olds and 51.1 percent of sixty-year-olds say they have not reviewed

Table 1. Percent of Centenarians, Eighty and Sixty-Year-Olds
Who Have Conducted a Life Review

| | Life Review | | |
Age	No ($n = 134$)	Yes ($n = 105$)	Currently Reviewing ($n = 50$)
100 ($n = 105$)	43.8% (46)	41% (43)	15.2% (16)
80 ($n = 94$)	44.7% (42)	41.5% (39)	13.8% (13)
60 ($n = 90$)	51.1% (46)	25.6% (23)	23.3% (21)

their lives. A chi-square test revealed that there were no significant differences among the three age groups ($x = 7.63038$, $df = 4$, $p = .1061$).

The question, "Are you satisfied with your past life?" was answered by 278 respondents of whom 243 or 87.4 percent answered yes. Thirty-five or 12.6 percent either said "no" or indicated they weren't totally satisfied with comments such as "there are things I would change," or "not 100 percent, no," or "could have done better." As can be seen in Table 2, being satisfied with one's past life appears independent of having conducted a life review. Of the thirty-five not satisfied with their past, twenty-two (13 "yes" plus 9 "currently reviewing") or 62.8 percent report having reviewed or are currently reviewing their lives; of the 115 who are satisfied with their past, 47.3 percent report *not* having reviewed their lives. A chi-square analysis revealed that there were no significant differences among groups ($x = 2.3424$, $df = 2$, $p = .3094$).

Respondents who had conducted a life review were asked what caused them to begin reviewing their lives. A wide range of answers was reported. For a few, the life review was caused by a major life event such as "husband's death," "children grew up and left," or "retirement." For others, the life review was precipitated by being prompted in some way ("prayer," "when young people ask questions," or "when someone mentions someone I know"), or by a generalized need ("thinking how life could get better," "not being able to do things for myself," "making important decisions," "life changes"). A number of respondents indicated that for them it was a continuous process. "Have done it since I was young," stated one centenarian; thinking about the past is an "ever-daily experience," said another. "Always have," stated an eighty-year-old. Others could identify no particular cause: "Don't know what causes it; I think about the past and present a lot;" "just getting older;" "things in daily life." No single "cause" was cited by the majority of respondents, and no one alluded, directly or indirectly, to his or her impending death as the reason for conducting a life review.

Table 2. Percent of Sample Who Have Reviewed Their Lives
and Who Are Satisfied With Their Past Lives

Past Life	Reviewed Life		
	No	Yes	Currently Reviewing
Satisfied ($n = 243$)	47.3% (115)	36.6% (89)	16.0% (39)
Not Satisfied ($n = 35$)	37.1% (13)	37.1% (13)	25.7% (9)

DISCUSSION

Results clearly call into question Butler's contention that the life review is a universal process. While a few previous studies [6, 7, 13] also report less-than-universal participation, it could be suggested that since the age range was younger, participants might still review their lives. That speculation is less convincing in this study where a third of the sample was 100 years and older and of them, 43.8 percent report not having reviewed their lives. Neither is Lewis' and Butler's contention that the life review is most intense in early old age, and then "abates in the 70s and 80s" [4, p. 169]. In this study, less than half (48.9%) of sixty-year-olds have reviewed or are currently reviewing their lives. Although not statistically significant, slightly more eighty and 100-year-olds have or are currently reviewing their lives (55.3% and 56.2% respectively).

That 46.4 percent of the study sample reported *not* having engaged in a life review could perhaps be explained as an inability to recall and/or unawareness of having conducted a life review. Lewis and Butler do speculate that awareness ranges from "fully aware" to "dimly conscious" to "totally unaware" [4, p. 166]. However, one of the criteria for participating in this study was that respondents be cognitively competent; furthermore, the life review questions were asked as part of a longer instrument on reminiscence such that participants would have been dealing with questions about recalling the past. A more likely explanation is that those who have not reviewed their lives have not felt the need to; they are satisfied with themselves and their past lives. In fact, of the 128 who did not review their lives (and who answered the question on satisfaction with past life), 115 or 89.8 percent report being satisfied with their past lives. Lieberman and Tobin who found that more than half of their sample (51%) had not reviewed their lives suggest yet another reason [7]. Noting that the theory emerged from a psychotherapeutic context, it might be "that the life review process—involving as it does a sorting out and restructuring of the past—is a task that demands high levels of inner skills not necessarily characteristic of most people" and that "perhaps we have been in error in assuming that the special skills needed to carry out a successful life review—a lifelong habit of introspection and heightened preoccupation with themes of mortality and immortality—are characteristic of most men and women" [7, pp. 309-310].

There has been an assumption in the life review literature that since older persons are nearer death than younger persons, older people will more likely have reviewed their lives. This assumption springs from Butler linking life review with the realization of approaching death. This connection was not supported in this study. Centenarians who are very close to death (there is a 50% mortality rate) were no more likely than either eighty-year-olds or sixty-year-olds to have reviewed their lives. Furthermore, when those who had reviewed their lives were asked what had caused them to begin doing so, awareness of one's own death was never alluded to. Neither were life crises (another motivator mentioned by Butler [1]) cited with any more frequency than more casual motivators such as "prayer" or "do it all the time." Perhaps acknowledgment of approaching death is difficult to articulate and a response such as "getting old" is the closest one can come. However, the range of responses to this question suggests just that—that there are many precipitators of the life review.

The assumption that conducting a life review leads to positive outcomes was not tested in this study. The only sense we have of this is whether or not those who reviewed their lives were satisfied with their past lives. As was discussed above, there appears to be no discernable pattern with regard to reviewing one's life and whether or not one feels satisfied with his or her past life.

In summary, findings from this study of the life review, because it focused on centenarians, calls into question at least two assumptions about the life review: First, the life review does not appear to be a universal process; second, the life review does not appear to be precipitated by approaching death. Neither was there any support for linking age, approaching death, and the life review. These assumptions have been challenged by findings from a few previous studies, and supported by findings from other studies. However, no previous studies of the life review were found that included an analysis focusing on centenarians. It would seem that the results of this study would suggest modifying the claims related to life review. It would be more fruitful to consider how the life review might function for those who have a need to engage in it. In addition to this therapeutic/psychological model, research on the life review might also be approached from a cultural transmission/educational or historical/political perspective [7, 11, 12].

REFERENCES

1. R. N. Butler, The Life Review: An Interpretation of Reminiscence in the Aged, *Psychiatry, 26,* pp. 65-76, 1963.
2. R. N. Butler, Successful Aging and the Role of the Life Review, *Journal of the American Geriatric Society, 22,* pp. 529-535, 1974.
3. R. N. Butler, The Life Review: An Unrecognized Bonanza, *International Journal of Aging and Human Development, 12,* pp. 35-38, 1980-81.
4. M. I. Lewis and R. N. Butler, Life Review Therapy: Putting Memories to Work in Individual and Group Psychotherapy, *Geriatrics, 29,* pp. 1615-173, 1974.
5. R. N. Butler and M. I. Lewis, *Aging and Mental Health,* The C. V. Mosby Company, St. Louis, 1982.
6. M. Romaniuk and J. G. Romaniuk, Looking Back: An Analysis of Reminiscence Functions and Triggers, *Developmental Aging Research, 7,* pp. 477-489, 1981.
7. M. A. Lieberman and S. S. Tobin, *The Experience of Old Age,* Basic Books, New York, 1983.
8. L. B. Taft and M. F. Nehrke, Reminiscence, Life Review, and Ego Integrity in Nursing Home Residents, *International Journal of Aging and Human Development, 30,* pp. 189-196, 1990.

9. S. Thornton and J. Brotchie, Reminiscence: A Critical Review of the Empirical Literature, *British Journal of Clinical Psychology, 26,* pp. 93-111, 1987.

10. V. W. Marshall, *Last Chapters: A Sociology of Aging and Dying,* Brooks/Cole Publishing, Monterey, California, 1980.

11. H. R. Moody, Twenty-five Years of the Life Review: Where Did We Come From? Where are We Going?, *Journal of Gerontological Social Work, 12,* pp. 7-21, 1988.

12. V. I. Tarman, Autobiography: The Negotiation of a Lifetime, *International Journal of Aging and Human Development, 27,* pp. 171-191, 1988.

13. J. E. Gorney, Experiencing and Age: Patterns of Reminiscence Among the Elderly, unpublished doctoral dissertation, University of Chicago, 1968.

14. W. Boylin, S. K. Gordon, and M. F. Nehrke, Reminiscence and Ego Integrity in Institutionalized Elderly Males, *The Gerontologist, 16*:2, pp. 118-124, 1976.

15. J. M. Holden and C. Guest, Life Review in a Non-Near Death Episode: A Comparison with Near-Death Experiences, *Journal of Transpersonal Psychology, 22,* pp. 1-15, 1990.

16. R. Noyes and R. Kletti, Panoramic Memory: A Response to the Threat of Death, *Omega Journal of Death and Dying, 8,* pp. 181-194, 1977.

17. W. Borden, Life Review as a Therapeutic Frame in the Treatment of Young Adults with AIDS, *Health and Social Work, 14,* pp. 253-259, 1989.

18. J. Pickre, Tell Me Your Story: Using Life Review in Counseling the Terminally Ill, *Death Studies, 13,* pp. 127-135, 1989.

19. S. Malde, Guided Autobiography: A Counseling Tool for Older Adults, *Journal of Counseling and Development, 66,* pp. 290-293, 1988.

20. B. K. Haight, The Therapeutic Role of a Structured Life Review Process in Homebound Elderly Subjects, *Journal of Gerontology, 43,* pp. 40-44, 1988.

21. J. M. Giltinan, Using Life Review to Facilitate Self-Actualization in Elderly Women, *Gerontology and Geriatrics Education, 10,* pp. 75-83, 1990.

22. P. G. Coleman, Measuring Reminiscence Characteristics From Conversation as Adaptive Features of Old Age, *International Journal of Aging and Human Development, 5,* pp. 281-294, 1974.

23. H. M. Miller, Life Review as an Intervention: A Comparison of a Systematically Induced Life Review and Non-Specific Factors Groups with Elderly Adults, unpublished doctoral dissertation, University of Kansas, 1985.

24. S. Fishman, An Investigation of the Relationships Among an Older Adult's Life Review, Ego Integrity, and Death Anxiety, unpublished doctoral dissertation, New York University, 1988.

25. M. L. Aubell, Adjustment to Senior Citizens Apartment Hotel and the Effectiveness of Life Review: A Comparison Between Senior Citizens Who Have the Opportunity for Life Review and Those Who Do Not, unpublished doctoral dissertation, St. Louis University, 1986.

26. G. E. Shute, Life Review: A Cautionary Note, *Clinical Gerontologist, 6,* pp. 57-58, 1986.

27. J. Lesser et al., Reminiscence Group Therapy with Psychotic In-Patients, *Gerontologist, 21,* pp. 291-296, 1981.

28. E. M. Job, Retrospective Life Span Analysis: A Method for Studying Extreme Old Age, *Journal of Gerontology, 38,* pp. 369-374, 1983.

29. B. Cohler, Personal Narrative and the Life Course, in *Life-Span Development and Behavior,* P. Baltes and O. Brim (eds.), Vol. V, Academic Press, New York, 1983.
30. L. M. Gambia, Daydreaming About the Past: The Time Setting of Spontaneous Thought Intrusion, *Gerontologist, 17,* pp. 35-38, 1977.
31. B. Myerhoff, Life History Among the Elderly: Performance, Visibility, and Re-Membering, in *Life Course; Integrative Theories and Exemplary Populations,* K. Back (ed.), Westview Press, Boulder, Colorado, 1980.
32. C. Ryant, Comment: Oral History and Gerontology, *Gerontologist, 21,* pp. 104-105, 1981.
33. L. W. Poon (ed.), The Georgia Centenarian Study, *The International Journal of Aging and Human Development,* Special Issue, 1992.

Chapter 2

REMINISCING: THE STATE OF THE ART AS A BASIS FOR PRACTICE

Barbara K. Haight

This integrated review, from the years 1960 through March, 1990, presents the state of the art in reminiscing and life review. Three areas—reports, reviews, and research—classify the existing literature, which is analyzed for positive or negative outcomes. This classification sorts the varied articles and defines the use of the existing literature for practice. Perceptions and direction are garnered from previously published reviews. Reports are discussed, and, finally, the research literature is examined for its collective worth as a basis for practice. From this analysis of the work in reminiscing, conclusions may be drawn and suggestions made for the use of reminiscing by practitioners who work with older people. (A tabular listing of this integrated review appears as an Appendix on pages 32-48.)

The purpose of this chapter is to analyze the literature on reminiscing and life review with the intent of clarifying the existing results and setting guidelines for practice.

DATA COLLECTION

This search reviewed thirty years of literature, starting in 1960 and ending in March, 1990. Refereed journals originating in the United States were hand searched for references on life review and reminiscing. In addition, the Medical University of South Carolina's Mini-Medline database served as a computer resource in the search of the literature. The key words used for this search were: aging, reminiscing, remembering, and life review. Table 1 displays criteria for this search.

Strict guidelines were needed to limit the search. Some published articles were not included in this analysis, because they did not meet the criteria nor did they fit the purpose of the review. For example, articles on autobiography and oral history

Table 1. Criteria for Review

I. Years 1960-1990
II. Refereed Journals of the United States
III. Key Words: Reminiscing, Remembering, Aging, Life Review, History, and Oral History
IV. Benefit to the Reminiscer

were not included. Some of these dealt with the importance of recording life's stories rather than the effect the story telling had on the individual doing the reminiscing. Birrens', "The Best of All Stories," in *Psychology Today* is an example of such an article [1]. Though several good books exist (Kaminsky's book on life review [2] and Coleman's *Aging and Reminiscence Processes* [3]), they did not come under the guideline of a refereed journal and so were excluded. Dissertations and dissertation abstracts were also excluded, as were published abstracts indicative of presentations at national conferences. To summarize, the guidelines for this review include: manuscripts on reminiscing or life review published within the years 1960-1990, refereed journals of the United States, and key words as identified in Table 1. Table 2 displays the journals included in the search and the number of articles found in each journal.

REVIEW OF THE LITERATURE

Analysis and Interpretation

One of the most striking features of this review is the growth in interest in life review and reminiscing. Gerontologists in the 1960s published only three articles on the subject, growing to twenty articles in the 1970s, and finally multiplying in the 1980s with seventy-one articles. So many assumptions are made in these publications, it seems necessary to examine the literature critically and closely, dividing the work into type (report, review, research) and outcome (positive and negative). This division is necessary to give practitioners a clear picture of the past in order to guide future practice, which is the stated purpose of this review.

Seven manuscripts review the literature and offer a discussion, analysis, and direction for future work. Forty-nine of the articles are reports or case studies; ten report on groups; and thirty-nine report on the clinical impressions of practitioners. Researchers published a total of forty-two articles that should form a basis for the present practice of reminiscing modalities. Of these forty-two articles, twenty-one described research in groups, and twenty described research with individuals. Figure 1 represents the growth of interest in reminiscing, by decade, since 1960; Figure 2 presents a chart depicting the types of articles written.

Table 2. Journals Searched

Number of Articles	Journal
22	International Journal of Aging and Human Development
11	Journal of Gerontological Nursing
7	The Gerontologist
5	Journal of Gerontology
4	Clinical Gerontologist
4	Physical and Occupational Therapy in Geriatrics
3	Journal of Gerontological Social Work
2	Activities Adaptation and Aging
2	The American Journal of Nursing
2	The American Journal of Occupational Therapy
2	Experimental Aging Research
2	The Journal of Contemporary Social Work
2	Journal of Geriatric Psychiatry
2	Journal of Nursing Care
2	Social Work
1	Academic Psychology Bulletin
1	Advances in Nursing Science
1	American Health Care Association Journal
1	American Journal of Art Therapy
1	Archives of General Psychiatry
1	The Arts in Psychotherapy
1	Death Studies
1	Geriatric Nursing
1	Geriatrics
1	Gerontology and Geriatrics Education
1	International Forum of Logo Therapy
1	Issues in Mental Health Nursing
1	Journal of the American Geriatrics Society
1	Journal of the Nurse Practitioner
1	Journal of the Nursing Staff Development
1	Journal of Practical Nursing
1	Journal of Psychosocial Nursing and Mental Health Service
1	Nursing Mirror
1	Nursing Forum
1	Omega
1	Oral History Review
1	Perspectives in Psychiatric Care
1	Psychiatry
1	Psychological Reports
1	Provider
1	Social Work in Health Care

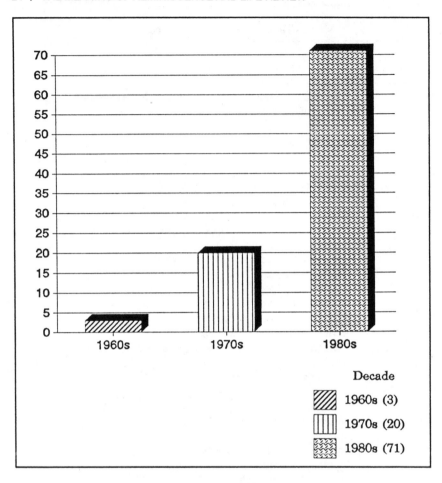

Figure 1. Number of articles by decade.

Reports

The seminal article on life review by Robert Butler stimulated an awareness of the process of life review in caregivers of elderly people [4]. As a result, the literature offers over sixty reports of reminiscing or life review on either an individual or a group basis. Many of the reports are one-shot case studies and therefore are either quite positive about life review or, at the least, nonevaluative. Hausman [5], a psychologist, related positive and chance reviewing in one of her clients as did Chubon [6] who used a novel to guide a patient through life review.

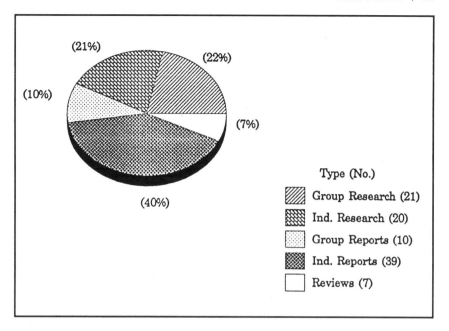

Figure 2. Types of articles.

Babb de Ramon [7] described the use of life review with a dying patient, while others, Butler [8, 9], Beaton [10], and Allen and Bennett [11] talked of the general benefit of reminiscing with elderly people. Still others portrayed reminiscing as healthy [11], therapeutic [12], adaptive [13], and integrative [14].

Using a "how to" approach Detzner reported the use of life review with students [15]. Holzberg [16], Keddy [17], Mintz [18], and Myerhoff [19] spoke of life histories, while Eisenberg presented logotherapy as an additional tool to enhance life review [20]. Perschbacher used life review in an innovative manner to describe a program where older people told their stories to a third-grade class [21], while Zeiger recommended the use of art in recalling memories [22]. Each of these individual reports are of interest and encourage practitioners to use reminiscence themselves. However, other than positive reports, there were no guidelines or instructions, no testing, and no differentiation of different types of reminiscing. Thus, others who wished to practice reminiscence on an individual basis did so by instinct alone.

Several people wrote about the use of reminiscence in groups. Ebersole [23] discussed potential problems in groups, while Baker [24] and Price [25] reported successful reminiscing group programs. The reported success of the reminiscing groups was observational and not subjected to the research process. Finally, Busch described the reminiscing process as one of the four main themes in older adult group psychotherapy [26].

Only one person reported negative findings. Nicholl studied the life reviews in five short stories and based his article on fictional work [27]. Despite the use of fiction, the author suggested real life application of his findings and stated that the literature should be used to support significant principles about the aging process. Again, practitioners received few guidelines. They did learn that groups enjoyed reminiscing as much as individuals.

Reviews and Discussions

Past reviews, though valuable, were not exhaustive and only reported selected parts of the literature. Because past reviews were selective, a clear and defined state of the art in reminiscing has never evolved. Past reviewers did offer varied and valuable suggestions, however. If researchers followed the suggestions, a true body of knowledge surrounding life review and reminiscence might be evolving today.

Another criticism of past reviews is that the reviewers did not describe the method used to conduct their reviews. They did not report facts, such as journals searched, key words, and years covered. Consequently, it is hard to evaluate the suggestions made by reviewers—the reviews may be based only on selected studies leading to inconclusive results.

Romaniuk conducted the first review of reminiscing in 1981 [28]. Through his review, he noticed the diversity of opinion regarding the relationship between reminiscence and adaptation. He determined that the idea of reminiscence needed rigorous examination, and that researchers should study the relationship of reminiscence to adaptation.

Hughston and Merriam reviewed the research on reminiscence in 1982 and concluded that the notion of reminiscence and its relationship to other affective processes was not clearly delineated [29]. Merriam stated that researchers needed to conceptualize the phenomenon of life review and concentrate on discovering the attributes of reminiscence. This way, an exploratory, inductive, theory-building methodology might generate insights that could later be operationalized and tested empirically. Merriam also suggested that researchers accumulate more descriptive data regarding the content, type, and amount of time spent in reminiscing.

Kiernat looked at reminiscing and life review as retrospection and examined this phenomena along with day dreaming about the past [30]. Kiernat created a different concept of recall by including day dreaming in her analysis and concluded that retrospection was complex and involved. She also stated that research regarding the use of retrospection was in a state of infancy.

A review of the literature by Molinari and Reichlin [31] examined the concept of life review. These two authors evaluated and interpreted much of the work on life review in the past twenty years. They reached interesting conclusions that may be a guide for future research on the subject. These authors proposed the following: a need for basic demographic data, a separation of life review and reminiscence in future research, a clarified process of life review, a division and clarification of intrapersonal and interpersonal reminiscence, an examination of life review differences in community versus institutional settings, longitudinal studies to examine long-term effects of life review, and, more collaboration between the clinical and research areas. Each of these suggestions is valuable and contributes to a clarification of the issues surrounding life review.

Kovach reanalyzed the research literature in 1989 and concluded that there was a weakness in the methodology and the definition of reminiscing, but that the modality might have a therapeutic effect [32].

A few authors analyzed the process of reminiscing and life review. LoGerfo is much cited for her categorization of types of reminiscence as informative, evaluative, and obsessive [33]. Webster and Young also made a distinct contribution in depicting the process variables in life review as recall, evaluation, and synthesis [34]. These analysts tried to give clear descriptions of reminiscing along with directions for others to use reminiscing and life review in their practice.

These five reviews and two discussion papers make a distinct contribution to the body of knowledge about reminiscence, but they have not defined the history or shaped the future of reminiscence. This may be because each reviewer examined the phenomena in a different way. Present practitioners and future researchers need a clear, objective, exhaustive report of all past work in order to gain a clear picture of the present state of the art of reminiscing. A close examination of all past research should help to build that picture.

Research

The body of research on reminiscing does not reflect the suggestions of the reviewers. Perhaps the reviews are too recent to have benefitted the researchers who have already published. The 1990s may be the decade for the clarification and full application of knowledge to the conducting of reminiscence and life review therapies. This analysis of the research literature to date will provide a beginning blue print for future scholars, but provide little guidance for practitioners.

Of the forty-one research reports published since 1960, twenty-one discuss reminiscing in groups, and twenty discuss reminiscing with individuals. Six of the research studies with individuals were conducted before the 1980s, and only four had positive results. McMahon and Rhudick's study is an often quoted classic in which the researchers determined that veterans who reminisced had high self-esteem [35].

Then in the 1970s, Lieberman and Falk looked at data from past interviews and concluded that reminiscence had little effect on adaptation [36]. Boylin, Gordon, and Nehrke also reported negative results in correlating ego adjustment to six questions asked about reminiscing in interviews [37]. Peter Coleman investigated functions of reminiscence and found the life review to be more beneficial than simple reminiscing [38]. Havighurst and Glasser used an interview schedule to explore reminiscence with thirty adults and discovered that the older participants reminisced both alone and with others, a little more with others [39]. Lewis analyzed a one-hour conversation and determined that reminiscers had a higher self-concept in times of stress, possibly using reminiscence as a defense mechanism [40]. Each of these research projects during the 1970s used only a one-hour intervention or an interview schedule and concluded that reminiscing was not therapeutic. The negative results may have been responsible for the mixed reviews on the efficacy of reminiscing.

Kiernat conducted life review research in groups with seventeen confused, nursing home residents and reported positive change in eleven of them [41]. Dietsche conducted a reminiscence group for fifteen weeks and found that shared life reviews helped to increase confidence and self-respect [42], while Emlet met one-hour, twice a week with institutionalized, aged adults and discovered an 80 percent improvement in some areas in all patients [43]. The group reminiscing interventions of the 1970s used lengthy interventions and produced positive outcomes. The 1970s research raises questions about the group versus the individual process and the length of the intervention. One may be led to believe that group modality is more effective than individual modality—when in fact, the longer intervention may have made the reminiscing more therapeutic.

In the 1980s, several authors examined reminiscing as therapy for individuals. Haight used a six-week, structured, life review intervention and achieved significant results [44, 45]. Hedgepeth and Hale [46] employed a one-hour, reminiscing intervention and had negative results as did Brennan and Steinberg [47]. Carlson [48] and Fallot [49] also used a one-hour intervention, but they obtained positive results. Job [50] looked at the process of life review for information about the reviewer, as did Bramwell [51]. Romaniuk [28, 52] analyzed the reminiscence function, and Wright and Payne [53] reported that males and females reminisced equally.

Research with groups in the 1980s almost always resulted in positive outcomes. Lesser, et al. [54], worked with psychotic, geriatric patients and discovered that reminiscence groups fostered cohesiveness. Matteson and Munsat [55] found their group made people more socially interactive, while Parson's [56] decreased levels of depression. Bergland [57], Lappe [58], and Ingersoll and Goodman [59] raised levels of self-esteem. Others' groups reduced state anxiety [60], decreased denial of death [61], improved cognitive function [29, 62], and improved mental adaptability [63]. Only one group interaction resulted in negative results: the group of

Table 3. Data on Outcomes of Reminiscing Processes

Area	Positive	Negative	Nonevaluative	Total
Report (Group)	8	0	2	10
Report (Individual)	31	1	7	39
Research (Group)	18	1	2	21
Research (Individual)	12	5	3	20
Review	1	0	6	7
Totals:	70	7	20	97

community residents run by Perrotta and Meacham [64]. Table 3 summarizes the outcomes, both positive and negative, for all reviews, reports, and research.

DISCUSSION

Reminiscence is a multi-varied concept. Each portion of the concept must be identified, labeled, and described. The processes for reminiscing are as varied as the types of reminiscing; these must be defined as well. To be more precise, group reminiscing must be separated from individual reminiscing, life review from random reminiscing, structured reminiscing from unstructured reminiscing, evaluative reminiscing from nonevaluative reminiscing, and external reminiscing from internal reminiscing. Only then will the process and its outcomes be measurable. The results from one type of reminiscing will not apply to the conduct of another type. The existing reports must be analyzed for differences in variables, process, and outcome.

Gerontologists must define the varied kinds of reminiscence and create a sound typology. Earlier reviewers identified varied ways of reminiscing and suggested labels. The labeling, however, is incomplete and inconsistent. Molinari and Reichlin suggested labels such as intrapersonal and interpersonal [31]; LoGerfo proposed informative, evaluative, and obsessive [33]; and Coleman recommended life review and simple reminiscing [38]. Each of these labels are a step in the right direction, but none have been adopted as a permanent framework.

Reminiscing is a great umbrella encompassing many types of reminiscing. One type of reminiscing may be interpersonal, another informative, and still another obsessive, as identified by past reviewers. As new researchers begin their projects, they should make an effort to describe and label the type of reminiscing that is taking place, using some of the descriptions and labels presented by past reviewers. Perhaps as researchers repeatedly use the suggested labels and explore the meanings of the labels, they will begin to define the type of process they are conducting. Then, only similar processes will be compared to one another, possibly yielding more similar and more sound results. When researchers reach consensus, as to the type of reminiscing they are testing, practitioners will begin to have a sound, practice base.

When examining process, the length of the intervention is important. Of the twenty studies conducted with individuals rather than groups, only three used a lengthy intervention. The highest number of visits for any intervention dealing with individuals was six. The other sixteen studies conducted with individuals used either one interview, a one-hour, reminiscing modality, a paper and pencil test, or an examination of past interview data. Of the twenty studies of reminiscence with individuals, only twelve studies attained positive outcomes, two other studies were nonevaluative, and five described negative outcomes. There is a positive note, however: the last three studies conducted with individual participants did achieve positive outcomes. So perhaps researchers are beginning to define and upgrade the process to an intervention rather than an interview. All five of the negative outcome studies used a reminiscing intervention of one hour or less.

In contrast, group research studies, twenty-one in all, seemed to be conducted in an opposite manner. Sixteen of the group research studies reported interventions ranging from four weeks to eleven months. Only two studies reported interventions of one hour, and three studies did not report the length of their interventions. Of the twenty group research studies, eighteen had positive outcomes, only one reached a negative outcome, and two were nonevaluative.

The research results from these studies may lead practitioners to believe that group reminiscing is more therapeutic than reminiscing on an individual basis— when in fact, as stated earlier, the success of group reminiscing may be attributed to the longer group intervention. Obviously, it is more costly both in time and money to conduct lengthy sessions with individuals rather than with groups. However, this one variable of length of intervention may skew the data in all the research.

Still another issue included in process is the essence of group versus individual process. Each has distinct characteristics. In the individual process, the reviewer may be more open and reveal more intimate details. The reviewer has an opportunity to establish a confidante type of relationship with the interviewer. The reviewer is able to work over the more painful details of life in a more intimate setting and so may get more of the hard work completed.

In the group process, the individual may achieve support from peers. This group type of process may be especially effective when an older person needs to form new relationships and establish new networks. Relocation and entry into a nursing home setting may be a time when the group process serves more than one purpose.

Perhaps in sharing like memories, people begin to find new grounds for communicating with one another. The process itself may establish common bonds.

Each type of process may be effective for different reasons. Most importantly, the process, when used in research, must be identified and the results compared only with similar processes. When practitioners base their practice on research results, they also must use similar processes as guidelines.

Emphasis placed on outcomes may divert the researcher and practitioner. Though outcomes are important, they have drawn the researcher's attention away from defining the process of reminiscence itself. Most of the forty-one research studies focused on outcomes. Clinicians know that reminiscence causes varied therapeutic outcomes, however, if reminiscence is to be used successfully in practice, researchers must first explain the type, the process, and the manner of conducting the reminiscence modality. If the process is clearly described and is therapeutic, the outcomes such as decreased depression and increased self-esteem may occur more often in practice. Perhaps after the researcher determines the process and outcome, a summary paragraph comparing the reported study, exclusively, to like studies will help the practitioner determine the usability of the study for practice.

CONCLUSIONS AND RECOMMENDATIONS

Researchers must examine the literature closely and decide which variables affect the process. They must separate the reports from the experimental data and from the theory building articles to make correct assumptions; they can then begin their own work on firmer foundations. Actually, the large number of published reports has clouded this intervention. Many of the articles add to the confusion, instead of clarifying the concept. Conceivably, with the evolution and clarification of a concept, a clear implementation will follow.

Future research must reflect the differences between life review and reminiscing and must contribute to a uniform and best way of conducting any reminiscence process. The work in reminiscing from 1960-1990 has been exemplary and has led to a point in the discovery process that should serve as a sound beginning. When one examines the literature as a whole much information has evolved. By the 21st century, gerontologists using this information will have established a research based method for conducting reminiscence. A typology must be established to guide this future research and practice and to identify differences in the process.

However, while the research continues, it is important for practitioners to continue to use the reminiscence process as a therapeutic modality for aging people. Reminiscing modalities must be reworked and refined by the theorists and researchers, while the practitioners continue to use this most effective tool. In conclusion, reminiscence may serve as a highly effective therapeutic intervention—the who, what, when, where, and why still need to be identified.

APPENDIX
Life Review

Research (Individual)

Article	Study Variables	Findings	*
Boylin, W., Gordon, S.K., & Nehrke, M.F. (1976). Reminiscing and ego integrity in institutionalized elderly males. The Gerontologist, 16(2), 118-124.	N=41 Institutionalized Males. Mean Age=64.37. The relationship of ego adjustment to reminiscing. Six questions asked about reminiscing in interviews.	Negative effect of reminiscing correlated moderately but significantly with ego integrity, fails to support that increased ego integrity is correlated with favorable attitude about past.	N
Bramwell, L. (1984). Use of the life history in pattern identification and health promotion. Advances in Nursing Science, 7(1), 37-44.	N=8. Age=65. Use of life review by nurses as a tool for identification of human patterning with potential for health promotion.	Qualitative study. Requires further investigation with larger, more diverse samples. A possibility of risk associated with consciousness expansion.	N
Brennan, P.L., & Steinberg, L.D. (1984). Is reminiscence adaptive? Relations among social activity level, reminiscence, and morale. International Journal of Aging and Human Development, 18(2), 99-109.	N=40 Females. Age=64-88. Is reminiscence adaptive? Its relation to social activity and morale. One-hour interview, correlational study.	Reminiscence was not positively related to morale or negatively related to activity level. Findings indicated that reminiscence may be a correlate of social activity.	N
Carlson, C.M. (1984). Reminiscing: Toward achieving ego integrity in old age. Journal of Contemporary Social Work, (2), 81-89.	N=8 Community Residents. Interview format to assess ego integrity and reminiscing. One-hour interview.	Reminiscing does serve an adaptive function in old age and correlates with ego integrity.	P
Coleman, P.G. (1974). Measuring reminiscence characteristics from conversation as adaptive features of old age. International Journal of Aging and Human Development, 5(3), 281-294.	N=48. Age=69-92. Mean Age=80. Adults living alone in sheltered housing. Purpose was to investigate functions of reminiscing. Interviewer had conversations that were taped and structured in average of six visits over 1½ to 2 years.	Describes two types of reminiscing. Life review was found to be of more significant benefit than simple reminiscing.	P

*P = Positive Outcome; N = Negative Outcome; NE = Nonevaluative

32

Reference	Sample	Findings	Outcome
David, D. (1990). Reminiscence, adaption, and social context in old age. International Journal of Aging and Human Development, 30(3), 175-188.	N=43. Age=68-95. Residents of two sectarian retirement communities. Interview format to determine social variations in the relationship between reminiscence and adaption.	Social context is an important variable that shapes the relationship between reminiscence and old age.	P
Fallot, R.D. (1980). The impact on mood of verbal reminiscing in later adulthood. International Journal of Aging and Human Development, 10(4), 385-400.	N=36 Females. Age=46-85. Impact of verbal reminiscing on self reports of mood. Intervention of one hour of reminiscing.	Reminiscing can serve as an adaptive function through decreased depression and shame in middle age as well as old age.	P
Haight, B.K. (1988). The therapeutic role of a structured life review process in homebound elderly subjects. Journal of Gerontology, 43(2), 40-44.	N=60. Examines the therapeutic role of a structured life review in homebound elderly people. Reminiscence intervention duration of six weeks.	Life satisfaction and psychological well-being improved significantly after the use of a structured life review process. Life review did not produce depression in the experimental group.	P
Haight, B.K. (1984). The therapeutic role of the life review in the elderly. Academic Psychology Bulletin, 6, 287-289.	N=12. Age=60 and over. Pilot study. Experimental and control group to assess the therapeutic role of life review. Six week intervention.	Study supports hypothesis of an increase in life satisfaction in those that participated in life review.	P
Havighurst, R.J., & Glasser, R. (1972). An exploratory study of reminiscence. Journal of Gerontology, 27(2), 245-253.	N=30. Interview schedule to ask about reminiscing experience.	Sixty-seven percent of respondents reminiscence when alone. Seventy-nine percent of respondents reminiscence when with others.	P
Hedgepeth, B.E., & Hale, D. (1983). Effect of a positive reminiscing intervention on affect, expectancy, and performance. Psychological Reports, 53, 867-870.	N=60 Females. Age=60-98. Reminiscence intervention of one hour.	Lack of significance suggests that reminiscing may not always be an effective intervention tool.	N
Job, E.M. (1983). Retrospective life span analysis: A method for studying extreme old age. Journal of Gerontology, 38(3), 369-374.	N=209. 62 Males, 142 Females. Age=over 80. People living in a suburb in Australia. Including private dwellers and institutionalized. One taped interview study for learning more about aged populations.	There should be more research into the "old-old." Retrospective accounts of life span experiences are far from worthless and many attain a surprisingly high standard of factual accuracy.	P

*P = Positive Outcome; N = Negative Outcome; NE = Nonevaluative

33

Research (Individual) (Cont'd)

Article	Study Variables	Findings	*
Lewis, C.N. (1971). Reminiscing and self-concept in old age. Journal of Gerontology, 26(2), 240-243.	N=24 Caucasian males. Age=65 and older. Study investigated whether reminiscers show an increased consistency of the self-concept following some form of stress. One hour conversation labeled as reminiscence if more than 40 percent of conversation was about the past.	Following stress, there was a significant increase in past-present self-concept correlation for reminiscers indicating the possibility of reminiscence as a defense mechanism.	P
Lieberman, M.A., & Falk, G.M. (1971). The remembered past as a source of data for research on the life cycle. The International Journal of Aging and Human Development, 14, 132-141.	N=180, Average Age 78. N=25, Average Age 49. Study the use of reminiscence in the aged and middle aged. Data from past interviews.	Failed to find empirical support for the proposition of a difference in adaptation of reminiscence involvement versus non-involvement.	N
McMahon, A.W., & Rhudick, P.J. (1964). Reminiscing: Adaptational significance in the aged. Archives of General Psychiatry, 10, 292-298, May 64.	N=25 Age 75-90. Reminiscing, not related to intellectual determinants. Non-depressed individuals reminisced more than depressed. Maintenance of esteem, frame of reference for social interchange. One hour interview.	Veterans who reminisced the most had high self-esteem.	P
Merriam, S.B. (1989). The structure of simple reminiscence. The Gerontologist, 29(6), 761-767.	N=25. Age=61-80. Mean Age=71. Taped interviews over a four week period.	Categories found in reminiscing: selection, immersion, withdrawal, and closure.	NE
Romaniuk, M., & Romaniuk, J. (1981). Looking back: An analysis of reminiscence functions and triggers. Experimental Aging Research, 1(4), 477-489.	N=91. Completed paper and pencil survey of reminiscence.	The relationship between reminiscence and adjustment may be due to measuring it inter-personally rather than intra-personally.	NE

*P = Positive Outcome; N = Negative Outcome; NE = Nonevaluative

34

Reference	Description	Outcome
Taft, L.B., & Nehrke, M.F. (1990). Reminiscence, life review, and ego integrity in nursing home residents. International Journal of Aging and Human Development, 30(3), 189-196.	N=30. Mean Age=84.13. The relationship of reminiscence frequency, the three dimensions of reminiscence, and ego integrity.	The use of life review was positively related to ego integrity, but not to the other two dimensions of reminiscence. Frequency showed no relationship.	P
Vickers, W.D. (1983). Project looking back: A structured reminiscence experience. Activities, Adaptation and Aging, 3(4), 31-38.	A structured reminiscence project. N=9. Average age=81 male in and out patients at a VA hospital. Four contacts with each patient. 1) Initial meeting, 2) History taping averaged one hour, 15 minutes with a structured format, 3) Post taping review of transcript, 4) Delivery of edited copy of history.	Quality of response suggested it was a worthwhile experience for participants and they expressed interest in further reminiscing with their families.	P
Wright, B.M., & Payne, R.B. (1985). Effects of aging on sex differences in psychomotor reminiscence and proficiency. Journal of Gerontology, 40(2), 179-184.	N=35 Males. N=34 Females. Reminiscence defined as time lag between task.	In elderly, no significant sex differences in reminiscence tendencies.	NE

*P = Positive Outcome; N = Negative Outcome; NE = Nonevaluative

Research (Group)

Article	Study Variables	Findings	*
Berghorn, F.J., & Schafer, D.E. (1987). Reminiscence intervention in nursing homes: What and who changes. International Journal of Aging and Human Development, 24(2), 113-127.	N=185 in 30 homes participated in reminiscing groups of the story telling type for approximately 3 months. Mental adaptability consisting of 8 variables was tested, pre and post intervention. Eight variables were categorized as: behavior patterns, mental functioning and attitudes.	Characteristics of persons were developed. Persons who are not adaptive and support values not supported by the social structure of the nursing home will benefit most from a reminiscence group intervention.	P
Bergland, C. (1982). The life review process in geriatric art therapy: A pilot study. The Arts in Psychotherapy, 9, 121-130.	N=14. One group=7 women in a state hospital long-term nursing home. One group=7 men and women in a private short-term psychiatric hospital. Art work and life lines done both before and after a life review. Met weekly 1½ hours for four months.	Though life review was seen as a positive influence on increased self-esteem the research was deemed to need further study with increased numbers.	P
Cook, J.B. (1984). Reminiscing: How it can help confused nursing home residents. The Journal of Contemporary Social Work, (2), 90-93.	N=6. Core group pilot study to interrupt excessive social isolation.	Group reminiscing decreased isolation and increased socialization and mental stimulation.	P
Dietsche, L.M. (1979). Know your community resources: Facilitating the life review through group reminiscences. Journal of Gerontological Nursing, 5(4), 43-46.	N=10. Mean Age=73.2. Forty to 60 minutes for 15 weeks. Specific, agreed upon topic for each session. Ambulatory geriatric day care center. All with known health problems.	Shared life review helped participants to restructure and gain an identity, with gains in confidence and self-respect.	P
Ellison, K.B. (1981). Working with the elderly in a life review group. Journal of Gerontological Nursing, 7(9), 537-541.	N=5 70-96 year old nursing home residents with no identified mental or emotional problems. One hour weekly for eight weeks.	Life review and reminiscing promote successful aging and the process in a small group setting is most helpful.	P
Emlet, C.A. (1979). Reminiscence: A psychological approach to institutionalized aged. American Health Care Association Journal, Sep 5(5), 19, 22.	Mean Age=83. Groups of 8. Met one hour twice a week for 8 weeks. A physical object bearing relationship to discussion topic brought to each session.	Eighty percent displayed some degree of improvement. Sixty percent improved in self-esteem in narrative section of evaluation. Twenty percent improved in every area of behavioral assessment.	P

*P = Positive Outcome; N = Negative Outcome; NE = Nonevaluative

Reference	Sample/Method	Outcome	
Froehlich, J., & Nelson, D.L. (1986). Affective meanings of life review through activities and discussion. The American Journal of Occupational Therapy, 40(1), 27-33.	N=22 Women. Age=60-85. Urban subsidized housing project; one hour session. Each participant assigned to one of two discussion groups.	Supports life review with peers as a positive experience for elderly, but does not answer question of whether life review is enhanced by activities or through discussion alone.	P
Georgemiller, R., & Maloney, H. (1984). Group life review and denial of death. Clinical Gerontologist, 2(4), 37-49.	N=63. Control and experimental group workshop conducted on life review. For 6, one hour sessions.	Treatment group significantly decreased in denial of death.	P
Goldwasser, A.N., Auerbach, S.M., & Harkins, S.W. (1987). Cognitive, affective, and behavioral effects of reminiscence group therapy on demented elderly. International Journal of Aging and Human Development, 25(3), 209-222.	N=27 demented elderly nursing home residents. Intervention consisted of ½ hour reminiscence groups 2 x week for 5 weeks.	Reminiscing group scored higher than the no-treatment and control group on measures of cognitive and affective function, but remained almost the same on ADL until follow up testing 6 weeks after the intervention. Amount of depression increased 6 weeks later.	P
Holzberg, C.S. (1984). Anthropology, life history, and the aged: The Toronto Baycrest Centre. International Journal of Aging and Human Development, 18(4), 255-275.	N=25. Age=70-95. Memoirs group of aged Jews at an integrated geriatric facility. Met once a week for 11 months. Anthropologist interviews and private tapes to preserve story of Canadian Jewish immigration experiences.	Writing memoir enabled elderly to achieve final phase of personal growth and had value as life offering and self validity experience to preserve important historical data.	P
Hughston, G.A., & Merriam, S.B. (1982). Reminiscence: A non-formal technique for improving cognitive functioning in the aged. International Journal on Aging and Human Development, 15(2), 139-149.	N=105 Volunteers. Residents of public housing complex. Does reminiscence affect cognition of reminiscence group of four weeks duration?	Structured reminiscence can improve cognitive function in women.	P
Ingersoll, B., & Goodman, L. (1980). History comes alive: Facilitating reminiscence in a group of institutionalized elderly. Journal of Gerontological Social Work, 2(4), 305-319.	N=10 Jewish residents. Age=69-98. Group intervention of six sessions. To facilitate reminiscing among institutionalized elderly. No measure.	Leaders and participants felt it was a positive experience. Feelings of self-worth increased, enhanced identity and social utilization.	P

*P = Positive Outcome; N = Negative Outcome; NE = Nonevaluative

Research (Group) (Cont'd)

Article	Study Variables	Findings	*
Kiernat, J.M. (1979). The use of life review activity with confused nursing home residents. _The American Journal of Occupational Therapy_, 33(5), 306-310.	N=23 Nursing Home Residents. Men=2. Women=21. No severe visual or hearing loss. Charted as confused at least three months. Three groups met twice a week for ten weeks, 45 minutes to one hour. Three died during sessions. Two leaders at each session. One constant at all sessions was occupational therapist for each group.	11 Showed definite improvement in behavior during life review. Seven showed no change. Two members showed minimal behavior change. Three died. Life review activity is a valuable intervention technique.	P
Lappe, J.M. (1987). Reminiscing: The life review therapy. _Journal of Gerontological Nursing_, 13(4), 12-16.	N=83. Mean Age=82.6 years. Ten weeks intervention. Four private long-term care institutions with two groups in each institution. One discussing current events, one utilizing reminiscing. Four groups met once a week, four groups met twice a week.	Reminiscing increases self-esteem of elderly institutionalized to a greater degree than discussion of current events.	P
Lesser, J., Lazarus, L.W., Frankl, R., & Havasg, S. (1981). Reminiscence group therapy with psychotic geriatric inpatients. _The Gerontologist_, 21(3), 291-296.	N=45. Average Age=69.7. Clinical case group study. All clients were psychotic, structured group of 45 men, two times a week; numerous sessions.	Reminiscence group promoted stronger cohesiveness, and fostered patient accessibility to therapeutic intervention.	P
Matteson, M.A., & Munsat, E.M. (1982). Group reminiscing therapy with elderly clients. _Issues In Mental Health Nursing_, 4(3), 177-189.	N=7. Age 75-85 men and women in intermediate care facility. Six categorized as mildly to severely depressed. One non-depressed. Eight weekly sessions of 30 minutes. Two leaders at each session.	Goals were met though only partially in some instances. Participants appeared to become more socially active. This group study was very difficult for leaders physically and emotionally and it would be beneficial to use collaborative leadership model for mutual support and encouragement.	NE
Parsons, C.L. (1986). Group reminiscence therapy and levels of depression in the elderly. _Journal of Nurse Practitioner_, 11(3), 68-76.	N=6 Females. Does group reminiscence have an effect on depression? Intervention of six weeks of structured reminiscence topics.	Levels of depression did decrease in all subjects. Reminiscence increased. Social interaction could play a role in the findings.	P

*P = Positive Outcome; N = Negative Outcome; NE = Nonevaluative

38

Reference	Description	Findings	Outcome
Perrotta, P., & Meacham, J.A. (1982). Can a reminiscing intervention alter depression and self-esteem? International Journal on Aging and Human Development, 14(1), 23-30.	N=21 community residents placed in groups of 7. Mean Age=77. Structural reminiscence intervention of 5 weeks, 45 minutes per week.	Reminiscence was not found to be an effective short-term therapeutic intervention. Neither depression nor self-esteem were affected.	N
Orten, J.D., Allen, M., & Cook, J. (1989). Reminiscence groups with confused nursing center residents: An experimental study. Social Work in Health Care, 14(1), 73-86.	N=56. Age 58-101. Mean of 82.6. Nursing home residents broken down into 6 groups: 3 experimental and 3 control. Met for 45 minutes a week for 16 weeks. Group discussion used to determine social behavior.	Results were varied in experimental groups. Suggest that skilled leadership in group discussion is useful.	NE
Rattenbury, C., & Stones, M.J. (1989). A controlled evaluation of reminiscence and current topics discussion groups in a nursing home context. The Gerontologist, 29(6), 768-771.	N=24. Average age in each group 85, 83, and 87. Nursing home residents. A pre-post design over 8 weeks was used. Topics by group reminiscence, current events, control group.	Reminiscence and current events groups showed greater psychological well-being.	P
Scates, S.K.II, Randolph, D.L., Gutsch, K., & Knight, H.V. (1986). Effects of cognitive behavioral, reminiscence, and activity treatments on life satisfaction and anxiety in the elderly. International Journal on Aging and Human Development, 22(2), 141-146.	N=50. N=17 In reminiscence setting. N=16 In Cognitive behavioral. N=17 In activities. Life Satisfaction, state anxiety and trait anxiety were studied. Six one-hour sessions for three weeks.	Reminiscence may be related to a decrease in state anxiety. Results not significant, but reminiscence group improved more than others.	P

*P = Positive Outcome; N = Negative Outcome; NE = Nonevaluative

Reports (Individual)

Article	Study Variables	Findings	*
Allen, C., & Bennett, A. (1984). Healing memories. Nursing Mirror, 158(15), vi-vii.	Benefits of reminiscing in elderly.	Reminiscing is normal, healthy, and can be encouraged.	P
Asnes, D.P. (1983). Psychotherapy of the elderly: The life validation approach in psychotherapy with elderly patients. Journal of Geriatric Psychiatry, 16(1), 87-97.	Reports the use of life validation in therapy which is a combination of Erikson's and Butler's work as well as historical events.	Requires more active participation of therapist than usual life review. Most often well received.	P
Babb de Ramon, P. (1983). The final task: Life review for the dying patient. American Journal of Nursing, 13(2), 44, 46-49.	Value and objectives of nurses using life review with dying patients.	It is a means of helping patient end life with peace of mind.	P
Baum, W. (1980). Therapeutic value of oral history. International Journal of Aging and Human Development, 12(1), 49-53.	Method of collection of oral history.	Therapeutic value of oral history is related to how vigorous a historical effort it is.	P
Beaton, S.R. (1980). Reminiscence in old age. Nursing Forum, 19(3), 271-283.	Report on reminiscence and implications for nursing.	The functions of reminiscence: validating, integrating, guiding, and connecting can enrich the data gathering process.	NE
Butler, R.N. (1980). An unrecognized bonanza. International Journal of Aging and Human Development, 12(1), 35-38.	Report on value of doctors taking comprehensive oral histories from patients.	Taking time to attentively listen to reflections of past will advance understanding of human aging and expand repertoire of mechanisms useful in clinical practice.	P
Butler, R.N. (1974). Successful aging and the role of the life review. Journal of the American Geriatrics Society, 22(12), 529-535.	Report on the role of life review.	Life review and life cycle group therapy are two forms of useful psychotherapy to older adults.	P

*P = Positive Outcome; N = Negative Outcome; NE = Nonevaluative

Reference	Description	Outcome	Rating
Butler, R.N. (1963). The life review: An interpretation of reminiscence in the aged. Psychiatry, 26, 65-76.	Report on the presence of life review in elderly clients.	The author perceives life review as a natural, universal mental occurrence which is conscious.	NE
Chubon, S. (1980). A novel approach to the process of life review. Journal of Gerontological Nursing, 6(9), 543-546.	Report on a patient with end-stage renal disease who had life review with help of fiction.	Fictional life stories can aide those with similar life histories to life review.	P
Detzner, D.F. (1981). Models and content implications: Teaching life review to the introductory student. Gerontology and Geriatrics Education, 2(2), 119-122.	Report on life review assignment given to students in an introductory course in sociocultural gerontology.	Technique for life review is easily learned and proves beneficial for the student and the person interviewed.	P
Eisenberg, M. (1981). Life review and life preview. International Forum of Logo Therapy, 4(1), 49-51.	Report on use of logo therapy.	Provides an additional tool to enhance life review.	P
Greene, R. (1983). Life review: A technique for clarifying family roles in adulthood. Clinical Gerontologist, 1, 59-67.	Case studies discussing life review as an adaptive mechanism for role change within families.	Practitioner is key to using reminiscing to the adaptational advantage of the client.	P
Haight, B.K., & Olson, M. (1989). Teaching home health aids the use of life review. Journal of Nursing Staff Development, 5(1), 11-16.	Report on a class of life review for nursing home aids.	Life review does not influence attitudes toward the elderly, but was shown to be successful in teaching health aids.	P
Hamner. M.L. (1984). Insight, reminiscence, denial, projection: Coping mechanisms of the aged. Journal of Gerontological Nursing, 10(2), 66-81.	Report on insight, reminiscence, denial and projection as coping mechanisms.	Reminiscence can be used to help the elderly to maintain and/or achieve integrity.	P
Harris, R., & Harris S. (1980). Therapeutic uses of oral history techniques in medicine. International Journal of Aging and Human Development 12(1), 27-34.	Report on use of oral history technique in clinical medicine.	This technique adds a new approach to inner therapeutic healing process and may provide unexpected answers.	P

*P = Positive Outcome; N = Negative Outcome; NE = Nonevaluative

Article	Study Variables	Findings	*
Hasselkeis, B.R. (1982). Use of a monthly newsletter for life review: Case illustration. Physical and Occupational Therapy in Geriatrics, 2(1), 53-55.	Report on an induced life review with 81 year-old war veteran in a nursing home.	Provided renewed sense of self-worth and connection with the outside world.	P
Hauseman, C.P. (1980). Life review therapy. Journal of Gerontological Social Work, 3(2), 31-37.	Clinical case study using life review.	Life review therapy is one modality useful in helping the elderly achieve ego integrity.	P
Holzberg, C.S. (1984). Anthropology, life histories, and the aged: The Toronto Baycrest Centre. International Journal of Aging and Human Development, 18(4), 255-275.	Anthropologist reports project in Canada with 25 Jewish women, ages 75-90, recording their life's stories.	Project raised self-esteem and self-worth and gave participants a new identity. Also, recorded cultural and non-stereotypical differences in Jewish emigres to Canada.	P
Kaminsky, M. (1978). Pictures from the past: The uses of reminiscence in casework with the elderly. Journal of Gerontological Social Work, 1(1), 19-32.	Discussion of diagnostic and treatment implications of reminiscence.	Gives an accurate assessment of client's psychosocial problems and gives four ways in which reminiscence is effective in coping with the problems of old age.	P
Keddy, B.A. (1988). Getting to know you: The benefits of oral histories. Geriatric Nursing, May-Jun, 170-171.	Describes the benefit of oral histories to the historian and to the listener.	Historian found their own lives interesting and fascinating.	P
King, K.S. (1982). Reminiscing psychotherapy with aging people. Journal of Psychosocial Nursing and Mental Health Service, 20(2), 21-25.	Report on reminiscence.	Reminising begins at approximately age 10. In the elderly, it aids in personal and social growth.	P
Lewis, C.N. (1973). The adaptive value of reminiscing in old age. Journal of Geriatric Psychiatry, 6, 117-121.	Report on reminiscing as coping mechanism.	Reminiscing is viewed in two ways; 1) interest are redirected inward to accomplish review, 2) extended grief reaction of life loss.	NE

*P = Positive Outcome; N = Negative Outcome; NE = Nonevaluative

Citation	Description	Outcome[*]
Lewis, M.I., & Butler, R.N. (1974). Life review therapy: Putting memories to work in individual and group psychotherapy. Geriatrics, 29(11), 165-173.	Report on experiments with life review in individual and group therapy.	P
Liton, J., & Olstein, S.C. (1969). Therapeutic aspects of reminiscence. Social Casework, 5(May, Vol 50), 263-268.	Case studies of four senile elderly patients reminiscing with a social worker.	P
McMordie, W.R., & Blom, S. (1979). Life review therapy: Psychotherapy for the elderly. Perspectives in Psychiatric Care, 17, 162-166.	Report on Life Review.	NE
Mintz, S.W. (1979). The anthropological interview and the life history. Oral History Review, 18-26.	Report on life histories.	NE
Myerhoff, B.G., & Tufte, V. (1975). Life history as integration: An essay on an experiential model. The Gerontologist, 15, 541-543.	Anthropology students conducted case studies by obtaining life histories.	P
Nicholl, G. (1984-1985). The life review in five short stories about characters facing death. Omega, 15(1), 85-96.	Report of five modern short stories about people facing death, illustrating acceptance and the use of the life review.	N
Perschbacher, R. (1984). An application of reminiscence in an activity setting. The Gerontologist, 24(4), 343-345.	Report on a program of the elderly in a long-term care setting using their life experience to teach a history class to 3rd graders.	P
Pickrel, J. (1989). Tell me your story: Using life review in counseling the terminally ill. Death Studies, 13(2), 127-135.	Report on various forms of life review in dealing with terminally ill patients of all ages.	P

*P = Positive Outcome; N = Negative Outcome; NE = Nonevaluative

43

Reports (Individual) (Cont'd)

Article	Study Variables	Findings	*
Pincus, A. (1970). Reminiscence in aging and its implication for social work practice. Social Work, 47-53.	Review of prior work on reminiscing related to social work practice.	Possible adaptive mechanism for use by social workers.	NE
Ryden, M.B. (1981). Nursing intervention in support of reminiscence. Journal of Gerontological Nursing, 7(8), 461–463.	Report on reminiscence.	Developmental age criterion for intervention use. Open ended questions trigger reminiscence, reinforce reminiscence, avoid ridicule and help in dealing with feelings.	NE
Safier, G. (1976). Oral life history with the elderly. Journal of Gerontological Nursing, 2(5), 17-23.	Clinical case studies on use of oral histories.	Clients stated they felt better after oral histories. Gives client opportunity to organize thoughts, feelings, and experiences in a meaningful way.	P
Schnase, R.C. (1982). Therapeutic reminiscence in elderly patients. The Journal of Nursing Care, (2), 15-17.	Report on reminiscence.	Innovative programs could be designed for meaningful reminiscence in any institutional setting.	P
Sullivan, C.A. (1982). Life review: A functional view of reminiscence. Physical and Occupational Therapy in Geriatrics, 2(1), 39-52.	Discusses functions and benefits of reminiscence as well as responsibility of the therapist using the modality.	Reminiscence needs to be seen as successful adaptation to old age, not senility, and used by therapists for more successful treatment.	P
Viney, L.L., Benjamin, Y.N., & Preston, C. (1989). Mourning and reminiscence: Parallel psychotherapeutic processes for elderly people. International Journal of Aging and Human Development, 28(4), 239-249.	Report on using personal construct theory as a means to explain mourning and reminiscence in the elderly.	By exploring personal constructs, the bereaved can face the implications of loss, reestablish identity, and reevaluate future directions.	P

*P = Positive Outcome; N = Negative Outcome; NE = Nonevaluative

Citation	Description	Outcome*
Weiner, M.B. (1979). Caring for the elderly: Mental health in the elderly. The Journal of Nursing Care, 12(6), 34.	Report on understanding aging process in elderly patient.	Need to understand inner/outer person to best help them and this can be done by listening to them reminisce on past life and past ways of coping.	P
Wysocki, M.R. (1983). Life review for the elderly patient. American Journal of Nursing, (2), 46-49.	Clinical case studies using life review with dying patients.	Life review offers the dying patient an opportunity to deal with unfinished business.	P
Zeiger, B.L. (1976). Life review in art therapy with the aged. American Journal of Art Therapy, 15, 47-50.	Two patient experiences in recalling memories through art.	Positive way to enhance memory and allow patients to visualize past.	P

*P = Positive Outcome; N = Negative Outcome; NE = Nonevaluative

45

Reports (Group)

Article	Study Variables	Findings	*
Baker, N.J. (1985). Reminiscing in group therapy for self-worth. Journal of Gerontological Nursing, 11(7), 21-24.	Report on a six-week period of reminiscence group therapy with the mentally impaired.	Improvement in verbal interaction, eye contact, touching and smiling, and participation.	P
Burnside, I., Rodriguez, A., & Trevino, E. (1989). Reminiscence therapy offers many advantages. Provider, 15(8), 17-19.	Report on developing a group for reminiscing. The how to's and how not's are discussed.	Reminiscence group therapy can be a positive experience; helps to improve the quality of life.	P
Busch, C.D. (1984). Common themes in group psychotherapy with older adult nursing home residents: A review of selected literature. Clinical Gerontologist, 2(3), 25-38.	Selected report of literature pertaining to older adult group psychotherapy. Includes analysis of life review.	There are four main themes in older adult group psychotherapy: Social Interaction, Orientation of Group Participants to Reality, Life Review Process, and Remotivation.	NE
Byrne, L.A. (1982). Music therapy and reminiscence: A case study. Clinical Gerontologist, 1(1), 76-77.	Listening to music combined with reminiscence groups at a senior day care center.	One person was tested with the GDS with a pretest of 17 decreasing to a post-test of 8 at end of seven sessions.	P
Ebersole, P. (1976). Problems of group reminiscing with the institutionalized aged. Journal of Gerontological Nursing, 2(6), 23-27.	Report of aged group problems.	Reported problems were hopelessness, helplessness, caretaker's needs, timing, sensory deprivation, and personality conflicts.	NE
Harwood, K.J. (1989). The effects of an occupational therapy reminiscence group: A single case study. Physical and Occupational Therapy in Geriatrics, 7(4), 43-57.	Case study of a 92 year old female schizophrenic in interaction with group therapy.	Subject became more spontaneous. Shared significant events of her life.	P
Kibbee, P.E., & Lackey, D.S. (1982). The past as therapy: An experience in an acute setting. Journal of Practical Nursing, 32(9), 29-31.	Group=6 - 8. Group approach to reminiscence and life review with acute geriatric patients in a psychiatric inpatient setting.	Can foster personal growth and development in this population.	P

*P = Positive Outcome; N = Negative Outcome; NE = Nonevaluative

46

Citation	Description	Outcome
Lowenthal, R.I., & Marrazzo, R.A. (1990). Milestoning: Evoking memories for resocialization through group reminiscence. _The Gerontologist_, 30(2), 269-272.	Report on the value of milestoning (a directional and selective technique biased toward positive experiences in life) with disturbed elderly people.	Milestoning can be used effectively on mental hospital residents in the retrieval of positive memories. P
Osborn, C.L. (1989). Reminiscence: When the past eases the present. _The Journal of Gerontological Nursing_, 15(10), 6-12.	Report on how to set up and run a group for reminiscing.	Can be positive means for fostering coping skills and behaviors in the elderly. P
Price, C. (1983). Heritage: A program design for reminiscence. _Activities, Adaptation, and Aging_, 3(3), 47-52.	A program development in a 120-bed intermediate and skilled care facility with reminiscing for stimulating group activity rather than for individual counseling.	Reminiscence within a structured program provides a meaningful activity at individual, group and facility levels. P

*P = Positive Outcome; N = Negative Outcome; NE = Nonevaluative

47

Reviews and Discussions

Article	Study Variables	Findings	*
Hughston, G.A., & Merriam, S.B. (1982). Reminiscence: A non-formal technique for improving cognitive functioning in the aged. International Journal of Aging and Human Development, 15(2), 139-149.	Reviewed all work in reminiscing.	Concept of reminiscence and its relationship to other affective processes was not clearly delineated. Need exploratory theory building methodology.	NE
Kiernat, J.M. (1984). Retrospection as a life span concept. Physical and Occupational Therapy in Geriatrics, 3(2), 35-48.	Review of literature on daydreaming about the past, reminiscing, and the life review.	Retrospection is complex and involved, and research regarding it is in an infancy state.	NE
Kovach, C.R. (1989). Promise and problems in reminiscence research. The Journal of Gerontological Nursing, 16(4), 10-14.	A review of literature on reminiscence research.	Theoretical frameworks are weak when used and methodology is generally weak. Reminiscence must be more clearly defined. May be helpful in improving mood, self-esteem, and life satisfaction.	NE
LoGerfo, M. (1980-81). Three ways of reminiscence in theory and practice. International Journal of Aging and Human Development, 12(1), 39-48.	Theoretical analysis of literature on reminiscence.	Literature and practice suggest three distinct though overlapping categories of reminiscence; informative, evaluative, and obsessive.	NE
Molinari, V., & Reichlin, R.E. (1984-85). Life review reminiscence in the elderly: A review of the literature. International Journal of Aging and Human Development, 20(2), 81-92.	Reviewed and evaluated work in past 20 years.	Need to separate life review from reminiscence, examine differences in samples as well as long-term effects and clarify interpersonal and intrapersonal reminiscence.	NE
Romaniuk, M. (1981). Reminiscence and the second half of life. Experimental Aging Research, 7(3), 315-336.	Review of reminiscence.	Suggests rigorous examination of the dimensions of reminiscence and the study of the relationships of reminiscence to adaptation.	NE
Webster, J.D., & Young, R.A. (1988). Process variables of the life review: Counseling implications. International Journal of Aging and Human Development, 26(4), 315-232.	Discusses the process variables in life review identified as recall evaluation and synthesis. Talks about implications for counseling.	Well done report of the process of life review. Showing the process of life review to be much different from other forms of reminiscing.	P

*P = Positive Outcome; N = Negative Outcome; NE = Nonevaluative

48

REFERENCES

1. J. E. Birren, The Best of All Stories, *Psychology Today, 21*:5, pp. 91-92, 1987.
2. M. Kaminsky, *The Uses of Reminiscence: New Ways of Working with Older Adults,* Haworth Press, New York, 1984.
3. P. G. Coleman, *Ageing and Reminiscence Processes: Social and Clinical Implications,* J. Wiley and Sons, New York, 1986.
4. R. N. Butler, The Life Review: An Interpretation of Reminiscence in the Aged, *Psychiatry, 26,* pp. 65-76, 1963.
5. C. P. Hausman, Life Review Therapy, *Journal of Gerontological Social Work, 3*:2, pp. 31-37, 1980.
6. S. Chubon, A Novel Approach to the Process of Life Review, *Journal of Gerontological Nursing, 6*:9, pp. 543-546, 1980.
7. P. Babb de Ramon, The Final Task: Life Review for the Dying Patient, *American Journal of Nursing, 13*:2, pp. 44, 46-49, 1983.
8. R. N. Butler, Successful Aging and the Role of the Life Review, *Journal of the American Geriatrics Society, 22*:12, pp. 529-535, 1974.
9. R. N. Butler, An Unrecognized Bonanza, *International Journal of Aging and Human Development, 12*:1, pp. 35-38, 1980.
10. S. R. Beaton, Reminiscence in Old Age, *Nursing Forum, 19*:3, pp. 271-283, 1980.
11. C. Allen and A. Bennett, Healing Memories, *Nursing Mirror, 158*:15, pp. vi-vii, 1984.
12. W. Baum, Therapeutic Value of Oral History, *International Journal of Aging and Human Development, 12*:1, pp. 49-53, 1980.
13. R. Greene, Life Review: A Technique for Clarifying Family Roles in Adulthood, *Clinical Gerontologist, 1,* pp. 59-67, 1983.
14. M. L. Hamner, Insight, Reminiscence, Denial, Projection: Coping Mechanisms of the Aged, *Journal of Gerontological Nursing, 10*:2, pp. 66-81, 1984.
15. D. F. Detzner, Models and Content Implications: Teaching Life Review to the Introductory Student, *Gerontology and Geriatrics Education, 2*:2, pp. 119-122, 1981.
16. C. S. Holzberg, Anthropology, Life History, and the Aged: The Toronto Baycrest Centre, *International Journal of Aging and Human Development, 18*:4, pp. 255-275, 1983-1984.
17. B. A. Keddy, Getting to Know You: The Benefits of Oral Histories, *Geriatric Nursing,* pp. 170-171, May-June, 1988.
18. S. W. Mintz, The Anthropological Interview and the Life History, *Oral History Review,* pp. 18-26, 1979.
19. B. G. Myerhoff and V. Tufte, Life History as Integration: An Essay on an Experiential Model, *The Gerontologist, 15,* pp. 541-543, 1975.
20. M. Eisenberg, Life Review and Life Preview, *Interactional Forum of Logo Therapy, 4*:1, pp. 49-51, 1981.
21. R. Perschbacher, An Application of Reminiscence in an Activity Setting, *The Gerontologist, 24*:4, pp. 343-345, 1984.
22. B. L. Zeiger, Life Review in Art Therapy with the Aged, *American Journal of Art Therapy, 15,* pp. 47-50, 1976.
23. P. Ebersole, Problems of Group Reminiscing with the Institutionalized Aged, *Journal of Gerontological Nursing, 2*:6, pp. 23-27, 1976.

24. N. J. Baker, Reminiscing in Group Therapy for Self-Worth, *Journal of Gerontological Nursing, 11*:7, pp. 21-24, 1985.
25. C. Price, Heritage: A Program Design for Reminiscence, *Activities, Adaptation, and Aging, 3*:3, pp. 47-52, 1983.
26. C. D. Busch, Common Themes in Group Psychotherapy with Older Adult Nursing Home Residents: A Review of Selected Literature, *Clinical Gerontologist, 2*:3, pp. 25-38, 1984.
27. G. Nicholl, The Life Review in Five Short Stories about Characters Facing Death, *Omega, 15*:1, pp. 85-96, 1984-85.
28. M. Romaniuk and J. Romaniuk, Looking Back: An Analysis of Reminiscence Functions and Triggers, *Experimental Aging Research, 1*:4, pp. 477-489, 1981.
29. G. A. Hughston and S. B. Merriam, Reminiscence: A Non-formal Technique for Improving Cognitive Functioning in the Aged, *International Journal of Aging and Human Development, 15*:2, pp. 139-149, 1982.
30. J. M. Kiernat, Retrospection as a Life Span Concept, *Physical and Occupational Therapy in Geriatrics, 3*:2, pp. 35-48, 1984.
31. V. Molinari and R. E. Reichlin, Life Review Reminiscence in the Elderly: A Review of the Literature, *International Journal of Aging and Human Development, 20*:2, pp. 81-92, 1984-85.
32. C. R. Kovach, Promise and Problems in Reminiscence Research, *The Journal of Gerontological Nursing, 16*:4, pp. 10-14, 1989.
33. M. LoGerfo, Three Ways of Reminiscence in Theory and Practice, *International Journal of Aging and Human Development, 12*:1, pp. 39-48, 1980-81.
34. J. D. Webster and R. A. Young, Process Variables of the Life Review: Counseling Implications, *International Journal of Aging and Human Development, 26*:4, pp. 315-232, 1988.
35. A. W. McMahon and P. J. Rhudick, Reminiscing: Adaptational Significance in the Aged, *Archives of General Psychiatry, 10*, pp. 292-298, May 1964.
36. M. A. Lieberman and G. M. Falk, The Remembered Past as a Source of Data for Research on the Life Cycle, *The Journal of Aging and Human Development, 14*, pp. 132-141, 1971.
37. W. Boylin, S. K. Gordon, and M. F. Nehrke, Reminiscing and Ego Integrity in Institutionalized Elderly Males, *The Gerontologist, 16*:2, pp. 118-124, 1976.
38. P. G. Coleman, Measuring Reminiscence Characteristics from Conversation as Adaptive Features of Old Age, *International Journal of Aging and Human Development, 5*:3, pp. 281-294, 1974.
39. R. J. Havighurst and R. Glasser, An Exploratory Study of Reminiscence, *Journal of Gerontology, 27*:2, pp. 245-253, 1972.
40. C. N. Lewis, Reminiscing and Self-Concept in Old Age, *Journal of Gerontology, 26*:2, pp. 240-243, 1971.
41. J. M. Kiernat, The Use of Life Review Activity with Confused Nursing Home Residents, *The American Journal of Occupational Therapy, 33*:5, pp. 306-310, 1979.
42. L. M. Dietsche, Know Your Community Resources: Facilitating the Life Review through Group Reminiscences, *Journal of Gerontological Nursing, 5*:4, pp. 43-46, 1979.

43. C. A. Emlet, Reminiscence: A Psychological Approach to Institutionalized Aged, *American Health Care Association Journal, 5*:5, pp. 19, 22, September 1979.
44. B. K. Haight, The Therapeutic Role of the Life Review in the Elderly, *Academic Psychology Bulletin, 6,* pp. 287-289, 1984.
45. B. K. Haight, The Therapeutic Role of a Structured Life Review Process in Homebound Elderly Subjects, *Journal of Gerontology, 43*:2, pp. 40-44, 1988.
46. B. E. Hedgepeth and D. Hale, Effect of a Positive Reminiscing Intervention on Affect, Expectancy, and Performance, *Psychological Reports, 53,* pp. 867-870, 1983.
47. P. L. Brennan and L. D. Steinberg, Is Reminiscence Adaptive? Relations among Social Activity Level, Reminiscence, and Morale, *International Journal of Aging and Human Development, 18*:2, pp. 99-109, 1984.
48. C. M. Carlson, Reminiscing: Toward Achieving Ego Integrity in Old Age, *Journal of Contemporary Social Work, 2,* pp. 81-89, 1984.
49. R. D. Fallot, The Impact on Mood of Verbal Reminiscing in Later Adulthood, *International Journal of Aging and Human Development, 10*:4, pp. 385-400, 1980.
50. E. M. Job, Retrospective Life Span Analysis: A Method for Studying Extreme Old Age, *Journal of Gerontology, 38*:3, pp. 369-374, 1983.
51. L. Bramwell, Use of the Life History in Pattern Identification and Health Promotion, *Advances in Nursing Science, 7*:1, pp. 37-44, 1984.
52. M. Romaniuk, Reminiscence and the Second Half of Life, *Experimental Aging Research, 7*:3, pp. 315-336, 1981.
53. B. M. Wright and R. B. Payne, Effects of Aging on Sex Differences in Psychomotor Reminiscence and Proficiency, *Journal of Gerontology, 40*:2, pp. 179-184, 1985.
54. J. Lesser, L. W. Lazarus, R. Frankl, and S. Havasg, Reminiscence Group Therapy with Psychotic Geriatric Inpatients, *The Gerontologist, 21*:3, pp. 291-296, 1981.
55. M. A. Matteson and E. M. Munsat, Group Reminiscing Therapy with Elderly Clients, *Issues in Mental Health Nursing, 4*:3, pp. 177-189, 1982.
56. C. L. Parsons, Group Reminiscence Therapy and Levels of Depression in the Elderly, *Journal of Nurse Practitioner, 11*:3, pp. 68-76, 1986.
57. C. Bergland, The Life Review Process in Geriatric Art Therapy: A Pilot Study, *The Arts in Psychotherapy, 9,* pp. 121-130, 1982.
58. J. M. Lappe, Reminiscing: The Life Review Therapy, *Journal of Gerontological Nursing, 13*:4, pp. 12-16, 1987.
59. B. Ingersoll and L. Goodman, History Comes Alive: Facilitating Reminiscence in a Group of Institutionalized Elderly, *Journal of Gerontological Social Work, 2*:4, pp. 305-319, 1980.
60. S. K. H. Scates, D. L. Randolph, K. Gutsch, and H. V. Knight, Effects of Cognitive Behavioral, Reminiscence, and Activity Treatments on Life Satisfaction and Anxiety in the Elderly, *International Journal of Aging and Human Development, 22*:2, pp. 141-146, 1986.
61. R. Georgemiller and H. Maloney, Group Life Review and Denial of Death, *Clinical Gerontologist, 2*:4, pp. 37-49, 1984.
62. A. N. Goldwasser, S. M. Auerbach, and S. W. Harkins, Cognitive, Affective, and Behavioral Effects of Reminiscence Group Therapy on Demented Elderly, *International Journal of Aging and Human Development, 25*:3, pp. 209-222, 1987.

63. F. J. Berghorn and D. E. Schafer, Reminiscence Intervention in Nursing Homes: What and Who Changes, *International Journal of Aging and Human Development, 24*:2, pp. 113-127, 1987.
64. P. Perrotta and J. A. Meacham, Can a Reminiscing Intervention Alter Depression and Self-Esteem? *International Journal of Aging and Human Development, 14*:1, pp. 23-30, 1982.

Chapter 3

REMINISCENCE, ADAPTATION, AND SOCIAL CONTEXT IN OLD AGE

Debra David

The adaptiveness of reminiscence in old age has been the subject of considerable debate, but research on this issue has produced mixed results. One reason for inconsistent findings may be the failure to consider social variables shaping the content and context of the act of reminiscing. The results of an exploratory study of social correlates of reminiscence and adaptation in old age supports this contention. The relationship between various aspects of the contents and process of memories and current life satisfaction, self-esteem, and social integration revealed strikingly different patterns among single (never-married) women, widowed women, and widowed men.

Early psychoanalytic writings held that personal memories in old age were regressive [1, 2]; studies by Reichard [3] and Clark and Anderson [4] linked high past orientation with poor adaptation, supporting this negative view. Other writers suggested that reminiscence may serve a variety of adaptive functions. Butler's well-known formulation of the life review proposes that reminiscence facilitates the reconciliation of past conflicts [5]. Coleman found support for this life review function only among respondents who reported dissatisfaction with the past [6]. Erikson views reminiscence as central to the task of developing ego integrity in old age [7]; research by Boylin, et al. [8] supports Erikson. Lieberman and Falk [9] and Chiriboga and Gigy [10] report that reminiscing is associated with coping with transitions. Miller and Lieberman [11], Havighurst and Glaser [12], Grunes [13], and Lieberman and Tobin [14] link reminiscing with comfort and gratification. The role of reminiscence in the maintenance or enhancement of the self-image has been discussed by Lewis [15], Castelnuovo-Tedesco [16], Grunes [13], Revere and Tobin [17], and Lieberman and Tobin [14] . Several writers, including McMahon and Rhudick [18], Pincus [19], Coleman [6], and Myerhoff [20], suggested that reminiscence with others may promote social exchange or integration.

Inability to reminisce has been linked to depression by McMahon and Rhudick [18] and to poor adaptation to relocation by Miller and Lieberman [11]. Several authors including Butler [5], McMahon and Rhudick [18], Postema [21], LoGerfo [22], and Molinari and Reichlin [23], noted that the adaptiveness or reminiscence may be variable depending on its quality, type, or setting.

Recent reviews of the literature on reminiscence in old age agree that empirical evidence on its adaptiveness in old age is inconclusive [14, 22-24]. Research studies have been exploratory and have used differing methods and operational definitions. Summarizing their own work and the work of others, Lieberman and Tobin concluded that they were:

> . . . unable to determine whether . . . there are any universal processes involving reminiscence in old age; or . . . whether there are systematic and predictable differences in the use of the past among individuals [14, p. 310].

SOCIAL CONTEXT AND REMINISCENCE

In his seminal article on memory and childhood amnesia, psychiatrist Schachtel argued that memory, especially "autobiographical memory" of past experience, is highly conventionalized and social:

> One might say that, while all human experience, perception, and thought are eminently social—that is, determined by socially pervailing ways of experiencing, perceiving, and thinking—memory is even more socialized, to an even higher degree dependent on the commonly accepted categories of what and how one remembers [25, p. 291] .

A number of psychologists have developed a "contextual" model of memory that emphasizes the dialectical relationship between personal and social determinants of memory [26-30].

Sociologists Berger and Luckmann saw the recollection of autobiographical experience as reciprocally related to social structure [31]. On one hand, the individual makes sense of personal experiences in terms of society's symbolic universe, which gives them meaning and order; on the other hand, individual subjective biography is the original source of the symbolic universe. Memories shared with others and legitimated by consensus provide the basis for the emergence of the institutionalized conception of social reality.

Although these works are cited widely in their respective disciplines, their insights have not been tested systematically, perhaps because they do not explicitly use the term "reminiscence." They do, however, provide theoretical support for including social variables in examining reminiscence in old age.

Empirical findings on social variability of reminiscence in old age have been noted in several studies. Lieberman and Falk [9] found that respondents on a waiting list for admission to an old-age home reminisced more extensively than respondents residing in more stable situations in the community or the old-age home, but they found no relationship between reminiscence and subsequent adaptation. Tobin found more themes of loss in the earliest memories of the institutionalized respondents of the same sample [32]. Postema reported that men residing in the community reminisced more extensively and more positively than those in institutions [21]. In their review of research on life-review reminiscence in old age, Moliriari and Reichlin suggested that reminiscence may be positive for community elders, but that "institutionalized individuals would be seen as lacking the opportunity to resolve the conflict that arises in the course of reminiscence given that their environment tends to reflect a failure of autonomy" [23, p. 86]. Several studies reported sex differences in theme, with women's memories focusing more on others and men's on self [6, 12, 33]. Coleman also found age-related differences between old men and women in the frequency of "storytelling" memories [6]. Among men, age was positively related to storytelling; among women, the opposite was true.

In contrast to findings linking social factors with reminiscence in old age, other studies failed to fmd expected associations. Coleman found no relationship between reminiscence and either role loss or environmental change [6]. Oliveira reported no differences in memories by sex or level of social activity [34].

The interaction between social factors, reminiscence, and adaptation has not been examined directly in previous work. The research described below is an effort to explore that interaction.

RESEARCH FOCUS AND DESIGN

Based on dialectical models of memory, the present study sought to identify social variations in the relationship between reminiscence and adaptation. It was based on further analysis of data collected for a broader study of socially-shaped variations in the content, process, and relationship to the present of reminiscence [35]. Because of-the virtual absence of similar studies, the purpose was to generate, rather than test, hypotheses.

Reminiscence was defined as the conscious recall of autobiographical experiences. It was viewed as a *social act in the present*, related to social factors in the person's current life and to the interview situation itself.

The sample was comprised of forty-three residents of two sectarian retirement communities in northeastern Ohio, including fourteen single women, sixteen widowed women, and twelve widowed men. All respondents were Protestant, native-born of European lineage, high school graduates, from the middle class, and able to function independently. Ages ranged from sixty-eight to ninety-five.

During taped interviews, respondents were asked to describe "three memories that you've been thinking about lately." The narration was not interrupted except for factual clarification. An informal, conversational tone was maintained. The intent was to solicit memories without any specific direction so that respondents would select ones which were personally salient and spontaneous. This approach to studying reminiscence is less naturalistic than participant observation or completely unstructured interviews, but preferable to standardized questions for particular kinds of memories or structured life histories used by many previous researchers.

Following the memories, respondents were asked more specific, semistructured questions about their memories and experiences of reminiscing. Information was also obtained on current activities. The next section explored social involvement, which was viewed as a potentially salient correlate of both reminiscence and adaptation. Following sections covered adaptation (including two structured scales on life satisfaction and self-esteem, described below) and socio-demographic information.

Measures

Eight ordinal scales were constructed to assess key dimensions of content and process for each memory:

1. Evaluation—a high score reflects the respondent's positive assessment of both the remembered experience and his/her own role in it;
2. Feelings—a high score indicates high past and current satisfaction with the memory;
3. Victimization—this measure rates the degree to which a memory involves loss that is blamed on external causes;
4. Importance of others—a high score means that the respondent emphasized relatedness to others in the memory;
5. Self-focus—this scale measures the extent to which the memory is about the respondent rather than others;
6. Elaboration—a high score indicates extensive detail and digression in recounting the memory;
7. Reviewing—this scale rates the extent to which the respondent spontaneously made evaluative comments in recounting the memory; and
8. Connection to present—a high score means that the respondent reported meaningful links between the memory and his/her current experience.

Three independent coders rated the memories; differences were reconciled by discussion. Scores were summed for the three memories.

In addition to the memory scales, the analysis included three items which asked respondents to rate their life overall (life evaluation), enjoyment of reminiscing alone (enjoyment alone), and enjoyment with others (enjoyment with others).

Social involvement was measured by ten items rating contact and satisfaction with friends, neighbors, formal groups, and family. The eight items on friends, neighbors, and groups were sufficiently similar in their relationship to reminiscence to combine into a single index of peer contact. The two family items comprised an index of family contact.

Causal linkages between reminiscence, adaptation, and social involvement were not specified and could not be directly tested with this exploratory research design.

RESULTS

Reminiscence and Adaptation Scores across Subgroup

Scores on the measures of reminiscence and adaptation were compared across single women, widowed women, and widowed men using the Mann-Whitney test—a nonparametric statistic appropriate for ordinal-level data and small samples. No significant differences were found on any scales except for life satisfaction. Single women had significantly higher life satisfaction scores than widowed men ($p > .05$).

Reminiscence and Adaptation within Subgroup

Associations between reminiscence and adaptation were computed separately for single women, widowed women, and widowed men using Kendall's tau-a nonparametric correlation measure appropriate for ordinal-level data and sample sizes as small as eleven. Results are presented in Table 1.

The strongest associations are found among the widowed women. As one might expect, memories with positive evaluations, low victimization, and meaningful connections to the present are related to high self-esteem. However, those widowed women whose memories minimize the importance of others and maximize self-focus and those who report not enjoying reminiscing with others also have high self esteem. Memories involving negative feelings and limited elaboration are related to high life satisfaction. Examination of the actual memories shows that widowed women with the highest life satisfaction and self-esteem tended to report a "short and sweet" experience or experiences which they reported as valuable but unpleasant. While the actual number of significant others mentioned did not differ from those mentioned by widowed men (and showed a trend toward positive association with life satisfaction), women with high adaptation scores generally saw themselves as central and in control of the situation; the opposite was true for poor adaptors. Widowed women with high adaptation scores were more likely than others to spontaneously comment that they seldom spend time thinking about the past in response to the interviewer's request for reminiscence.

In general, reminiscence and adaptation among the single women show similar patterns to those found among the widowed women. Elaboration of memories and feelings are, however, unrelated to adaptation scores for this group. Reviewing is

Table 1. Relationship between Reminiscence and Adaptation:
Total Sample and Subgroups
(Kendall's Tau Correlation)

Reminiscence Scale	Adaptation Scale	Group			
		Total (N = 43)	Single Women (N = 14)	Widowed Women (N = 16)	Widowed Men (N = 13)
Evaluation	Life satisfaction	.14	.12	.19	.24
	Self-esteem	.26**	.50**	.33*	.02
Feelings	Life satisfaction	-.13	.00	-.31*	.02
	Self-esteem	.14	.15	.20	-.09
Victimization	Life satisfaction	.00	.05	-.21	.32*
	Self-esteem	-.21*	-.24	-.40**	.02
Importance of Others	Life satisfaction	-.17*	-.33*	-.23	.14
	Self-esteem	.05	-.22	-.38**	.37*
Self-focus	Life satisfaction	.11	.02	.27	.12
	Self-esteem	.25**	.33*	.50**	.00
Elaboration	Life satisfaction	-.27**	.02	-.47**	-.09
	Self-esteem	.18*	.04	.00	.44**
Reviewing	Life satisfaction	-.16*	-.22	-.27	.03
	Self-esteem	-.11	-.35*	-.20	.24
Connection to Present	Life satisfaction	.20*	.23	.24	-.12
	Self-esteem	.24**	.55**	.40**	.02
Life evaluation	Life satisfaction	-.07	.03	.13	-.30
	Self-esteem	.03	.02	.00	-.10
Enjoyment alone	Life satisfaction	.01	.11	-.01	.08
	Self-esteem	.00	.00	-.22	.35
Enjoyment with Others	Life satisfaction	-.12	-.27	-.38**	.20
	Self-esteem	-.03	-.46**	-.19	.36

NOTE: Life satisfaction scores were missing for one single woman; self-esteem scores were missing for two widowed men.

* $p < .10 > .05$.

** $p < .05$.

negatively associated with self-esteem among single women (and shows trends in that direction among the widows). The most prevalent theme of the memories of the single women with high life satisfaction and self-esteem was of past personal or work challenges successfully mastered. These women appeared to experience considerable pleasure in recalling the past but not to be intensely absorbed in the process.

Few associations show statistical significance for the widowed men (partially due to the small sample size), but those few are in the opposite direction from those found among the women. High elaboration and high importance of others are related to high self-esteem, while victimization is associated with positive life satisfaction. High enjoyment of reminiscing alone and with others and negative life evaluation fall just short of significance as correlates of self-esteem or life satisfaction. Memories of men with high adaptation scores tended to focus on satisfactions and losses in past relationships with parents or wives; the feelings expressed were often bittersweet. These men seemed to be highly absorbed in experiencing and evaluating the past. They often gave extensive detail, idealized others, and were likely to digress.

Strong male/female differences can be found in the direction and strength of many of the relationships between reminiscence and adaptation. Most striking are differences for victimization, importance of others, elaboration, reviewing, and enjoyment with others, which are all negatively linked with life satisfaction and/or self-esteem for women but positively lillked with those measures for men. Self-focus, connection to present, and evaluations are strongly associated with self-esteem for women but not men. Enjoyment alone and a negative evaluation of one's life are correlated with adaptation among men but not women. These findings suggest sharp gender differences in the function of reminiscence in later life.

Reminiscence and Social Interaction

Single women had less family contact than the two widowed subgroups, but the subgroups were similar in level of peer contact. As with the adaptation measures, however, there were sharp differences in the correlations between social involvement—particularly peer contact—and reminiscence among the subgroups. The results are presented in Table 2.

Among the single women, high peer contact is correlated with positive evaluation and feelings, low victimization, high connection to present, positive life evaluation, and low enjoyment of reminiscing with others. High family contact is correlated with high elaboration and low self-focus. In sum, peer contact is associated with reminiscence patterns that are generally adaptive for women. Although family contact is unrelated to most reminiscence scales, it is associated with a negative pattern (low self-focus) and a "neutral" one (high elaboration).

High peer contact has a very different link to reminiscence among the widowed men. It is associated with negative evaluation and feelings, high victimization,

Table 2. Relationship between Reminiscence and Social Involvement:
Total Sample and Subgroups
(Kendall's Tau Correlation)

Reminiscence Scale	Social Involvement Scale	Group			
		Total (N = 43)	Single Women (N = 14)	Widowed Women (N = 16)	Widowed Men (N = 13)
Evaluation	Peer contact	.05	.48**	.08	-.35*
	Family contact	-.03	.13	.00	.04
Feelings	Peer contact	.11	.58**	.05	-.34*
	Family contact	.02	.07	.05	-.06
Victimization	Peer contact	-.07	-.31*	-.06	.29*
	Family contact	.07	.12	.09	.10
Importance of Others	Peer contact	-.05	-.16	-.28*	.33*
	Family contact	.14	-.06	.12	.18
Self-focus	Peer contact	.20*	.20	.33*	.10
	Family contact	-.15	-.32*	-.27*	.16
Elaboration	Peer contact	-.02	-.07	-.11	.42**
	Family contact	.10	.50**	-.05	-.22
Reviewing	Peer contact	.00	-.22	-.09	.35*
	Family contact	.06	-.05	.00	.25
Connection to Present	Peer contact	.00	.48**	.11	-.21
	Family contact	.14	.11	.05	-.18
Life Evaluation	Peer contact	-.08	.39*	.02	-.39**
	Family contact	.14	-.02	.09	-.02
Enjoyment alone	Peer contact	-.10	.06	-.31*	.09
	Family contact	-.05	.30	-.18	-.30
Enjoyment with Others	Peer contact	-.06	-.43*	-.30*	.45**
	Family contact	-.05	.02	.30*	-.16

* $p < .10 > .05$.
** $p < .05$.

importance of others, elaboration, reviewing, negative life evaluation, and high enjoyment of reminiscing with others. In almost every comparison with single women, peer contact has an *opposite* effect on memory among the widowed men. Family contact is unrelated to reminiscence. For widowed men, as for single women, peer contact is associated with gender-linked adaptive reminiscence patterns.

Neither peer nor family contact is strongly associated with reminiscence patterns among the widowed women. High peer contact is generally associated with adaptive memories, however, while family contact is either "neutral" or negative.

To summarize, high peer contact is associated with adaptive memories, particularly among the single women and widowed men, but the direction of the link between peer contact and memory is reversed between the sexes. Family ties are less likely to be linked with reminiscence, but tend to be neutral or maladaptive.

DISCUSSION

What might account for these striking differences across the subgroups? Several factors (not mutually exclusive) may be involved. The gender differences in the adaptativeness of reminiscence may be a reflection of *developmental changes in gender roles* that have been found by several researchers, including Gutmann [38], Lowenthal, et al. [33], Maas and Kuyper [39], Neugarten [40], and Turner [41]. For both sexes there appears to be a "return of the repressed," an increase in behaviors that were inhibited in early adulthood to fit socially expected gender-role norms in work and family. Gutmann attributes these developmental changes to the end of a "parental imperative." Projective data suggest that women become more assertive, egocentric, dominant, and unsentimental, and men become more affiliative, nurturant, religious, and expressive. Self-concepts of independence and assertiveness for women and of nurturance and sensitivity to others for men have been linked to positive adaptation.

The gender-role perspective would lead us to expect that the memories of older women would be more egocentric and less expressive, and the memories of older men would be more focused on others and more expressive. In this study, egocentricity may be related to self-focus and low importance given to others in memories; expressiveness may be related to elaboration, reviewing, and enjoyment of reminiscing. Although the subgroups did not differ in their distribution of scores on these scales, those individuals within subgroups who scored in the direction predicted by the gender-role perspective were better adapted. Single women were similar to widowed women although the associations were slightly weaker. The small differences between these two subgroups may simply be due to chance, but they are consistent with the expectation that gender-role changes would be smaller among women who did not become mothers. A larger, longitudinal research design would be necessary to examine this directly.

A more contemporaneous factor influencing reminiscence and adaptation may be the social composition of the retirement communities. The concept of "social homogeneity" suggests that the meaning of past and present life experiences is shaped by the extent to which a person shares similar characteristics with others and feels part of a community (see Blau [42], Gubruim [43], and Messer [44]). Present, in contrast with remembered, experience may be more salient to those who identify with the dominant social group; conversely, memories may be more salient to minority social groups. There may also be subgroup differences in norms about reminiscence in social situations.

The results are consistent with the social-homogeneity perspective. In the study communities, widowed women were 60 percent of the population; single women, 16 percent; and widowed men, 7 percent. (Married men and women comprised the remaining 17 percent; only two single men were found.) Although both single women and widowed men were "deviants," the single women were less deviant numerically and by sex. Elaborating, reviewing, and enjoying the past were adaptive for men but not for women. The homogeneity concept may also help to explain the differential effects of social interaction upon the three groups. We would expect peer interaction to have a greater impact on reminiscence among the two deviant subgroups and that high peer interaction would be associated with adaptive patterns, as was found. Family interaction based primarily on inter-generational ties rather than homogeneity did not have similar effects on reminiscence.

Still another possible factor that may help explain social differences in the adaptiveness of reminiscence is that of continuity. Several researchers, including Chiriboga and Gigy [10], Falk [45], and McHugh [46], have found that people tend to reconstruct their memories more extensively under conditions of change. As noted previously, the inability to draw on past experience has been associated with depression, death, and poor adaptation to relocation [11, 18] . This perspective suggests that people who experience greater discontinuity between past and present role and situations reminisce more extensively, reflecting on the meaning of the past for coping with the present. Negative views of the past probably indicate more successful adaptation to discontinuity.

The actual amount of continuity was not measured. Perceived continuity in the past five years and since age fifty was not clearly related to reminiscence. More adequate measures of continuity are necessary to explore this factor. On a conceptual level, it appears that the single women have experienced the most continuity between past and present: unlike the widowed subgroups, they have not experienced the greatest discontinuity, not only because of their desolation, which is shared by the widowed women, but because of their relative decline in power and status within this community of women. If this reasoning is accurate, then memories of single women (and perhaps widowed women) that are positive, involving little review, and connected to the present would be adaptive; the opposite would hold for widowed men. The positive association among women, but not among men, between self-esteem and the memory scales of connection to present, evaluation, and low victimization fits this interpretation.

To what extent do these results reflect the dynamics of "real-life" reminiscence? Since older adults do not usually recount memories to interviewers, the research situation is not a direct measure of natural reminiscing. The unstructured, conversational format of most of the interview, however, was intended to be reasonably natural. Although respondents were not explicitly asked about the role of reminiscing in their everyday lives, their comments provide indirect evidence that their usual patterns paralleled their behavior in the research context. For example, those whose memories involved low elaboration, digression, and evaluation often mentioned that they did not usually spend much time reminiscing and viewed themselves as present or future oriented. Several women who reported elaborate memories and scored low on the adaptation scale expressed unhappiness about the fact that they tended to dwell too much on the past, while several men who also gave elaborate memories but scored high on life satisfaction and self esteem noted that reminiscence, alone and/or with friends, was a frequent and satisfying activity in their lives.

CONCLUSION

The results of this exploratory study clearly support the contention that social context is an important variable shaping the relationship between reminiscence and adaptation in old age. The particular functions of reminiscence, such as maintaining a positive self-image, coping with transitions, or reconciling past conflicts, may vary according to relatively enduring social characteristics of the individual, life-history events, group norms, and/or current social circumstances. From a sociological perspective, it would be particularly interesting to explore the use of reminiscing as a means of social interaction or exchange.

The present data are insufficient to test the possible explanations outlined above. Systematic studies of larger samples including a full range of settings and social characteristics are needed.

REFERENCES

1. S. Atkin, Discussion, *American Journal of Orthopsychiatry, 10,* pp. 79-84, 1940.
2. R. Kaufman, Old Age and Aging: The Psychoanalytic Point of View, *American Journal of Orthopsychiatry, 10,* pp. 73-79, 1940.
3. S. Reichard, F. Livson, and P. G. Peterson, *Aging and Personality: A Study of Eighty-Seven Older Men,* John Wiley and Sons, New York, 1962.
4. M. Clark and B. G. Anderson, *Culture and Aging: An Anthropological Study of Older Americans,* Charles C. Thomas, Springfield, Illinois, 1967.
5. R. N. Butler, The Life Review: An Interpretation of Reminiscence in the Aged, *Psychiatry, 26,* pp. 65-76, 1963.

6. P. G. Coleman, Measuring Reminiscence Characteristics from Conversations as Adaptive Features of Old Age, *International Journal of Aging and Human Development, 5,* pp. 281-294, 1974.

7. E. H. Erikson, *Childhood and Society,* W. W. Norton, New York, 1959.

8. W. Boylin, S. K. Gordon, and M. F. Nehrke, Reminiscing and Ego Integrity in Institutionalized Elderly Males, *Gerontologist, 16,* pp. 118-124, 1976.

9. M. A. Lieberman and J. M. Falk, The Remembered Past as a Source of Data for Research on the Life Cycle, *Human Development, 14,* pp. 132-141, 1970.

10. D. Chiriboga and L. Gigy, Perspective on the Life Course, in *Four Stages of Transitions, M.* F. Lowenthal, M. Thurnher, and D. Chiriboga (eds.), Jossey-Bass, San Francisco, 1975.

11. D. Miller and M. A. Lieberman, The Relationship of Affect State and Adaptive Capacity to Reactions to Stress, *Journal of Gerontology, 20,* pp. 492-497, 1965.

12. R. J. Havighurst and R. Glasser, An Exploratory Study of Reminiscence, *Journal of Gerontology, 27,* pp. 245-253, 1972.

13. J. M. Grunes, Reminiscences, Regression, and Empathy—A Psychotherapeutic Approach to the Impaired Elderly, in *The Course of Life: Psychoanalytic Contributions Toward Understanding Personality Development, Volume III: Adulthood and the Aging Process,* S. I. Greenspan and G. H. Pollock (eds.), Government Printing Office, Washington, D.C., 1980.

14. M. A. Lieberman and S. S. Tobin, *The Experience of Old Age,* Basic Books, New York, 1983.

15. C. N. Lewis, *Reminiscence and Self Concept in Old Age,* Ph.D. Dissertation, Boston University Graduate School, 1970.

16. P. Tedesco-Castelnuovo, Reminiscence and Nostalgia: The Pleasure and Pain of Remembering, in *The Course of Life: Psychoanalytic Contributions Toward Understanding Personality Development, Volume III: Adulthood and the Aging Process,* S. I. Greenspan and G. H. Pollock (eds.), Government Printing Office, Washington, D.C., 1980.

17. V. Revere and S. S. Tobin, Myth and Reality: The Older Person's Relationship to His Past, *International Journal of Aging and Human Development, 12,* pp. 15-25, 1980-81.

18. A. W. McMahon and P. J. Rhudick, Reminiscing in the Aged: An Adaptational Response, in *Psychodynamic Studies on Aging: Creativity, Reminiscing, and Dying,* S. Levin and R. J. Kahana (eds.), International Universities Press, New York, 1967.

19. A. Pincus, Reminiscence in Aging and Its Implications for Social Work Practice, *Social Work, 15,* pp. 47-53, 1970.

20. B. Myerhoff, Life History among the Elderly: Performance, Visibility, and Re-membering, in *Life Course: Integrative Theories and Exemplary Populations,* K. W. Black (ed.), Westview Press, Boulder, Colorado, 1980.

21. L. J. Postema, *Reminiscing, Time Orientation, and Self-Concept in Aged Men,* Ph.D. Dissertation, Michigan State University, 1970.

22. M. LoGerfo, Three Ways of Reminiscence in Theory and Practice, *International Journal of Aging and Human Development, 12,* pp. 39-48, 1980-81.

23. V. Molinari and R. E. Reichlin, Life Review Reminiscence in the Elderly: A Review of the Literature, *International Journal of Aging and Human Development, 20,* pp. 81-92, 1984-85.

24. S. Merriam, The Concept and Function of Reminiscence: A Review of the Research, *Gerontologist, 20*, pp. 604-609, 1980.
25. E. G. Schachtel, *Metamorphosis: On the Development of Affect, Perception, Attention, and Memory*, Basic Books, New York, 1959.
26. F. C. Bartlett, *Remembering: A Study in Experimental and Social Psychology*, University Press, Cambridge, 1932.
27. S. Kvale, The Temporality of Memory, *Journal of Phenomenological Psychology, 5*, pp. 7-31, 1974
28. S. Kvale, Dialectics and Research on Memory, in *Life-span Developmental Psychology: Dialectical Perspective on Experimental Research*, N. Datan and H. Reese (eds.), Academic Press, New York, 1977.
29. J. A. Meacham, Continuing the Dialogue, Dialectics and Remembering, *Human Development, 19*, pp. 304-309, 1976.
30. H. W. Reese, Models of Memory Development, *Human Development, 19*, pp. 291-303, 1976.
31. P. L. Berger and T. Luckmann, *The Social Construction of Reality: A Treatise in The Sociology of Knowledge*, Doubleday, Garden City, New York, 1966.
32. S. S. Tobin, The Earliest Memory as Data for Research, in *Research, Planning, and Action for the Elderly: The Power and Potential of Social Science,* D. P. Kent, R. Kastenbaum, and S. Sherwood (eds.), Behavioral Publications, New York, 1972.
33. M. F. Lowenthal, M. Thurnher, D. Chiriboga, and Associates, *Four Stages of Life,* Jossey-Bass, San Francisco, 1975.
34. D. H. Oliveira, *Understanding Old People: Patterns of Reminiscing in Elderly People and Their Relationship to Life Satisfaction*, Ph.D. Dissertation, University of Tennessee, 1977.
35. D. D. David, *The Uses of Memory: Social Aspects of Reminiscence in Old Age*, Ph.D. Dissertation, University of California at Berkeley, 1981.
36. R. J. Havighurst, B. L. Neugarten, and S. S. Tobin, Disengagement and Patterns of Aging, in *Middle Age and Aging*, B. L. Neugarten (ed.), University of Chicago Press, Chicago, 1968.
37. C. Gordon, Self Conceptions Methodologies, *Journal of Nervous and Mental Disease, 148*, pp. 328-364, 1969.
38. D. Gutmann, The Parental Imperative Revisited: Toward a Developmental Psychology of Adulthood and Later Life, in *Contributions to Human Development, Volume 14*, S. A. Meacham (ed.), Karger, New York, 1985.
39. H. S. Maass and J. A. Kuypers, *From Thirty to Seventy,* Jossey-Bass, San Francisco, 1974.
40. B. L. Neugarten and Associates, *Personality in Middle and Late Life: Empirical Studies,* Atherton Press, New York, 1964.
41. B. F. Turner, The Self-Concepts of Older Women, *Research on Aging, 1*, pp. 464-480, 1979.
42. Z. S. Blau, *Old Age in a Changing Society*, New Viewpoints, New York, 1973.
43. J. F. Gubrium, *The Myth of the Golden Years: A Socio-Environmental Theory of Aging*, Charles C. Thomas, Springfield, Illinois, 1973.
44. M. Messer, The Possibility of Age-Concentrated Environment Becoming a Normative System, *Gerontologist, 7*, pp. 247-250, 1967.

Section II

Research into the Role of Life Review

Chapter 4

LIFE PATTERNS AND AGE STYLES IN OLDER ADULTS

Peter Martin

The biographical approach has been used to conceptualize the life-span of the individual in general [1, 2] and more specifically after the experience of significant life events [3, 4]. Life experiences often serve as life markers [5] and can further be related to broader individual life themes [6, 7]. The purpose of this study was to explore the relationship of life events, life themes, personality, and intelligence in a sample of older individuals. The interaction of life experiences, life themes, personality, and intelligence is thought to build life patterns in the retrospective construction of the life course.

The smallest experiential unit in the biography of individuals relates to life experiences. Such life experiences are commonly defined as events that disrupt or threaten to disrupt an individual's usual activities, requiring readjustment in that individual's behavior [8].

In her biographical studies of 1,311 persons, Lehr [6] found that while only a minority of events were related to broad event categories, many experiences related to very individual personal experiences such as: meeting a special person, a relationship, discussions with parents, and friendship. Numerous other studies have pointed out the relationship between critical life events and developmental outcomes [8-10]. While most life-event studies emphasize the nature and consequences of critical life events few studies have investigated life events over the total life-span. Thomae used the concept of life events to describe lives that either were characterized by many crises or few crises over the life-span [11]. This research attempted to extend Thomae's work by exploring the relationship between life events, life themes, personality, and intelligence.

Life events can be classified in terms of broader biographical units, namely as life themes [7]. Thomae [7] defined life themes as repeatedly mentioned thoughts, wishes, fears, and/or hopes. Themes are referred to as personal representations of life processes that individuals are concerned with and to which they react. Thomae emphasized the importance of assessing themes through biographic methods. Personal biographies of individuals were thought of as theme oriented. Thomae [7] found that when reflecting upon their lives, individuals expressed biographical themes, such as the importance of maintaining or increasing social contacts (activation, expansion), relatedness to past life contacts (occupation, family), or the finitude of life. In her intergenerational studies, Hagestad also identified certain themes that pervade human experience: views on social issues; work, education, and money; health and appearance; daily living; and interpersonal relations [12]. Berman [3] suggested three ideas from the Florida Scott-Maxwell [13] Journal, *The Measure of My Days*: experience of old age, individuation of late life, and successful aging.

The conceptual basis for this study stems from Thomae's cognitive theory of aging [7], which emphasizes the importance of life experiences, life themes, as well as individual characteristics, such as cognitive functioning and personality for the overall development of individuals. Life experiences and more general life themes are thought of as age fates; critical features experienced over the life-span. Intelligence and personality, on the other hand, are thought of as individual age styles that contribute to the way events and life themes are interpreted.

Thomae made a distinction between age fates and age styles [7]. Age fates are defined as critical experiences and themes over the life-span. An example of an age fate would be a person who has expressed many critical events and focused on health concerns as a personal, major life theme. Age styles are thought of as individual characteristics that contribute to the way events and life themes are interpreted. Intelligence, personality, and level of activity are examples of individual life styles. Finally, life patterns are defined as a combination of specific age fates and age styles. A person who has experienced many life crises, who has focused on health concerns as a major life theme, and who is extremely intelligent and active may serve as one idiographic example of a life pattern.

The interaction between individual and environment makes up thematic units or aspects of life relating meaning to unique individuals. By creating themes of existence, individuals give themselves orientation points or goals and meaningful personal experiences [14, 15]. Meaning is subjective and related directly to Dasein in the sense that a particular situation becomes "fitting" or meaningful [16]. Biographical studies enable researchers to detect "life themes" [14, 17], existential projects [2], or world views [8]. They may also contribute to the process of individuation [3].

The establishment of a life theme in relationship to life events may well depend on individual characteristics, such as personality and intelligence. Hultsch and Plemons [10] and Filipp [19] in their models on life course events highlighted this relationship. Much has been written on the relationship between personality and events [20, 21], but little attention has been focused on the relationship between life events and intelligence and between life themes, personality, and intelligence.

Personality and intelligence are considered age styles, which may interact with life events and life themes.

In analyzing biographies, it becomes apparent how different the life paths of individuals can be [11, 22]. Thomae [11] in particular stressed the importance of developing typologies of what he calls "aging fates" (*Altersschicksale*) and "aging styles" (*Alternsstile*). He linked the number of critical events experienced over the life-span to various degrees of life satisfaction and called this constellation aging fates. Within a particular aging fate, individuals were differentiated from each other in terms of specific individual characteristics, such as activities and competence—aging styles. A summary of this classification is contained in Table 1. Thomae's classification can be carried further. If life experiences determine the age fate of individuals, then among those life events certain theme patterns may be detected to form a general biographical life pattern. While Thomae used life satisfaction as a description of age fates, thereby concentrating on current states, one may also explore more general themes in the life of individuals.

This research attempted to explore, through extensive interviews, biographical typologies of older individuals that define age fates (i.e., experiences and themes) as they relate to age styles (i.e., intelligence and personality). A typology of age fates and age styles was thought to contribute to the discussion of individual differences in later life.

CASE HISTORIES

Fifteen older individuals, (age 60–90, mean age 79 years) recruited from a retirement community in central Pennsylvania, were extensively interviewed for this exploratory study. Most participants were well educated individuals; ten were female, five male. Because of the limited sample size, its middle-class characteristics, and the self-selection process, the case histories presented here are, of course, not representative of the general population of older adults. However, the primary goal of this research was to explore individual differences in biographies, and it therefore seemed justified to assess life patterns and age styles first with a relatively small and self-selected sample.

In order to assess life themes connected to life events, participants were invited for an in-depth, semi-structured interview in which both a personal event of the past year and a historical event of their lifetime were explored. Most personal experiences related to work- and family-related events. Historical events most often mentioned included the Great Depression, World Wars I and II, and President Kennedy's assassination. The procedure of this exploration used many features of the "focused interview" described by Merton, Fiske, and Kendal [23] and although the focus was on recent personal experiences, participants were not restricted in their interests from reflecting upon the more distant past.

Participants were asked to describe: how they experienced the event, how it influenced them personally, whether it confined or expanded their lives, whether

Table 1. Aging Fates and Aging Styles [11]

Age Fate A	Many life conflicts, High life satisfaction
Style A1:	High activity, high competence
Style A2:	High activity, low competence
Style A3:	Low activity, high competence
Style A4:	Low activity, low competence
Age Fate B	**Many life conflicts, Low life satisfaction**
Style B1:	High activity, High competence
Style B2:	High activity, low competence
Style B3:	Low activity, high competence
Style B4:	Low activity, low competence
Age Fate C	**Few life conflicts, High life satisfaction**
Style C1:	High activity, high competence
Style C2:	High activity, low competence
Style C3:	Low activity, high competence
Style C4:	Low activity, low competence
Age Fate D	**Few life conflicts, Low life satisfaction**
Style D1:	High activity, high competence
Style D2:	High activity, low competence
Style D3:	Low activity, high competence
Style D4:	Low activity, low competence

they saw it as threatening or challenging, what meaning it had for them, and how it related to past experiences. The interview closed with a question on "values in life." The interview focused specifically on life events and biographies, although the evaluation assessed themes mentioned most often with regard to these life experiences.

Life themes were assessed with regard to the domains of each significant event and followed the definition suggested by Thomae [7]. Life-theme categories included: engagement activities, seeking and maintaining social contacts, concern with physical problems, family themes, concern with finitude of life, concern with home/residence, religious themes, work-related themes, concern with daily living, and concern with missing opportunities. Three independent remarks in relation to one of the themes were necessary to call it a representative theme in the life of the individual [12].

In addition, participants engaged in a task of sorting 223 life event cards. The events were selected from common life-event lists [24-26]. Participants had to sort out those events that had happened in their lives and rate them in terms of perceived overall importance. Participants mentioned an average of fifty-eight events as having occurred in their lives. This procedure was chosen to obtain a detailed analysis of events over the biography of participants and allowed for an assessment of significant life events or, in Thomae's words, age fates [11].

Finally, participants filled out the 16 PF personality inventory [27] to assess individual personality differences. The 16 PF assessed the following fifteen personality factors: warmth, emotional stability, dominance, impulsivity, conformity, boldness, sensitivity, suspiciousness, imagination, shrewdness, insecurity, radicalism, self-sufficiency, self-discipline, and tension. In addition, this test provided a rough measure of intellectual functioning. High scorers on this factor are characterized as having high general mental ability, as insightful, fast learning, and intellectually adaptable. Low scorers on this factor are characterized as having low mental capacity and are unable to handle abstract problems [28]. Estimates of reliability based on test-retest correlations reportedly range from .63 to .88. Convergent validity between the 16 PF and the MMPI is moderate. The instrument was appropriate for this research, since it provided the possibility of differentiating age styles with regard to differing personalities.

LIFE PATTERNS AND AGE STYLES

The purpose of this analysis was to link personality and event variables with life themes to obtain biographical life patterns. Idiographic life patterns were introduced, which included the major life theme of individuals, the number of life events experienced, and personality and intelligence in relation to particular life themes.

Table 2 summarizes three suggested life patterns corresponding to various life themes. The most common theme mentioned in the interview related to social contacts ($N = 6$), engagement in activities ($N = 5$) and concern with physical problems ($N = 4$) were also noted as major themes among the participants, however. Each life pattern was subdivided into age styles, differentiating the number of events experienced over the life-span, as an indicator for a more or less eventful life [11], and personality traits.

As can be seen in this summary of individual life patterns, a wide variety of different personality styles related to personal themes. Similar to Orbach, Iluz, and Rosenheim's [29] findings, interpersonal relationships in this study also turned out to be the most important theme or concern.

Table 2. Life Patterns and Age Styles in Biographies

PATTERN A $N = 6$

Life Theme:	Seeking and Maintaining Social Contacts
	Very eventful life ($M = 81$ events)
Style A1:	extremely controlled, very intelligent (Mr. A)
Style A2:	extremely controlled, intelligent (Mr. B)
Life Theme:	Seeking and Maintaining Social Contacts
	Somewhat eventful life ($M = 59$ events)
Style A3:	submissive, group dependent (Mrs. C)
Style A4:	extremely controlled, very intelligent (Mrs. D)
Life Theme:	Seeking and Maintaining Social Contacts
	Not very eventful life ($M = 44$ events)
Style A5:	extremely sober, astute, conservative
Style A6:	controlled, very intelligent (Mrs. F)
	emotionally labile, sensitive, shrewd (Mrs. G)

PATTERN B $N = 5$

Life Theme:	Engagement in Activities
	Somewhat eventful life ($M = 64$ events)
Style B1:	extremely venturesome, astute, conservative, very intelligent (Mrs. H)
Style B2:	extremely suspicious, tense, very intelligent (Mrs. J)
Style B3:	extremely astute, controlled (Mrs. K)
Life Theme:	Engagement in Activities
	Not very eventful life ($M = 43$ events)
Style B4:	extremely suspicious, astute, moderately intelligent (Mrs. L)
Style B5:	extremely humble, controlled, very intelligent (Mrs. M)

PATTERN C $N = 4$

Life Theme:	Concern with Physical Problems
	Very eventful life ($M = 76$ events)
Style C1:	extremely conforming and suspicious, self-sufficient, moderately intelligent (Mr. N)
Style C2:	extremely tender-minded, astute, controlled, very intelligent (Mrs. O)
Life Theme:	Concern with Physical Problems
	Not very eventful life ($M = 32$ events)
Style C3:	extremely emotional, astute, controlled, (Mrs. P)
Style C4:	extremely humble, practical, moderately intelligent (Mrs. R)

Within these life patterns and compared to the average number of life events reported over the life-span, some reported very eventful lives, others less eventful lives. Personality traits and intelligence further distinguished the participants from each other. Although the sample was quite small, a number of gender difference trends were apparent: while more male participants mentioned activity-related themes than would have been expected (40%), more female participants (75%) mentioned physical problems than would have been expected by their sample representation. In addition, more males indicated very eventful lives (75% male, 25% female), while more women (83%) indicated not very eventful lives than would have been expected by their sample representation.

With regard to age differences, those individuals who predominantly mentioned social contact themes were on average seventy-four years of age, while individuals classified as concerned with activities had a mean age of eighty years, and those with physical-related themes had a mean age of eighty-two years. No age difference, however, was obtained with regard to the nature of life events experienced over the life-span. The mean age for participants with very eventful lives and somewhat eventful lives was both seventy-eight years, while the mean age for informants with not very eventful lives was only slightly higher at seventy-nine years.

The following sections will highlight three examples of individuality for each of the life-pattern groups. Individuals with the strongest representation of particular life themes were chosen as examples.

Case 1: Seeking and Maintaining Social Relations

Mr. A's (born 1908) personality profile can be characterized by high scores (i.e., upper 30% of norm tables) on warmth, intelligence, impulsivity, boldness, sensitivity, self-sufficiency, self-discipline, and tension. Low scores (i.e., lower 30% of norm tables) were obtained for emotional stability and dominance. Mr. A perceived his life as having been very eventful (73 events), with most events relating to work (24.3%) and social relations (20.3%). With regard to the whole life-span, the dense areas of experiences fell between the ages of sixty-three and eighty, a somewhat different pattern when compared to most other participants. As one of the significant events in his life, he reported his wife's sickness and ensuing death. During the same time, he reported the support of a good friend as one of the twenty most important events in his life.

In the interview, Mr. A first reflected upon his involvement in a "marketing tour" for a resident community. "It got me out of my own little circle," he reported. He also wanted "the people to know what D.N. (retirement community) was like."

As the interview proceeded, Mr. A went on to tell of comparisons to his work as a minister:

> As a clergyman, I do a selling job all the time . . . I have been accustomed to it all my life. The only thing I . . . have said is that I prefer a larger group of people to a smaller group of people. . . . Speaking to an audience I'd much rather talk to seventy-five people than to ten. . . . An audience is inspiring, you get feedback from people, there is no doubt about it. I feel very strongly, and not only by numbers, you get a sense whether people are paying attention to you, or whether they couldn't care less. . . . I've heard actors say the same thing that they sense the audience, and I know this is true, you get a sense of what is going on in people's minds. . . . Before we started our presentation, we were wondering, "What would these people be like," and "these people look like they are interesting.". . . People are always a challenge, I think. I like people, generally, some people I don't like, but I like working with people.

The life theme of this individual is apparent from this interview passage. He has always enjoyed working with people, and his commitment to the retirement community is determined by his interest in social relations.

His life theme became even more apparent in an interview passage, which came up during talk about a historical event. At one point he talked about war as an experience, linking a personal experience that could well be labeled a "key event" of his later life:

> In every war you get down to the people, you discover that they are just people, just good, nice people. . . . My greatest crusade would be to get rid of bigotry and prejudice. I feel so strongly about this . . . I think that has probably been the purpose [of my life] as much as anything else, even more than any theological purpose, that has been the purpose of my ministry. . . .
>
> I was a minister in R. when the racial change took place, and I just felt it was my purpose to get my people ready for this, and it worked. The complexity of my church changed dramatically. Later on I was invited back to give a speech, and it was the thrill of my life to get up on the pulpit and look upon a church full of people, they were black, but they were people. . . .
>
> And I get so angry at bigotry. Unfortunately, my ministry ended with a very terrible, terrible experience. About Christmas time, I had a young woman stop in the church who wanted to know whether I was willing to baptize her baby, she was pregnant, and I talked to her about it and about the importance of coming to church, and she said they wanted to become a part of the church, but it was a mixed marriage (which to me had always meant catholic/protestant marriage); as she talked I began to realize that her husband was black, and I said, it did not make any difference to me, I said everybody is welcomed in church. . . . She came to church and her husband came to church with her, and a couple of the officials of the church got bitter about it. . . . Finally, a meeting of the board was called, and I presented the case to them, and one by one I told them what kind of a church it would be that did not let people in, but they decided against it . . . a terrible, terrible experience. So I got in touch with my superintendent and told him that I would not go back.

Little needs to be added to this statement. The importance of social relations came out in almost every topic that was covered in the interview. This last example also indicates a strong link to the extreme score on the self-discipline (upper 7%) factor of the personality inventory. For this individual, having relations to people almost meant to be in control, be it in small or large groups. Mr. A summed up his regard for people in an answer to the question about values in life: "Recognizing the truth about and having respect for people."

Case 2: Engagement in Activities

Mrs. K's (born 1901) personality profile can be characterized by high scores on intelligence, conformity, sensitivity, shrewdness, and self-discipline. Low scores were obtained for dominance, impulsivity, suspiciousness, radicalism, and tension. Mrs. K also perceived her life as having been very eventful (71 experiences reported). Her life-span profile was typical with dense areas around ages eighteen and thirty-five and a second peak between ages seventy-two and eighty. Events that occurred during her young-adult years were also considered the most important ones, and she reported her marriage and the death of her father as having been particularly important during that time. Mrs. K reported an unusually high number of school-related events (15.2%), which was only outnumbered by work-related experiences (22.7%). During the interview, Mrs. K chose to talk about her recent trip to Europe. She had always been interested in Europe ever since she was a child. She felt it was "romantic to go and see these places." She explained how she had not been able to go to Europe for so many years, but then, "I was getting to Europe, at last . . . 83 years old, going on a trip: I made it, and it was wonderful."

The trip to Europe in itself, however, was not the only evidence of her high level of activity:

> I am already writing my illustrative diary of the trip. . . . There is the map, here is the plane. . . . Yes I drew this. I painted this man at the gas station: he had purple overalls on and a lavender shirt. . . . I made notes of everything I saw. Now I am already starting to wonder. Is this really how it was? I would like to go back and check! Now I have to stop and do my Christmas cards, because I make them every year.

Her interest in activities are closely linked to learning which perhaps explains the high number of school experiences:

> This picture on the wall is about an artist's colony. I spent many vacations there, watching the artists, and wishing I could learn to do water color painting, wishing with my whole heart, but so afraid, the teacher would charge me more than I could pay, because I did not have money when I was working and going on vacation; then after my husband died, I took a water-color class . . . and it's the biggest joy in my life, I am able to express myself, and the frustration after all these years.

It is interesting to note that the general theme of "engagement in activities" proved itself to be very specific for Mrs. K: her dream was to be able to paint in water colors. While the interview went on to other topics (most of them again turning to her interest in activities), the talk eventually came back to one of her major life themes:

> Life has been adventurous and good. Whatever came along, I made it an adventure. I have loved life . . . met a lady who did water color painting; and I said, "Will you teach me," and she said, "No, but I will work with you," she was delighted to have company and we painted together, so I took her to N . . . we were gone six weeks . . . we painted every day.

For Mrs. K, the very high scores on shrewdness (upper 2%) and self-discipline (upper 7%) of the 16 PF fit very well with the description of her life themes. Individuals who score high on shrewdness prefer to be around "polished, sophisticated people" [30, p. 9], and this factor often corresponds to high levels of behavior control. However, what stood out was not only the activities pursued but also the enjoyment of them:

> Isn't it marvelous the way I am blossoming, since I am on my own, since I don't have to strive for a living. . . . I am up at six every morning and the days aren't long enough.

Case 3: Concern with Physical Problems

Mr. N's (born 1907) personality profile can be characterized by high scores on conformity, suspiciousness, radicalism, self-sufficiency, and tension. Low scores were obtained for warmth, intelligence, impulsivity, and shrewdness. Mr. N perceived his life as having been very eventful (79 events reported). For this participant there was an important difference between the number of life events and the perceived importance of them. In terms of the number of overall critical experiences, most of his significant experiences occurred during young adulthood (age 18 to 26; 17.2%) and middle adulthood (age 45 to 53; 19%). However, the most important personal experience evidently occurred during later parts of the life-span (age 63 to 80).

Most of Mr. N's life events were related to work (20%) and health (15%). Health-related items were more often mentioned than by most other participants in the study. It is necessary to note, however, that Mr. N did not rate these experiences as particularly important events.

Mr. N's concern with physical problems might well have started during his young- and middle-adult years. He mentioned the death of his pastor, when he was seventeen years old; later he became an army chaplain (age 36) and listed the experience of shellfire at the same age as a significant event. Several years later (age 44 and 45), both of his parents died within a very short time interval. Perhaps it was those significant events that helped form a life theme that could be called "concern with physical health."

During the interview, Mr. N focused on a recent prostate operation: "It wasn't a particular problem; it was just something that needed to be done." He clearly down played the importance of this health-related experience and signs of denial became apparent. When he was asked why he had decided to have the operation at that particular time, Mr. N answered:

> I had thought about it for some time; it was necessary and I was here about three years and I just thought it was a good time; I just prodded myself that I had come through this many years without any operation, so I thought we will make a seventy-five year landmark.

Later on in the interview, Mr. N "remembered" that he once was hospitalized for a bleeding ulcer:

> I had a bleeding ulcer, I guess it was twenty years ago. . . and I had an operation; they made me sign the paper, I lost about two thirds of my blood. . . . I didn't have any trouble until it broke loose one night.

And even later in the interview:

> The treat is there . . . especially with the ulcer, and also with this kid . . . well that's another one, I was in for a kidney stone and that was an operation, too. . . . Now that was more threatening, because the kidney stone is terrific pain, that happened before I came here. . . . That's the only time I have been in the hospital, nothing too serious.

The cognitive representation of the health-related events is clearly dominated by processes of devaluation. On the other hand, it is apparent, how meaningful these experiences were for Mr. N. This participant was chosen as a representative for the health-related life themes in order to illustrate that life themes might not always be obvious for the interviewer, nor for the individual reporting. Only when the meaning of particular events is explored, might their relatedness to life themes be revealed:

> I guess, like for everybody, operations provoke anxiety. . . . The doctors talked with me very frankly and often very particularly; so I learned a lot through it, and I know many people worry about their operations. Probably the greatest risk in operations is taking an anesthetic, because they keep you hanging just between life and death, they almost suffocate you . . . with that stuff in your blood, so everybody wonders, and I probably even a little more, because . . . the effect it has on your heart, because they check your heart, and I have always had a strong heart, but nevertheless you know that; I think I had more anxiety over the ulcer . . . just two weeks before I went to the hospital we had an illustrative lecture, showing what the body does when you bleed internally . . . it says there is a point of no return, so I was wondering whether I would get to that point of no return.

The connection between this particular life theme and extreme scores on certain personality factors is striking: extreme scores were obtained for conformity (upper 2%), suspiciousness (upper 2%) and self-sufficiency (upper 7%). Suspiciousness has been discussed as an important health risk factor [31]. High scores reportedly show consistent relationships to coronary heart disease and higher frequencies of general illness. Similarly, high scores on self-sufficiency have been associated with "incidence of coronary heart disease, hypertension, and certain physical syndromes such as tuberculosis and peptic ulcers" [30, p. 9].

The extremely high scores on conformity also deserve a brief comment. High-scoring people on this factor are said to "set unrealistically high standards for themselves. . . . Flexibility is not a part of their behavioral repertoire, and this may lower the individual's ability to cope with extreme stress" [30, p. 7]. This personality description seems to fit the pattern of resistance and denial in Mr. N's comments about his past health problems.

CONCLUSIONS

The author has used an idiographic approach to illustrate life patterns and age styles, while linking life events and personality with more general themes of an individual's life. Gaining insight into individual lives provides a complementary perspective that focuses directly on older adults' experiences [3]. Three life themes emerged as central in the interviews: "seeking and maintaining social contacts," "engagement in social activities," and "concern with physical problems." The individual patterns reported in this study clarified the relationship between experiences, life themes, and individual characteristics. The specific constellation of life patterns and age styles may reveal processes of individuation and continued identity formation [3].

The approach used in this study provides an opportunity to investigate individual differences in later life. The classification of differences into life patterns and age styles allows for a more differential view of aging [11, 22] that may be useful in clinical work with older adults. Specific patterns may also be used as predictors or criteria for further research. For example, does one pattern predict life satisfaction of mental health in older adults more than another pattern? Life patterns may be useful as individual difference variables in further research and practice.

These results were obtained from a self-selected volunteer group of older individuals who were mostly female, white, middle class and well educated. One should be cautious, therefore, in generalizing these results to other populations. Indeed, it may be assumed that other life themes and personality factors play a role in different subgroups of a population. This research should be replicated with larger samples, without losing the focus on individual differences.

REFERENCES

1. D. N. Bertaux, *Biography and Society*, Sage, Beverley Hills, 1981.
2. M. Freeman, History, Narrative, and Life-Span Developmental Knowledge, *Human Development*, 27, pp. 1-19, 1984.
3. H. J. Berman, To Flame with a Wild Life: Florida Scott-Maxwell's Experience of Old Age, *The Gerontologist*, 26, pp. 321-324, 1986.
4. S. Kaufman, Illness, Biography, and the Interpretation of Self Following a Stroke, *Journal of Aging Studies*, 2, pp. 217-227, 1987.
5. B. Hardcastle, Midlife Themes of Invisible Citizens: An Explosion into How Ordinary People Make Sense of Their Lives, *Journal of Humanistic Psychology*, 25, pp. 45-63, 1985.
6. W. Lehr, Zur Frage der Gliederung des menschlichen Lebenslaufes, *Aktuelle Gerontologie*, 6, pp. 337-345, 1976.
7. H. Thomae, *Das Individuum und seine Welt* (2nd Edition), Hogrefe, Göttingen, 1988.
8. P. A. Thoits, Dimensions of Life Events That Influence Psychological Distress: An Evaluation and Synthesis of the Literature, in *Psychosocial Stress: Trends in Theory and Research*, H. B. Kaplan (ed.), Academic Press, New York, pp. 33-103, 1983.
9. L. H. Cohen *Life Events and Psychological Functioning: Theoretical and Methodological Issues*, Sage, Newbury Park, 1988.
10. D. F. Hultsch and J. K. Plemons, Life Events and Life-Span Development, in *Life-Span Development and Behavior*, Vol. 2, P. B. Baltes (ed.), Academic Press, New York, 1979.
11. H. Thomae, *Alternsstile und Altersschicksale*, Huber, Bern, 1983.
12. G. H. Hagestad, The Continuous Bond: A Dynamic, Multigenerational Perspective on Parent-Child Relations between Adults, in *Minnesota Symposium on Child Psychology*, Vol. 17, M. Perlmutter (ed.), Lawrence Erlbaum Associates, New Jersey, 1984.
13. F. Scott-Maxwell, *The Measure of My Days*, Penguin, New York, 1968.
14. C. Buhler, The Human Course of Life in Its Goal Aspects, *Journal of Humanistic Psychology*, 4, pp. 1-17, 1964.
15. W. B. Frick, The Symbolic Growth Experience: Paradigm for a Humanistic-Existential Learning Theory, *Journal of Humanistic Psychology*, 77, pp. 400-423, 1978.
16. F. C. Bartlett, *Remembering: A Study in Experimental and Social Psychology*, Cambridge University Press, Cambridge, 1932.
17. M. Csikszentmihalyi and O. Beattie, Life Themes: An Empirical and Theoretical Exploration of Their Origins and Effects, *Journal of Humanistic Psychology*, 19, pp. 45-63, 1979.
18. S. L. Klineberg, Social Change, World Views, and Cohort Succession: The United States in the 1980's, in *Life-Span Developmental Psychology: Historical and Generational Effects*, K. A. McCluskey and H. W. Reese (eds.), Academic Press, New York, 1984.
19. S. H. Filipp, *Kritische Lebensereignisse und ihre Bewältigung,* Urban and Schwarzenberg, Munchen, 1981.
20. O. W. Schonecke, H. Schuffel, M. Schafer, and K. Winter, Assessment of Hostility in Patients with Functional Cardiac Complaints, *Psychotherapy and Psychosomatics*, 20, pp. 272-281, 1977.

21. J. Suls, J. Gastorf, and Witenberg, Life Events, Psychological Distress and the Type A Coronary-Prone Behavior Pattern, *Journal of Psychosomatic Research, 23*, pp. 315-319, 1979.
22. G. L. Maddox, Aging Differently, *The Gerontologist, 27*, pp. 557-564, 1987.
23. R. K. Merton, M. Fiske, and P. L. Dendall, *The Focused Interview*, Free Press, Glencoe, 1956.
24. B. D. Dohrenwend, A. R. Askenasy, C. Krasnoff, and B. P. Dohrenwend, Exemplification of a Method for Scaling Life Events: The PERI Life Events Scale, *Journal of Health and Social Behavior, 19*, pp. 205-229, 1978.
25. T. H. Holmes and R. H. Rahe, The Social Readjustment Rating Scale, *Journal of Psychosomatic Research, 11,* pp. 213-218, 1967.
26. H. W. Reese, and M. A. Smyer, The Dimensionalization of Life Events, in *Life-Span Developmental Psychology: Non-normative Life Events*, J. Callahan and K. A. McCluskey (eds.), Academic Press, New York, 1983.
27. R. B. Cattell, *Sixteen Personality Factor Questionnaire*, Institute for Personality and Ability Testing, Champaign, Illinois, 1982.
28. R. B. Cattell, H. W. Eber, and M. M. Tatsuoka, *Handbook for the Sixteen Personality Factor Questionnaire*, Institute for Personality on Ability Testing, Champaign, Illinois, 1970.
29. I. Orbach, A. Iluz, and E. Rosenheim, Value Systems and Commitment to Goals as a Function of Age, Integrations of Personality, and Fear of Death, *International Journal of Behavioral Development, 10*, pp. 225-239, 1987.
30. S. E. Krug, *Interpreting 16 PF Profile Patterns*, Institute for Personality and Ability Testing, Champaign, Illinois, 1981.
31. J. L. Sherman and S. E. Krug, Personality-Somatic Interaction: The Research Evidence, in *Psychological Assessment in Medicine*, IPAT, S. E. Krug (ed.), Champaign, Illinois, 1977.

Chapter 5

INDIVIDUAL DIFFERENCES IN REMINISCENCE AMONG OLDER ADULTS: PREDICTORS OF FREQUENCY AND PLEASANTNESS RATINGS OF REMINISCENCE ACTIVITY

P. S. Fry

Research studies of reminiscence activity [1-4] have found a relatively high frequency of reminiscence among older adults. A wide range of benefits, including self-esteem development, psychological well-being, and adaptive functioning, have been attributed to the frequency of reminiscence [5, 6] and its related therapeutic effects [3-6]. The significance of the adaptive function of reminiscence has been operationalized in a number of studies through the relationship between frequency of reminiscence and levels of life-satisfaction, psychological well-being, purpose for living, and activities of daily living.

For example, some life-cycle theorists [2, 7] contend that the frequency of reminiscence activity may be linked to personality traits such as histrionic or exhibitionistic traits reflected in story telling, and the individual's specific tendency to mythicize or dramatize past experiences. Other researchers [7] have shown that prolific reminiscers are significantly more articulate about their perceptual experiences and show greater capability for utilizing pleasant imagery in reminiscing. These researchers suggest that an individual's capacity for experiential openness and sensory awareness may be strongly linked with the frequency of reminiscence activity and the resulting associations with pleasantness. Still other researchers [4, 8] have argued that the degree of satisfaction with one's past life and the degree of ego-integrity achieved may be influentially linked with frequency of reminiscence activity [9, 10]. However, the direction of the association between the frequency and pleasantness ratings of reminiscence activity and the degree of satisfaction with one's past or present is still undetermined [4, 6, 8].

Lack of meaning and purpose in life, or lack of goals, has generally been shown to correlate significantly with a variety of psychosocial adjustments or problems of adjustment in late life [11-14]. It is speculated therefore that the absence of meaning or purpose may contribute to certain individuals engaging in a greater frequency of reminiscence about past fulfillments, problems, and dissatisfactions [15, 16]. Prolific reminiscers have been observed by Butler [15] to engage in frequent self-evaluations in association with a motivation for self-understanding precipitated by a philosophical concern about the meaning of life [1, 17-19]. There is evidence that some traits and characteristics of elderly adults and their background factors are differentially associated with the responsiveness of these individuals to the reminiscence process, but no systematic or integrated attempt has been made thus far to study the direction of linkages between the personality and background characteristics of elderly adults and the frequency of their reminiscence activity. Nor has there been any previous attempt to study the independent contribution of these factors as predictors of individual differences in the frequency of reminiscence.

The present study, using subjective indices of life-satisfactions, daily functioning, personality characteristics, and goals and purposes in life, was designed to examine the psychosocial correlates of the frequency and pleasantness ratings of reminiscence in a sample of elderly persons. The major objective was to identify psychosocial factors and personality characteristics of elderly adults that are significant predictors of the frequency of reminiscence and the pleasantness associated with the reminiscence activity. It was postulated that the data obtained from this study would be helpful to mental health professionals who are concerned about the responsiveness of elderly persons to the reminiscence process.

METHODOLOGY

Community Sample

The community sample was gathered from residents living in semi-sheltered housing. Residents in semi-sheltered housing are a particularly suitable group to study. Previous studies [20, 21] have shown that this population has experienced many social and emotional losses and changes in old age (e.g., death and bereavement, separation from family and friends, dislocation from familiar environments), and they can be easily assessed on objective indices of physical health status [22], social support [20], and health services utilization. Such individuals are also amenable to interviews because of the relative lack of mental deterioration [20] and the privacy in living arrangements.

The community sample comprised seventy individuals (35 women and 35 men), between the ages of sixty-seven and eighty-two years, living alone in semi-sheltered housing developments for seniors in four Alberta communities. These men and women were selected randomly from a comprehensive list of Meals-on-Wheels recipients; some of whom were also receiving home care services. Of the 100 individuals invited, eighty agreed to participate. Of the twenty who did not participate, eight were ineligible due to moderate degrees of cognitive impairment on the mini-mental status assessment administered during the first meeting. Another six individuals, although not cognitively impaired, had speech impediments and difficulty in communicating. The remaining six persons were not interested. Ten individuals (6 men and 4 women) out of the original sample dropped out after volunteering because of unforeseen personal and family concerns. Complete data were obtained on seventy individuals.

Although no precise information was available on the financial or economic status of those living in the semi-sheltered housing development, by their own self-reportings the participants rated their financial status as "very comfortable" (21%), "comfortable" (53%), and "not so good" (26%). It is safe to conclude that the residents in this sample represented a low to low-middle income group, since the mandate of the semi-sheltered housing development was to serve this particular socio-economic group (see Table 1 for additional demographic details).

Nursing Home Sample

The nursing home sample was drawn from four free-standing nursing home units representing intermediate, extended, and rehabilitative care for inpatients residing in multi-level nursing homes in four western Alberta communities. The

Table 1. Demographic Data on Community-based Residents

Age (*M, SD*):	72 yrs. ± 5.5 yrs.
Race:	72% White; 25% Orientals/Asians; 3% Blacks
Education (*M, SD*):	8-9 yrs. ± 4.5 yrs.
Occupational Status:	92% Retired; 8% Employed
Length of Stay (*M, SD*):	14 days ± 19 days
Hospitalization in Past 5 Years (*M, SD*):	1.4 ± 2.5
Perceived Health Severity Assessment (Rated on 7-Point Scale) (1-Least Severe—7=Very Severe) (*M, SD*):	3.6 ± 1.9

four nursing homes approached were randomly selected from a directory of sixteen private nursing homes.

A sample of nursing home residents was considered essential to this study on reminiscence activity for two reasons. First, nursing home residents are generally more homogeneous in their case mix than are community samples with respect to disability, physical health status, and self-reported depressive states (see Waxman, McCreary, Weinrit, and Carner [23]; Murrell, Himmelfarb, and Wright [16] for a discussion of differences between inpatient and outpatient participants). Second, objective indices of physical health status [24], activities of daily living capability (ADL), and negative life experiences are easier to assess in nursing home residents.

After consultation with the coordinators of the nursing homes, ninety individuals were judged to be eligible participants. These individuals were identified by the nursing staff as having little or no cognitive impairment and relatively little difficulty in verbal communications. Fifty women and forty men are encouraged by the nursing staff to participate in the study. However, a total of thirty-five men and thirty-five women agreed to participate; complete data were obtained on these seventy individuals.

Although no precise information was available on the financial or economic status of the nursing home residents, by their own self-reportings participants rated their financial status as "very comfortable" (18%), "comfortable" (62%), and "not so good" (20%). It is safe to conclude that the nursing home sample represented a low-middle to middle income group, since the private nursing homes selected for this study were financed by the province to serve this particular socio-economic group of clients. (See Table 2 for details of additional demographic data on subjects).

Hypothesized correlates of the frequency of reminiscence were measured using a number of scales.

1. *Scale of perceived physical health status.* Health was assessed by including fifty-six selected items of the *Cornell Medical Health Index* [22, 24] that requires an individual to provide self-rated indices of their cardiovascular, musculoskeletal, respiratory and nervous system, fatiguability levels, and general ratings of whether the individual perceives physical health as being *excellent, reasonably good,* or *poor.*

2. *A social support score* was computed for each individual based upon answers to six questionnaire items related to marital status, living alone or with someone else, and number of close friends helping in daily activities— the higher the score the greater the social support capability. This scale was adapted from one used by Waxman et al. [23].

3. *Activities of daily living (ADL)* were measured by fifteen questions from the OARS (Older American Resources and Services) Multi-dimensional Assessment Form [20]. OARS has been used extensively as a total scale to

Table 2. Demographic Data on Nursing Home Residents

Age (M, SD):	69 yrs. ± 6 yrs.
Race:	76% White; 19% Orientals/Asians; 5% Blacks
Education (M, SD):	10-11 yrs. ± 4 yrs.
Occupational Status:	95% Retired; 5% Employed
Length of Stay (M, SD):	78 days ± 42 days
Hospitalization in Past 5 Years (M, SD):	4.2 ± 1.9
Perceived Health Severity Assessment (Rated on 7-Point Scale) (1-Least Severe—7=Very Severe) (M, SD):	5.4 ± 2.2

assess the functional well-being and the capability for daily life activities of elderly persons. OARS is scored from 0 to 2, with 0 denoting the least functional individual. Scores can range from 0 to 30, with 30 denoting the most functional individual.

4. The frequency of negative life events was assessed by means of Sarason, Johnson, and Siegel's *Life Experiences Survey* [21] scale—the higher the score the greater the frequency of stressful and negative life events experienced in the past.

5. Mood disturbance was assessed by means of a mood assessment scale containing thirty items adapted from the *Geriatric Depression Scale* designed by Brink, Yesavage, Rose, Lum, et al. [25].

6. Ego-strength (ES) was assessed by the *ES* scale of the *MMPI*.

7. Exhibitionism, understanding, and sentience scales were adapted from the Personality Research Form. This scale is the only one of its kind preferred for use with nonpsychiatric older adults. Most scales include items of neuroticism and depression in the assessment of openness and sentience and are therefore not appropriate for use with elderly adults in the community [25].

8. Psychological well-being was assessed by Bradburn's Affect Balance Scale [26]. This scale tests an individual's position on two independent measures of positive affect (e.g., happiness, joy, and peace of mind) and negative affect (e.g., sadness, anxiety, and fear). It measures the transitory nature of well-being proposed by Liang [27]. Tests of this scale for internal validity result in correlations ranging from .86 on positive affect items to .97 on negative

affect items. The scale has been recommended by Mangan and Peterson [28] for use with older adults. Positive items were scored with a +1, and negative items with a -1; 10 was added to the total score, providing a range of 0 to 20, with highest score denoting the most positive affect.

9. Meaning and purpose in life was assessed by the *Life Attitude Profile*—a forty-six-item seven-point Likert scale developed by Reker and Peacock [29]. This scale consists of seven factorially derived dimensions and provides separate scores for factors such as Goal Seeking, Future Meaning, Existential Vacuum, Death Acceptance, Life Purpose, Life Control, and Will to Meaning. The *Life Attitude Profile* has been validated with several different age groups [30].

10. Reminiscence activity was measured using Havighurst and Glasser's *Reminiscence Questionnaire* [1]. Participants completed a reminiscence questionnaire that defined reminiscence as follows:

All of us from time to time look back over our lives, recalling people, events, thoughts, and feelings. Sometimes such recall comes unexpectedly, as idle thoughts and daydreams. Sometimes we purposely look back, trying to remember and reconstruct. Such retrospection, both purposive and spontaneous, may be called reminiscence [1, p. 245].

In the present study, the following two questions assessing the frequency and affective quality of reminiscence were examined:

1. "Some of us reminisce more than others. Looking back over the last several few weeks, would you say you have done a great deal, some, or very little reminiscing?"

2. "Events or experiences you recall during reminiscence may be pleasant, unpleasant, or neutral in affect. Would you most often characterize your reminiscence activities as most pleasant, pleasant, or unpleasant?"

RESULTS

In response to an item asking the respondents in both the nursing home and community samples how often they reminisce, 16 percent responded "very little," 52 percent responded "sometimes," and the remaining 32 percent responded "a great deal." An analysis of variance test conducted on these ratings suggest that while aged persons vary widely in their use of reminiscence, the older adults residing in nursing home settings and community settings did not differ significantly in the frequency of self-reported reminiscence ($F(1,138) = 2.23$).

In response to an item asking respondents in both samples to characterize their reminiscence activity as pleasant or unpleasant, 44 percent of the total sample described their reminiscence activity to be "most pleasant," 37 percent said "pleasant," while 19 percent said "unpleasant." An analysis of variance test conducted on these ratings showed that older adults residing in nursing home and community settings did not differ significantly in their ratings of the pleasantness of the reminiscence activity (F (1,138) = 1.95). As a result, the two groups were collapsed into one for all further analyses.

Correlation coefficients of the frequency of reminiscence and the pleasantness ratings of reminiscence are presented in Tables 3, 4, and 5. The correlation coefficients attest to the wide complex of interrelationships between the frequency of reminiscence and the pleasantness ratings of reminiscence with the twenty-one variables selected for the study. Overall, however, one notable finding is that the frequency of reminiscence and the pleasantness ratings of reminiscence emerged as independent factors and did not correlate significantly with each other.

Hierarchical multiple regression analyses were performed to test a predictor model assessing the independent contribution of each of the hypothesized predictors (i.e., personality measures, meaning and purpose in life measures, and objective measures of negative life events, activities of daily living, social support and health status) to the self-reported frequency of remiscence activity (see Table 6).

Table 3. Zero-Order Correlations (Two-tailed) between Dependent Variables of Frequency and Pleasantness Ratings of Reminiscence Activity and Study Variables Related to Personality Traits and States

Variables	1 PLS	2 MD	3 ES	4 SN	5 UNS	6 EX	7 PWB	8 PRR	9 RAL
1. Past Life Satisfaction (PLS)	—								
2. Mood Disturbance (MD)	−.35*	—							
3. Ego-Strength (ES)	−.48**	−.48**	—						
4. Sentience (Openness) (SN)	.45**	.11	−.12	—					
5. Understanding (UNS)	−.09	.06	.04	.51	—				
6. Exhibitionism (EX)	.03	−.07	.14	.29*	.46**	—			
7. Psychological Well-Being (PWB)	.27*	.28*	.25*	.44**	.26*	.14	—		
8. Pleasantness Ratings of Reminiscence Activity (PRR)	.32*	−.29*	.08	.44**	.14	.36*	.26*	—	
9. Reminiscence Activity (RAL) (Frequency Levels)	−.24*	.29*	−.29*	.51***	.37**	.30*	−.56***	.16	—

*$p < .05$
**$p < .01$
***$p < .001$

Table 4. Zero-Order Correlations (Two-tailed) between Dependent Variables
of Frequency and Pleasantness Ratings of Reminiscence Activity
and Study Variables Related to Perceived Meaning and Purpose in Life

Measures	1 GS	2 FM	3 EV	4 DA	5 LP	6 LC	7 WM	8 PRR	9 RAL
1. Goal Seeking (GS)	—								
2. Future Meaning (FM)	.27*	—							
3. Existential Vacuum (EV)	.14	.16	—						
4. Death Acceptance (DA)	.04	.09	.02	—					
5. Life Purpose (LP)	.32*	.24*	.08	.06	—				
6. Life Control (LC)	.23*	.11	.04	.04	.32*	—			
7. Will to Meaning (WM)	.24*	.26*	.14	.09	.34**	.18	—		
8. Pleasantness Ratings of Reminiscence Activity (PRR)	.18	.16	−.26*	.18	.32*	.23*	.44**	—	
9. Reminiscence Activity (RAL)	.37*	−.29*	.47**	.11	−.54***	.44**	.39*	.14*	—

*$p < .05$
**$p < .01$
***$p < .001$

Table 5. Zero-Order Correlations (Two-tailed) between Dependent Variables
of Frequency and Pleasantness Ratings of Reminiscence Activity
and Study Variables Related to Subjects' Objective Indices

Variables	1 NLE	2 HS	3 LHS	4 EL	5 ADL	6 PHS	7 SSI	8 PRR	9 RAL
1. Number of Negative Life Events (NLE)	—								
2. Hospitalizations in Past Five Years (HS)	.08	—							
3. Length of Stay in Hospital (LHS)	.29*	.11	—						
4. Education Levels (EL)	.04	.09	.06	—					
5. Activities of Daily Living (ADL)	.11	.19	.16	.02	—				
6. Perceived Health Severity (PHS)	.23*	.12	.14	.04	.24*	—			
7. Social Support Index (SSI)	.18	.14	.09	.03	.27*	−.16	—		
8. Pleasantness Ratings of Reminiscence Activity (PRR)	−.42**	−.23**	−.16	.02	.24*	.27*	.11	—	
9. Reminiscence Activity (RAL) (Frequency Levels)	.54	.18	.29*	.17	−.51***	−.12	−.49***	.15	—

*$p < .05$
**$p < .01$
***$p < .001$

As shown in Table 6, significant predictors ($p < .05$) of the self-reported frequency of reminiscence in older adults emerged as follows:

— Past Life Satisfaction (percentage of variance accounted for = 1.5)
— Mood Disturbance (percentage of variance accounted for = 1.4)
— Sentience (percentage of variance accounted for = 2.2)
— Psychological Well-Being (percentage of variance accounted for = 1.9)
— Goal Seeking (percentage of variance accounted for = 2.1)
— Future Meaning (percentage of variance accounted for = 1.6)
— Existential Vacuum (percentage of variance accounted for = 2.1)
— Life Purpose (percentage of variance accounted for = 1.8)
— Life Control (percentage of variance accounted for = 2.1)
— Will to Meaning (percentage of variance accounted for = 1.9)
— Number of Negative Life Events (percentage of variance accounted for = 2.7)
— Activities of Daily Living (percentage of variance accounted for = 1.8)
— Social Support Index (percentage of variance accounted for = 1.4)

Table 6. Hierarchical Multiple Regression Analysis on Study Variables as Predictors of Frequency of Reminiscence

Variables (df = 20,119)	R SQ. Change	F	p	Beta
1. Past Life Satisfactions (PLS)	.015	5.8	<.05	−5.26
2. Mood Disturbance (MD)	.014	5.6	<.05	−4.55
3. Ego-Strength (ES)	.006	2.1	NS	−1.66
4. Sentience (SN)	.022	12.7	<.001	5.21
5. Understanding (UNS)	.005	2.6	NS	−1.01
6. Exhibitionism (EX)	.006	1.9	NS	1.61
7. Psychological Well-Being (PWB)	.019	9.6	<.01	−4.78
8. Goal Seeking (GS)	.021	6.6	<.05	3.21
9. Future Meaning (FM)	.016	7.1	<.01	−3.98
10. Existential Vacuum (EV)	.021	10.9	<.01	5.11
11. Death Acceptance (DA)	.006	1.9	NS	1.21
12. Life Purpose (LP)	.018	7.6	<.01	−4.98
13. Life Control (LC)	.021	8.6	<.01	−5.21
14. Willing to Meaning (WM)	.019	15.1	<.001	5.78
15. Number of Negative Life Events (NLE)	.027	13.7	<.001	6.01
16. Number of Hospitalizations (HS)	.003	1.1	NS	1.31
17. Length of Stay in Hospital (LHS)	.004	0.9	NS	0.99
18. Education Levels (EL)	.006	2.0	NS	1.41
19. Activities of Daily Living (ADL)	.018	7.4	<.01	−5.21
20. Perceived Health Severity (PHS)	.006	2.5	NS	0.99
21. Social Support Index (SSI)	.014	5.8	<.05	−4.11
Total R^2 =	.287			

Hierarchical multiple regression analyses were performed to test a predictor model that assessed the *independent contribution* of each of the hypothesized predictors described earlier to the self-reported pleasantness ratings of the reminiscence activity (see Table 7).

As shown in Table 7, significant predictors ($p < .05$) of the self-reported pleasantness ratings of reminiscence activity emerged as follows:

— Past Life Satisfactions (percentage of variance accounted for = 1.8)
— Sentience (percentage of variance accounted for = 1.9)
— Exhibitionism (percentage of variance accounted for = 1.9)
— Psychological Well-Being (percentage of variance accounted for = 2.8)
— Existential Vacuum (percentage of variance accounted for = 2.7)
— Life Control (percentage of variance accounted for = 1.4)
— Will to Meaning (percentage of variance accounted for = 2.1)
— Number of Negative Life Events (percentage of variance accounted for = 2.2)
— Activities of Daily Living (percentage of variance accounted for = 1.9)

Table 7. Hierarchical Multiple Regression Analysis on Study Variables as Predictors of Pleasantness of Reminiscence Activity

Variables (df = 20,119)	R SQ. Change	F	p	Beta
1. Past Life Satisfactions (PLS)	.018	5.6	<.05	4.98
2. Mood Disturbance (MD)	.008	2.4	NS	1.01
3. Ego-Strength (ES)	.004	1.84	NS	−1.64
4. Sentience (SN)	.021	10.1	<.01	4.72
5. Understanding (UNS)	.006	1.0	NS	0.98
6. Exhibitionism (EX)	.019	4.9	<.05	3.95
7. Psychological Well-Being (PWB)	.028	9.2	<.01	4.95
8. Goal Seeking (GS)	.001	1.2	NS	1.12
9. Future Meaning (FM)	.000	1.9	NS	1.09
10. Existential Vacuum (EV)	.027	12.1	<.001	−6.01
11. Death Acceptance (DA)	.004	0.9	NS	−0.99
12. Life Purpose (LP)	.004	1.6	NS	1.81
13. Life Control (LC)	.014	5.1	<.05	3.76
14. Willing to Meaning (WM)	.021	9.9	<.01	4.69
15. Number of Negative Life Events (NLE)	.022	11.2	<.001	−5.21
16. Number of Hospitalizations (HS)	.006	2.5	NS	−1.61
17. Length of Stay in Hospital (LHS)	.005	1.9	NS	−1.05
18. Education Levels (EL)	.002	1.4	NS	1.08
19. Activities of Daily Living (ADL)	.019	7.1	<.01	4.22
20. Perceived Health Severity (PHS)	.006	2.2	NS	0.99
21. Social Support Index (SSI)	.005	1.8	NS	1.02
Total R^2 =	.240			

When multiple regression analyses of study variables for predicting the frequency of reminiscence activity and the pleasantness ratings of reminiscence activity were compared (see Tables 6 and 7), it was clear that among factors predicting both frequency of reminiscence and pleasantness of reminiscence, the following were significant: Past Life Satisfactions, Sentience, Psychological Well-Being, Existential Vacuum, Life Control, Will to Meaning, Number of Negative Life Events, and Number of Activities of Daily Life.

DISCUSSION

What then can be said of the relationship between reminiscence activity and the psychological characteristics of elderly persons?

First, it can be argued that older persons vary widely in the frequency of their reminiscence activity and the degree of pleasantness they associate with the reminiscence activity. Based upon the results of the present study, it can be concluded that the normative process of reminiscence in the naturalistic environment is frequent, pleasing, and gratifying for a large percentage of elderly adults. These findings support the results of earlier studies [5, 6] which concluded that a majority of elderly individuals find opportunities for reminiscence as not merely pleasant but as fulfilling the need to bolster self-esteem. However, consistent with the results of other empirical investigations [3, 16, 31], the findings of the present study also suggest that reminiscence activity in the natural environment has not been a consistent source of pleasantness for elderly adults.

Although no assumptions of causality are implied, it appears from the results as if elderly individuals who self-reportedly engage in a greater frequency of reminiscence are also individuals who have certain traits and characteristics that, perhaps, contribute to their greater responsiveness to the reminiscence process. For example, the significant association between the frequency of reminiscence and sentience or openness to experience argues that this particular personality trait may play an important role in determining the individual's capacity for reminiscence in the natural environment. The results of the multiple regression analyses confirming sentience or openness as one of the significant predictors of the frequency and pleasantness of reminiscence activity in the natural environment support earlier findings of Brennan and Steinberg [3] who found that sentience or openness is a significant characteristic of elderly persons having a desire to achieve self-awareness through the therapeutic process.

Extrapolating from the results of previous studies and the results of the present, it may be argued that, at least in the natural environment, sentience or openness promotes reminiscence. It is equally plausible that individuals having the "trait" of sentience or openness probably have more life experiences to reminisce about and, therefore, find the reminiscence activity to be more pleasant. However, since the present study did not collect information about the contents of the respondents' reminiscence, it is difficult to conclude whether it is the reminiscence process that is pleasant or whether the contents of the reminiscence of individuals having the sentience trait make the activity more pleasant for them. In either case, the fact remains that in the present study sentience is a significant predictor not only of the self-reported frequency of reminiscence but also of the pleasantness of the reminiscence activity.

The negative association between the frequency of reminiscence and the respondents' psychological well-being (defined as the presence of positive emotions of happiness and the absence of negative emotions such as fear and anxiety) and the number of activities of daily life suggests that perhaps it is the presence of negative affects such as depression and anxiety that plays a contributory role in bringing reminiscence activity to the fore in the natural environment. One plausible explanation for the finding of a negative correlation between the frequency of reminiscence and the respondents' psychological well-being and the frequency of reminiscence and the number of activities of daily life is that individuals who have positive perceptions of psychological well-being, and who are engaged in a number of activities in their daily functioning, are probably already involved in pursuits that provide ongoing significance and meaning to their lives. It is not surprising therefore that they resort to reminiscence less frequently than others who are either depressed or who have limited functional capabilities for engaging in a variety of activities.

The present findings of a negative association between self-reported frequency and the number of activities of daily living are also consistent with the earlier theoretical positions of activity theorists who argued that elderly persons' perceptions of psychological and physical well-being are causally related to higher levels of outgoingness and direct activity [31-33]. It can be speculated that, regardless of age, individuals with positive perceptions of well-being and past life satisfactions have more meaningful activity choices in the present and, hence, may have less time or interest in reminiscing about the past. This position is consistent with that of Shupe [31] who noted that perceptions of limited activity, limited life choices, and helplessness are frequently reflected in the reminiscences of many elderly persons both in the natural environment and in the therapeutic environment. It is important to note, however, that psychological well-being and the functional capability to engage in a number of activities of daily living are significant predictors of the frequency of reminiscence activity in elderly persons.

Finally, the negative correlation between the frequency of reminiscence and variables such as purpose in life, life control, and will to meaning suggests that, in the naturalistic environment, older individuals still struggling to find concrete meaning in personal existence are likely to resort more frequently to reminiscence activity. One explanation for this may be that a general "thoughtfulness" about life underlies both the reminiscence process and the search for will to meaning and purpose in life [34]. It is equally possible that the search for values and goals in later years triggers reminiscence in certain individuals with particular types of personality attributes [5]. One might also argue that older individuals having positive perceptions of life control, life purpose, and future meaning are probably involved in goal-directed activity in the present [29, 30] and, as a result, may have less need for or time to reminisce about the past. By contrast, based upon the present results, one might argue that reminiscence activity serves a more pressing need for individuals who are experiencing a sense of existential vacuum in the present or who lack a sense of life purpose or will to meaning [34]. As noted by Blazer and Williams [35] and Fry [36], individuals experiencing the anxiety of meaninglessness [18] or striving to find a life purpose may revert more frequently to recollections of previous positive events.

Although the present study made some attempt to examine the relationship of reminiscence and personality traits, background factors, and life attitudes, many issues concerning the causality and the direction of the relationship remain unsettled. Our current knowledge of individual differences that trigger the reminiscence function in respect to both frequency and pleasantness continues to be tentative and qualified. A more systematic study of individual variations or mediators of the reminiscence function is warranted.

Meanwhile, the results of the present study provide clear evidence of the independent contribution of factors such as openness, psychological well-being, will to meaning, and life purpose in predicting self-reported frequency, and the pleasantness of reminiscence activity in elders. Additionally, based on the present results it is safe to postulate that individuals who have more options in activities available to them in the present, or those who have experienced a number of negative life events in the past, will be less responsive to the reminiscence process.

Although the probable gap between elders' reminiscence in the naturalistic evironment and reminiscence in the therapeutic environment is recognized, the present results obtained in a naturalistic environment may have significant implications for mental health professionals concerned with using reminiscence as a therapeutic tool with elderly adults. A detailed discussion of these implications is beyond the purview of this article, however. It is safe to conclude that elderly individuals having a delicate balance of traits such as sentience or openness will probably be more responsive to reminiscence as a therapeutic process. Additionally, elderly individuals striving to achieve a will to meaning or purpose in life may be more responsive to reminiscence as a therapeutic process. In contrast, individuals who have experienced a number of negative life events in the past are less likely to find the reminiscence activity pleasant or contributing to self-esteem development in the present [3, 8].

REFERENCES

1. R. Havighurst and R. Glasser, An Exploratory Study of Reminiscence, *Journal of Gerontology, 27*, pp. 243-253, 1972.

2. M. Lieberman and J. Falk, The Remembered Past as a Source of Data for Research on the Life Cycle, *Human Development, 14*, pp. 132-141, 1971.
3. P. L. Brennan and L. D. Steinberg, Is Reminiscence Adaptive?, *International Journal of Aging and Human Development, 18*:2, pp. 99-110, 1983-1984.
4. W. Boylin, S. K. Gordon, and M. F. Nehrke, Reminiscing and Ego Integrity in Institutionalized Elderly Males, *The Gerontologist, 16*, pp. 118-124, 1976.
5. M. Romaniuk and J. G. Romaniuk, Looking Back: An Analysis of Reminiscence Functions and Triggers, *Experimental Aging Research, 7*, pp. 477-489, 1981.
6. P. G. Coleman, Measuring Reminiscence Characteristics from Conversation as Adaptive Features of Old Age, *International Journal of Aging and Human Development, 5*, pp. 281-294, 1974.
7. D. J. Sperbeck, Age and Personality Effects on Autobiographical Memory in Adulthood, Unpublished Dissertation, University of Rochester, 1982.
8. C. N. Lewis, Reminiscence and Self-concept in Old Age, *Journal of Gerontology, 26*, pp. 240-243, 1971.
9. B. G. Myerhoff and V. Tufte, Life History as Integration: An Essay on an Experiential Model, *The Gerontologist, 15*, pp. 541-543, 1975.
10. M. Thurnher, Goals, Values and Life Evaluations at the Preretirement Stage, *Journal of Gerontology, 29*, pp. 85-96, 1974.
11. J. G. Ouslander, Physical Illness and Depression in the Elderly, *Journal of the American Geriatrics Society, 30*, pp. 593-599, 1982.
12. P. S. Fry, Structured and Unstructured Reminiscence Training and Depression among the Elderly, *Clinical Gerontologist, 1*, pp. 15-37, 1983.
13. B. L. Padelford, Relationship between Drug Involvement and Purpose in Life, *Journal of Clinical Psychology, 30*, pp. 303-305, 1974.
14. B. F. Sheffield and P. R. Pearson, Purpose-in-Life in a Sample of British Psychiatric Out-patients, *Journal of Clinical Psychology, 30*, p. 459, 1974.
15. R. N. Butler, The Life Review: An Interpretation of Reminiscence in the Aged, *Psychiatry, 26*, pp. 65-76, 1963.
16. S. A. Murrell, S. Himmelfarb, and K. Wright, Prevalence of Depression and Its Correlates in Older Adults, *American Journal of Epidemiology, 117*:2, pp. 173-185, 1983.
17. C. Hauseman, Life Review Therapy, *Journal of Gerontological Social Work, 3*:2, pp. 31-37, 1980.
18. J. E. Ruffin, The Anxiety of Meaninglessness, *Journal of Counseling and Development, 63*, pp. 40-42, 1984.
19. V. Molinari and R. E. Reichlin, Life Review Reminiscence in the Elderly: A Review of the Literature, *International Journal of Aging and Human Development, 20*, pp. 81-92, 1984-1985.
20. *Multidimensional Functional Assessment: The OARS Methodology*, Duke University, The Center for the Study of Aging and Human Development, 1978.
21. I. G. Sarason, J. H. Johnson, and J. M. Siegel, Assessing the Impact of Life Changes: Development of the Life Experiences Survey, *Journal of Consulting and Clinical Psychology, 46*, pp. 932-946, 1978.
22. K. Brodman, A. J. Erdmann, I. Lorge, and H. G. Wolff, The Cornell Medical Index: An Adjunct to Medical Interview, *Journal of the American Medical Association, 140*, pp. 530-534, 1949.

23. H. M. Waxman, G. McCreary, R. M. Weinrit, and E. A. Carner, A Comparison of Somatic Complaints among Depressed and Non-depressed Older Persons, *The Gerontologist, 25*:5, pp. 501-507, 1985.
24. K. Brodman, A. J. Erdman, I. Lorge, and H. G. Wolff, The Cornell Medical Index-Health Questionnaire II as a Diagnostic Instrument, *Journal of the American Medical Association, 142*, pp. 152-157, 1951.
25. T. L. Brink, J. A. Yesavage, O. Lum, P. Heersema, M. Adey, and T. L. Rose, Screening Test for Geriatric Depression, *Clinical Gerontologist, 1*, pp. 37-43, 1982.
26. N. Bradburn, *Structure of Psychological Well-Being*, Aldine, Chicago, 1969.
27. J. Liang, Dimensions of the Life Satisfaction Index A: A Structural Formulation, *Journal of Gerontology, 39*, pp. 613-622, 1984.
28. D. Mangan and W. A. Peterson, *Research Instruments in Social Gerontology*, University of Minnesota Press, Minneapolis, 1982.
29. G. T. Reker and E. J. Peacock, The Life Attitude Profile (LAP): A Multi-dimensional Instrument for Assessing Attitudes toward Life, *Canadian Journal of Behavioural Science 13*, pp. 264-273, 1981.
30. G. T. Reker, E. J. Peacock, and P. T. P. Wong, Meaning and Purpose in Life and Well-Being: A Life-Span Perspective, *Journal of Gerontology, 42*, pp. 44-49, 1987.
31. D. R. Shupe, Perceived Control, Helplessness, and Choice, in *Cognition, Stress and Aging*, J. E. Birren and J. Livingston (eds.), Prentice-Hall, Englewood Cliffs, New Jersey, 1985.
32. J. Hendricks and C. Davis Hendricks, *Aging in Mass Society: Myths and Realities*, Little, Brown and Co., Boston, 1986.
33. B. Hedgepath and D. Hale, Effect of a Positive Reminiscing Intervention on Affect Expectancy and Performance, *Psychological Report, 53*, pp. 867-870, 1983.
34. L. B. Rubin, *Women of Certain Age: The Midlife Search for Self*, Harper & Row, New York, 1979.
35. D. Blazer and C. D. Williams, Epidemiology of Dysphoria and Depression in an Elderly Population, *American Journal of Psychiatry, 137*, pp. 439-444, 1980.
36. P. S. Fry, *Depression, Stress and Adaptations in the Elderly: Psychological Assessment and Interventions*, Aspen Publishers, Rockville, Maryland, 1986.

Chapter 6

IF YOU HAD YOUR LIFE TO LIVE OVER AGAIN: WHAT WOULD YOU DO DIFFERENTLY?

Mary Kay DeGenova

The study examines what elderly people would spend more or less time doing if they had their lives to relive. This idea assumes elderly people reflect back on their lives in an evaluative sense. This theory is supported by Butler's presumption that the life review of one's past is a natural process occurring in later life [1]. It is characterized by the progressive return to consciousness of past experiences and the resurgence of unresolved conflicts. Butler posited that negative perceptions of the past are relevant in daily life in later life, and that reflections of the past, unresolved conflicts, and regrets affect life satisfaction [1].

Butler and Lewis pointed out some of the positive results of life review as being a righting of old wrongs, making up with enemies, coming to an acceptance of mortal life, developing a sense of serenity, feeling pride in accomplishment, and gaining a feeling of having done one's best [2]. They argue the experience of reminiscence must be surveyed and reintegrated for old age to be met in an adaptive manner.

Coleman refers to Butler's idea of life review as closely linked to Erikson's last stage, ". . . as it suggests a process whereby acceptance of one's one and only life cycle is or is not achieved" [3, p. 46]. The idea of life review is similar to Erikson's theory of later life being a time when personal adjustment involves the ability to sort through the memories of one's life and pull them together into a meaningful whole [4]. Erikson indicates something of the hunger for a meaningful view in the last part of life, and the lack of more substantial and comprehensible alternatives [4]. Unfortunately, since his account was first written, the characteristics of 'integrity' that he describes: acceptance of one's past life without regrets, a harmonious view of past, present and future, and a loss of fear of death, are rarely achieved [5].

Do older people frequently think about the past? The literature on life review and reminiscence is inconclusive on whether older people participate more in this process than any other age group. Although Cameron [6] and Giambra [7] did not find older people to be more involved in reminiscence about the past than younger people, they found that older people do think about the past. They also found that age was not a factor in frequency of reminiscence.

Costa and Kastenbaum studied centenarians and found there is more engrossment in memories of the remote past than recent past [8]. Lieberman and Falk [9] and Revere and Tobin [10] found older people reminisce more than middle age people. Some studies report that two-thirds of elderly people interviewed stated they do reminisce about the past [11, 12].

Older people may or may not think more about the past than younger people, but from existing research one can assume that many do indeed think about the past. It is possible that everyone thinks about the past and the elderly are no different. It is certain, however, that whether they choose to think about the past or not, the better part of their lives can be viewed in retrospect at the age of sixty-five.

METHODS

For the purpose of this study, life revision is defined as a desire or wish to change certain past thoughts, feelings, actions, or accomplishments relative to some object, person, activity, or situation, if it was possible to relive one's past life.

One of the biggest problems in conducting this research was the lack of previous research on life revision in later life. Since there was no existing measure, an instrument was designed by the author.

The Life Revision Index consists of thirty-five questions dealing with what people would do differently if they could live their lives over again (Table 1). For example, "If you had your life to live over again, how much time would you spend with good friends?" The thirty-five questions are divided equally into seven subgroups: family, work, friendships, health, education, leisure, and religion. The participants were asked to indicate if they would do an activity much more, more, about the same, less, or much less. To the right of each question, participants circled a number indicating the desired response based on a five-point scale.

A total life revision score was calculated by adding the points from each question. The responses were recorded as follows: A great deal more = 10; more = 5; about the same = 0; less = -5; and a great deal less = -10. The absolute values were added together for scoring. Original values were added together to address the direction of the life revision, whether more or less activity was desired. Frequency distributions and multivariate statistics were used to analyze the data.

Table 1. Life Revision Index

If you had your life to live over again, how much time would you spend . . .	Much more (percent)	More (percent)	Same (percent)	Less (percent)	Much less (percent)
1. With good friends	9.8	29.5	59.0	1.6	0
2. Keeping up with good friends (letter writing, phone calls, visits)	4.9	45.1	48.4	1.6	0
3. In social activities	1.6	24.6	67.2	5.7	.8
4. Developing friendships	6.6	40.2	50.8	2.5	0
5. Getting to know more people	8.2	32.0	57.4	2.5	0
6. In family activities	16.4	39.3	43.4	.8	0
7. Keeping up with family members (letter writing, phone calls, visits)	9.0	40.2	50.0	.8	0
8. At home with your family	9.0	21.3	68.9	.8	0
9. Developing close relations with your children	8.2	33.6	58.2	0	0
10. Developing close relations with your siblings	6.6	23.0	67.2	3.3	0
11. Keeping up with the demands of work	.8	9.8	72.1	16.4	.8
12. In work activities	.8	4.1	78.7	16.4	0
13. Worrying about your job	0	0	40.2	50.0	9.8
14. Financially preparing for the future	13.9	31.1	52.5	1.6	.8
15. Developing your career	11.5	31.1	55.7	1.6	0
16. Keeping current on topics that interest you	4.9	32.8	61.5	.8	0
17. In learning activities	3.3	36.9	57.4	1.6	.8
18. Studying	7.4	34.4	56.6	1.6	0
19. Developing your mind or intellect	13.1	43.4	43.4	0	0
20. Pursuing your education	15.6	45.5	37.7	.8	0
21. Traveling	13.9	38.5	45.1	1.6	.8
22. Making sure you fit in leisure time or time for fun	5.7	45.1	47.5	1.6	0
23. Doing things you enjoy	9.8	49.2	39.3	1.6	0
24. Relaxing	4.9	35.2	54.1	5.7	0
25. Developing hobbies	5.7	33.6	55.7	4.1	.8
26. In devotion to a religion	9.0	35.2	54.1	1.6	0
27. In charitable activities	1.6	26.6	66.4	5.7	0
28. Developing your spirituality	9.0	32.8	53.3	4.1	.8
29. In prayer	15.6	33.6	50.0	.8	0
30. Studying a religion	8.2	34.4	52.5	4.9	0
31. Developing good eating habits	14.8	26.2	58.2	.8	0
32. Exercising	11.5	44.3	41.8	1.6	.8
33. Taking good physical care of your body	8.2	45.9	45.9	0	.8
34. On personal appearance	4.9	26.2	68.0	.8	0
35. Visiting the doctor	.0	4.1	84.4	10.7	.8

Each subject received an overall life revision score. The mean life revision score was ninety-two (range 0 to 290), out of a possible range of zero to 350. The higher the score on life revision, the more change desired.

It is difficult to measure the construct validity of this instrument since no instrument has attempted to measure life revision. Content validity was measured by gathering the opinions of elderly people and people in the field regarding the reasonableness of the measure. Items were reviewed according to the opinions of others. A group of twenty-five elderly persons, ten professors, and ten graduate students were involved in pretesting the instrument, and revisions were made accordingly.

Reliability for the Life Revision Index was measured using the coefficient alpha. The internal consistency reliability (alpha) of the sample for life revision was .84.

Sample Procedure

A random sample of 200 retired persons was drawn using the 1987 Lafayette, Indiana *City Directory* as the sampling frame. The directory lists occupations of everyone in the household, and retirement is a classification.

The selection process consisted of randomly selecting 200 pages from the *City Directory*. Every fifth name in these pages was recorded until 400 names of retired people were selected. A random list of 400 names, addresses, and phone numbers of retired people was compiled. The Lafayette phone book was used to acquire a phone number and recent address for each name. One hundred-twenty four of the 400 people listed were not found in the phone book and were removed from the list. Finally, 200 people randomly selected from the revised list were mailed a questionnaire to be filled out and returned in a postage-paid envelope. The response was 61 percent.

Participants

The sample consisted of 122 participants, eighty-one females and forty-one males. The ages of the participants ranged from fifty-four to ninety-one years of age, with a mean age of 72.1. The range for educational level was from three to seventeen plus years, with the mean being 12.5 years. In general, the respondents were either married or widowed. Sixty-eight percent were married, 28 percent were widowed, 2 percent were divorced or separated and 2 percent were never married. The income level varied from under $10,000 to over $50,000, with the majority of participants falling between the $10,000 to $30,000 range. Three people failed to report their income and this was treated as missing data. Only 9 percent of the respondents reported being in poor or very poor health. Twenty-five percent reported their health as sometimes good/sometimes not, 46 percent reported good health, and 21 percent very good health. Most of the respondents did not rate high in social activity; only 8 percent reported being very active.

Thirty-five percent responded as being active, 32 percent responded as being sometimes active/sometimes not, and 25 percent reported being not very active.

It should be noted that Lafayette, Indiana has a low ethnic population. Less than 3 percent of its population is either African-American, Hispanic, Asian, or Native American. This sample only allows for generalization to white, mostly middle class America.

RESULTS

Descriptive Analysis

The direction of life revision (whether more or less change was desired) was examined for each of the items. The particular areas that over 50 percent of participants have spent more or much more time in were: family activities; financially preparing for the future; developing a career; developing one's mind or intellect; pursuing one's education; traveling; doing things one enjoys; exercising; and taking good physical care of one's body. The only area that over 50 percent of the participants would have spent less or much less time in was worrying about one's job (see Table 1).

Although there was no significant difference in the amount of life revision experienced by men and women, there were some differences between men and women in what they would do differently if they had the chance. Men said they would spend more time pursuing their education. This was followed by, in order of importance: spending more time in family activities; financially preparing for the future; praying; developing a career; keeping up with family members; and developing friendships. Women would spend more time developing their minds or intellect. This was followed by spending more time: doing things they enjoyed; pursuing their education; in family activities; traveling; exercising; and praying.

Exploratory Analysis

Since education was the area with the highest desired changes, it was hypothesized that education would be an important predictor of life revision. Standard multiple regression analysis was conducted looking at the effects of education on life revision. Since health, social activity, and income are important predictors of life satisfaction in later life [13], they were entered into the equation as control variables. All the variables were entered together as one block. Outlying cases were removed from the analysis using a 2.5, z score criterion.

The results revealed that R for regression was significantly different from zero, $R2 = .44$, $F(4,117) = 23.7$, $p < .0000$ (see Table 2). The best predictor of life revision was education with an F value of 82.3, $p < .0000$. No other variable was significant in predicting life revision.

Table 2. Standard Multiple Regression Results Dependent
Variable: Life Revision

	b	Beta	sr2	F
Education	2.8	.64	.64	82.3***
Health	−8.6	−.15	−.18	4.0
Social	1.1	.01	.02	.80
Income	−.04	.01	−.01	.02
R = .67	R2 = .44	Adj R = .42	F = 23.8	Sig F = 0000

***$p < .0001$

Standard multiple regression analysis was also conducted looking at the relationship of health, income, social activity and educational level to areas with the highest desired change. Again, since education was the area with the most desired change, it was expected that educational level would be the most significant predictor. A separate regression analysis was run for each of the following dependent variables: developing one's mind or intellect; pursuing one's education; worrying about one's job; doing things one enjoys; and time spent in family activities.

Looking at the variable of how much time one would spend pursuing his or her education, R for regression was significantly different from zero, $R2 = .18$, $F(4,116) = 6.4$, $p < .0001$. The best predictor was educational level ($F = 19.04$, $p < .0000$). No other variables were significant predictors of how much time one would spend pursuing an education. The less education respondents had the more time they would spend pursuing education.

With "how much time one would spend doing things they enjoy" in the equation, R for regression was significantly different from zero, $R2 = .08$, $F(4,117) = 2.7$, $p < .05$. Educational level was the only significant predictor ($F = 8.3$, $p < .01$). The less education, the more time one would spend doing things one enjoys.

R for regression was not significantly different from zero when looking at how much time one would spend developing the mind or intellect, worrying about the demands of work, or participating in family activities. However, educational level was the only significant predictor of how much time one would spend developing the mind or intellect, $F(4,117) = 7.3$, $p < .01$. The less education, the more time one would spend developing their mind or intellect. Income was the most significant predictor of how much time one would spend worrying about their job, $F(4,117) = 8.2$, $p < .01$. The higher the income, the less time they would spend worrying about the demands of work. Nothing was significant for predicting time spent in family activities.

DISCUSSION

This study reveals that education is highly valued. If life could be lived over again, more time would be spent pursuing education and developing the mind and intellect for men and women, respectively, than in any other area. This identifies the value placed on both formal and informal education when reviewing one's life.

Education was also an overwhelming predictor of life revision in later life. What is it about education that is so important? It is possible that lack of education leads to missed or limited opportunities.

The high value placed on education among the elderly should not be taken lightly, especially in a time when the high school dropout rate is escalating. This study could be a subtle form of advice to the youth of today that education is an important investment. Education matters!

It is also interesting to note that people would have spent more time doing many different things, but they would have spent less time worrying about the demands of work. There is an unequal balance between more and less time spent. Where would people get all the extra time in life if they are only willing to spend less time in one area? It could be that they spent a large amount of time worrying about the demands of work, or the questionnaire did not adequately assess the areas they would have spent less time in, or life is just too busy to do everything. In retrospect, a question should have asked about the amount of time spent watching TV.

The incredible diversity, years of experience, and accumulation of wisdom through participation in life which the elderly have is a great resource of our day that is underutilized. What better way to learn what life is about than to ask someone who has lived it and is approaching its end?

Learning about the things people would do differently if they had the chance can be beneficial to the listeners and readers of this information. The reciprocal contributions of the life review process, which may be conceived of as a form of oral history [1], may include "a personal sense of life's flow from birth to death, personal solutions from encountering grief and loss regarding old age and death, and models for growing older and for creating meaningful lives" [14, p. 173]. As Coleman stated so well, "The significance of people and events, movements and philosophies can rarely be appreciated at the time, but only in the context of a retrospective view" [3, p. 3].

Limitations of the Study

It is important to remember that the average educational level of this sample was twelve years. Had this questionnaire been administered only to those elderly individuals who have a college education, the results could be different due to the increase in educational level. Also, the results could be due to a cohort effect. That generation might have spent more time with the family and less time pursuing an education than the young today. Fifty years from now if the same questionnaire is administered to the elderly, one might get different results.

REFERENCES

1. R. N. Butler, The Life Review: An Interpretation of Reminiscence in the Aged, *Psychiatry, 26*, pp. 65-76, 1963.
2. R. Butler and M. Lewis, *Aging and Mental Health: Positive Psychosocial and Biomedical Approaches*, Mosby, St. Louis, 1982.
3. P. Coleman, Issues in the Therapeutic Use of Reminiscence with Elderly People, in *Psychological Therapies for the Elderly*, I. Hanley and M. Gilhooly (eds.), Crome Hall, London, 1986.
4. E. H. Erikson, *Childhood and Society*, W. W. Norton, New York, 1963.
5. V. Clayton, Erikson's Theory of Human Development as It Applies to the Aged: Wisdom as Contradictive Cognition, *Human Development, 18*, pp. 119-128, 1975.
6. P. Cameron, The Generation Gap: Time Orientation, *The Gerontologist*, Part 1, pp. 117-119, Summer 1972.
7. L. M. Giambra, Daydreaming about the Past: The Time Setting of Spontaneous Thought Intrusions, *The Gerontologist, 17*:1, pp. 35-38, 1977.
8. P. Costa and R. Kastenbaum, Some Aspects of Memories and Ambitions in Centenarians, *Journal of Genetic Psychology, 12*, pp. 3-16, 1967.
9. M. Lieberman and J. Falk, The Remembered Past as a Source of Data for Research on the Life Cycle, *Human Development, 14*, pp. 132-141, 1971.
10. V. Revere and S. S. Tobin, Myth and Reality: The Older Person's Relationship to His Past, *International Journal of Aging and Human Development, 12*:1, pp. 15-26, 1980-81.
11. R. Havignurst and R. Glaser, An Exploratory Study of Reminiscence, *Journal of Gerontology, 27*, pp. 245-253, 1972.
12. W. Boylin, S. Gordon, and M. Nehrke, Reminiscing and Ego Integrity in Institutionalized Elderly Males, *The Gerontologist, 16*, pp. 118-124, 1976.
13. R. Larson, Thirty Years of Research on the Subjective Well-being of the Older Americans, *Journal of Gerontology, 33*:1, pp. 109-125, 1978.
14. R. Butler, Successful Aging and the Role of the Life Review, *Journal of American Geriatrics Society, 22*, pp. 529-525, 1974.

Chapter 7

A STUDY OF AUTOBIOGRAPHICAL MEMORIES IN DEPRESSED AND NONDEPRESSED ELDERLY INDIVIDUALS

Janet Anderson Yang
and
Lynn P. Rehm

Studying the relationship between mood and memories for past events among elderly individuals is an important pursuit because such study among depressed people may increase our understanding of factors associated with depression in this population and because such study among nondepressed elderly can contribute to our understanding of healthy coping processes in the face of age-related losses. Processes and organization in memory have been implicated both as playing an important role in contributing to depression and as forming coping resources in the face of negative events and circumstances. This article addresses aspects of memory for autobiographical events which are associated with depression and lack of depression.

Teasdale and his colleagues present a theory of reciprocal relationship between cognition and depression [1-5], based on Bower's semantic network model [6]. They suggest that depressed people have many memories of negative self-relevant experiences, and that their attention is more likely to be directed toward negative aspects of current experience. These cognitive processes encourage the person to interpret experiences more negatively and to expect negative things to happen in the future. Because of mood-congruent memory effects, when one depressing event or thought occurs, a person more easily accesses various thoughts and memories which were learned or active during previous depressed moods, and therefore the person will get caught in a cycle of thinking about the sad event, accessing memories of previously depressing events, and lose access to thoughts of anything which is not sad. This model posits that cognitions, including memories, exist in a semantic network composed of nodes and associations between nodes. A person's current mood activates specific associative networks, and current mood is likely to be negative when a person has experienced a meaningful loss. Rehm and Naus elaborate on Teasdale's model, proposing a self-structure composed of memories, facts, beliefs, feelings, and attitudes about the self existing in memory [7]. Affect is a salient feature of how memories are encoded, stored, and retrieved; access to a particular memory is facilitated by an affectively congruent emotional state. Depression is precipitated by negative personally-relevant events which increase access to depressive self-schemas, including sad memories. In depression prone people, negative self-schema are more easily accessed than in non-depression prone people because they are stronger, more extensive, and related to more concepts in memory. In non-depressed people, positive self-schemas are more extensive than negative ones, so following a negative personally-relevant event, access to memories will be redirected to positive memories.

Empirical research has documented an effect of increased accessibility of mood congruent memories. Studies have found that clinical depression or induced depressed mood is associated with increased latency to retrieve positive memories [3, 4, 8], decreased latency to retrieve negative memories [8], retrieval of fewer positive memories [2, 4, 5], and more negative memories [4, 5]. Few studies utilizing this research paradigm have been conducted with elderly participants. Hyland and Ackerman found that among normal participants, there was no correlation between the score on a mood measure and the proportion of pleasant versus unpleasant memories retrieved in response to a list of cue words [9].

Memories for personal events among elderly individuals have more often been looked at within the context of life review and reminiscence theories than in relation to depression. These theories propose ways in which an older person's processes of thinking about memories will contribute to satisfactory completion of developmental tasks and to well-being. Erikson theorized that the task in old age is to come to an "acceptance of one's one and only lifecycle as something that had to be and that, by necessity, permitted of no substitutions" [10, p. 268]; "the older person is to consolidate his understanding of the life he has lived, a process which includes a 'mourning' for the lost opportunities of each developmental stage" [11, p. 63]. Under favorable conditions this experience will create an integration of earlier stages, enabling the person to come to terms with death. Butler asserts that old age involves a naturally occurring process of reviewing one's life, such that past experiences, especially unresolved conflicts, progressively return to consciousness [12]. Memories of these experiences can be reintegrated leading to serenity and wisdom. However, the more intense the unresolved conflicts, the harder it is to reintegrate the memories, and life review may lead to states such as despair and depression.

Molinari and Reichlin present a model of reminiscence as "psychological action," proposing that reminiscence is a deliberately initiated action to consolidate and redefine the self-identity in face of experiences of aging which are incompatible with the person's self-identity [13]. They suggest that this process establishes a sense of continuity with the self known in previous years. When experiences of aging have a negative impact on the person's current sense of self, reminiscing about past experiences can redefine one's current sense of self in light of past achievements. Other researchers have also proposed that thinking and/or talking about past events operate as an adaptive mechanism to help an older person cope with the losses of aging [14-18]. Recall of previous successful and positive experiences is thought to help an older person maintain self-esteem in the face of age-related lost abilities. Several forms of this adaptive reminiscence have been noted, but the one most often suggested by different writers corresponds to Molinari and Reichlin's proposal, and will be discussed as "self-enhancement" reminiscence [17].

Several studies investigating the process of reminiscence and the efficacy of reminiscence therapy in elderly individuals have found a correlation between reminiscing and current mood or adaptation. It has been found that reviewing one's past, particularly when positive in tone, was associated with decreased depression [14, 16], increased life satisfaction [19, 20], and other positive outcomes [15, 21, 22]. However, methodological weaknesses detract from the strength of some of these findings, and a number of other studies have found no clear relationship between reminiscence and adaptation.

Cognitive models of depression make certain implications for depression in elderly individuals. Given the hypothesis that negative self-relevant experiences will cause increased access to negative self-schema, it would be expected that the increased losses in later life would normally precipitate a depressive cycle. Although nondepressed people are expected to redirect their thoughts away from negative self-schema following a sad experience, if the elderly person experiences many losses that have a negative, personally-relevant effect, it would be difficult for him/her to have the energy and opportunity to redirect thoughts away from negative self-schema. And yet, research finds that many elderly are not depressed. For example, Blazer, Hughes, and George, in a study of 1,304 community elderly persons, found that only 27 percent reported depressive symptoms, including only 2 percent who met DSM III criteria for dysthymia and 0.8 percent who met DSM III criteria for a major depressive episode [23]. Comparing prevalence rates across ages, Myers, Weissman, Tischler, Holzer, Leaf, Orvaschel, Anthony, Boyd, Burke, Kramer, and Stoltzman found that affective disorders were least frequent in people sixty-five years old and older, and most frequent in eighteen- to twenty-four-year-olds and twenty-five- to forty-four-year-olds [24]. An average across men and women from three different cities found that 5.7 percent of eighteen- to twenty-four-year-olds, 7.4 percent of twenty-five- to forty-four-year-olds, and 5.1

percent of forty-five- to sixty-four-year-olds evidenced an affective disorder, while 2.5 percent of those sixty-five and older evidenced an affective disorder. Cognitive models of depression could be amplified using the hypothesis of the reminiscence literature to describe ways in which older people avoid depression despite loss experiences. One possible explanation for the low frequency of clinical depression among elderly individuals corresponds to the concept of life review proposed by Erikson and Butler. Psychologically healthy older people may actively alter the semantic network in which their negative memories are stored, connecting them to more positive concepts and self-schema, whereas depression prone older people may passively recall unaltered negative memories and slip into depression. A second explanation corresponds to self-enhancement reminiscing, similar to the hypotheses of Molinari and Reichlin [13] and Romaniuk and Romaniuk [17], such that when older people reminisce, some may think largely about positive memories, which would balance the attention paid to memories of conflicts and increase self-esteem. Third, memories for past conflicts may be stored in semantic networks relatively independent from current self-schema, and may not make a significant impact on one's self-concept.

In addition to providing a valuable model, cognitive research in depression also offers useful research methodologies with which to study of the relationship between reminiscing and well-being in elderly individuals. The present study used methods from research on the semantic network models to investigate the relationship between processes of recalling past events, and depression versus lack of depression among older people. The probability of retrieval and latency to retrieve different types of memories were used as measures of accessibility. Negative memories were expected to be less accessible to nondepressed people but more accessible to depressed people. First, it was hypothesized that nondepressed people would be quicker to retrieve positive than negative memories, that depressed people would be quicker to retrieve negative than positive memories, and that nondepressed people would be quicker to retrieve positive memories and slower to retrieve negative memories than depressed people. Second, it was expected that nondepressed people would retrieve more positive and fewer negative memories than depressed people, nondepressed people would retrieve more positive than negative memories, and depressed people might retrieve more negative than positive memories. Third, it was expected that when recalling events which were negative at the time of occurrence, nondepressed people would report more events which were previously negative ("then") but currently ("now") felt to be less negative and/or less important to the self, while depressed people would rate experiences as more negative "now" than "then" because of current mood biasing evaluations. Fourth, it was expected that depressed people would rate negative events as more important to the self than nondepressed people.

METHOD

Participants

Participants were volunteers who responded to verbal announcements, written fliers, and staff recruitment in senior citizen retirement hotels. Sixty participants began the procedure; three became fatigued and refused to complete the study. Three additional participants were excluded because their score on the Folstein Mini Mental Status Exam fell below twenty-four, suggesting the presence of cognitive impairment [25]. The final sample consisted of fifty-four participants.

Participants were included in the depressed group if they scored eleven or above on the Geriatric Depression Scale (GDS) [26], and considered in the nondepressed group if they scored ten or below. The GDS is a thirty-item self-report questionnaire specifically designed for and validated on elderly individuals. Yesavage reports that a cutoff score of eleven has yielded 84 percent sensitivity and 95 percent specificity in correctly classifying normal and depressed elderly persons [27]. In his validation study, the depressed group consisted of mildly depressed elderly individuals (with an average of 3.4 R.D.C. criteria symptoms of depression) and severely depressed elderly individuals (with an average of 5.9 R.D.C. criteria symptoms); his normal group consisted of normal community residing elderly individuals. Yesavage and his colleagues suggest that a score of eleven or greater indicates mild depression. Because one question on the GDS could be confounded with the dependent variables of this study ("Do you worry a lot about the past?"), this question was not used to contribute to a participant's total GDS score. Sample GDS scores ranged from zero to twenty-five. Twenty-seven participants scored ten or less, and twenty-seven scored eleven or greater. Within the depressed group, the mean GDS score was 15.5 (standard deviation = 4.0), and within the nondepressed group, the mean GDS score was 6.2 (SD = 3.3).

Participants' age, sex, ethnicity, marital status, self-rated health, number of health problems, types of medications, income, education, and (previous) occupation were compared between groups (see Table 1).

Age across the whole sample ranged between sixty-six and ninety-three years. The mean age did not vary between groups. There were forty-six women and eight men in the entire sample, with no group differences in the number of either sex. Marital status, ethnicity, income, years of education, and occupational ratings did not differ between groups. Over the whole sample, forty-four were widowed, five were divorced, four were married, and one was never married. The sample was almost entirely Caucasian (n = 53), with one participant of Asian descent. Occupational status was rated with the Hollingshead Occupational Rating scale. When participants were housewives and had not worked outside the home, their husband's occupational status was rated. The average occupational rating was 2.81, where level two includes business managers, proprietors of medium sized businesses and lesser professionals, and level three includes administrative

Table 1. Demographic Characteristics of Participant Groups

	Nondepressed		Depressed		Total Sample	
Age	82.0	(7.1)	82.0	(5.3)	82.0	(6.2)
GDS score	6.2	(3.3)	15.5	(4.0)	10.8	(6.0)
MMSE score	26.8	(1.7)	26.6	(1.5)	26.7	(1.6)
Income level	3.9	(2.0)	4.6	(1.5)	4.3	(1.8)
Years of education	12.8	(2.5)	13.7	(2.5)	13.2	(2.5)
Occupation rating	3.0	(1.1)	2.6	(1.1)	2.8	(1.1)
Number of losses	2.1	(1.9)	1.6	(1.6)	1.9	(1.7)
Self-reported health	3.6	(0.9)	3.0	(0.8)	3.3	(0.9)
Number of health problems	1.7	(1.6)	2.5	(1.6)	2.1	(1.6)
Number of medications	1.9	(1.8)	3.3	(2.5)	2.6	(2.3)

personnel, proprietors of small independent business and minor professionals. The total number of losses experienced in the previous six months was assessed with a questionnaire asking for the presence or absence, and if present, the number of losses in eight categories. There were: change in residence, loss of financial resources, loss of occupation, personal illness or injury, illness or injury of family member or close friend, death of close family member, death of other family member or close friend, and loss by theft or legal problems. The total number of losses did not vary significantly between groups, and did not correlate significantly with depression.

The three measures of health status did vary between groups. Self-reported health was assessed on a five point scale: "very poor," "poor," "fair," "good,", or "excellent." The depressed group, on the average, rated their health as fair, whereas the nondepressed group rated their health as good. This difference was statistically significant ($T(52) = 2.24, p = .029$). Depressed people also had more specific health problems ($T(52) = -1.83, p = .073$) and were taking more medications ($T(52) = -2.22, p = .031$). This association between depression and health problems is consistent with the previous literature, which finds that impaired health is a significant correlate of depression [28, 29]. It was assumed that health would contribute significantly to depression, but not be a direct influence on memory processes, and that to factor out a health variable from the analyses would obscure meaningful effects of depression, so health rating was not statistically controlled in the analyses.

Procedure

Participants read and signed a copy of the informed consent, which described that the study involved a two- to three-hour interview and procedure seeking to understand their mood and their recollection of events. They were orally administered demographic questions, the Mini Mental Status Exam, and the Geriatric Depression Scale. Following these assessment questions, the memory task was conducted. Eight questions were then asked to assess losses. Finally, participants were debriefed and given $10.00 for participation, which they could choose to keep or have donated to a charity. The entire procedure was administered by the experimenter or a trained research assistant.

Memory Assessment Task

Participants were told that they would be read a list of words, and each time they heard a word, they were to try to remember a real life personal memory. They were told that when the experience came to mind, they were to inform the interviewer by raising their hand. Participants were told each memory should be real and specific, and should be one they could recall with some detail, i.e., one which occurred at a specific time and place. They were then asked to describe the memory briefly. A few of the participants' words were noted by the interviewer to be used later for the rating tasks. If a participant did not recall an experience within sixty seconds, this was noted and the next word presented. Three conditions for the type of memory were requested. In the "Unspecified Condition," similar to Clark and Teasdale [2] and Teasdale, Taylor, and Fogarty [4], the participant was asked to recall any experience in response to twenty-two words (two were used as practice trials). In addition, participants were asked to recall events which were sad at the time of the event in response to five prompt words and events which were positive at the time in response to five words, similar to Lloyd and Lishman [8] and Teasdale and Fogarty [3]. However, analyses comparing memories from these positive and negative conditions did not yield significant results, and will not be presented. Four alternate interview forms were prepared with the same words, each in a different random order. The words used as cues for retrieving memories were chosen from lists used in other similar studies [2, 8, 9]. From these words, ones which were found to be rated as most extreme in pleasantness by Toglia and Battig's participants were eliminated [30]. Fairly neutral prompt words were expected to minimize inter-participant differences in the emotional meaning of different words. Words were also chosen on the basis of fairly high ratings on imagery and concreteness in order to increase the likelihood of eliciting specific rather than abstract general memories [30]. The words were: flower, swimming, train, dollar, hand, letter, box, church, shoe, table, sign, station, face, shop, animal, wall, scissors, pen, doctor, money, hair, boat, road, telephone, fire, school, tunnel, street, bell, cooking, stone, and sound.

After the entire list was presented, participants were reminded of each memory by being read the description noted by the interviewer. The person was first asked to rate the experience in terms of how happy or sad he/she felt when the experience occurred ("then") on a seven point scale from -3 (extremely sad) to 0 (neutral or not sad and not happy) to +3 (extremely happy). Second, the participant was asked to rate each experience in terms of how personally important the event was to him/her at the time ("then") on a three point scale from 0 (not at all) to 2 (very important). Third, the participant was asked to rate each experience in terms of how happy or sad he/she feels about it "now,"looking back on the experience, on the same seven point scale. Fourth, the participant was asked to rate each experience in terms of how important it is to him/her "now." The procedure was tape recorded.

Latency between presentation of cue words and retrieval of memories was later timed from the tape recordings by a research assistant, blind to the hypotheses and depression ratings. They were timed to one-tenth of a second, using a stopwatch. When the participant raised his/her hand to indicate retrieval of the memory, the interviewer had said "ok," so that the coder knew when to stop the timing. When participants did not clearly indicate retrieval of the memory or did not respond with a specific memory, latency was not recorded.

RESULTS

Latency of Retrieval

Analyses were conducted comparing memories which had been self-rated as positive with memories self-rated as negative. A mixed design manova of the latency to retrieve memories which were rated as positive "then" and negative "then," compared across depression groups was not significant for the main effects of depression group (i.e., depressed versus nondepressed) ($F(1,48) = .54$, $p = .465$) or the interaction between depression and affect (i.e., positive versus negative) ($F(1,48) = .00$, $p = .961$). It was significant for the main effect of affect ($F(1,48) = 4.86$, $p = .032$), indicating that over both groups, people retrieved memories rated as positive slightly faster than memories rated as negative.

Probability of Retrieval

A priori hypotheses had proposed differences between how depressed and non-depressed participants viewed negative and positive memories "then" and "now." The data were summarized into the percent of memories rated as sad (-3, -2, or -1), percent rated as neutral (0), and the percent rated as happy (+1, +2, or +3), as done by previous investigators for "then" and "now" ratings [2, 4, 31]. A mixed design manova was performed to test for between and within group differences on the variables of percentage of memories rated positive "then," negative "then," positive "now," and negative "now." This manova was significant at the .05 level for the main effect of time ("then" versus "now"; $F(1,52) = 68.46$, $p < .001$), affect (positive versus negative memories; $F(1,52) = 25.91$, $p < .001$), the two-way interactions between depression group and affect ($F(1,52) = 4.87$, $p = .032$), and between time and affect ($F(1,52) = 4.12$, $p = .047$) and the three way interaction

Table 2. Percentage of Memories Rated Positive and Negative
"Then" and "Now"

	Nondepressed		Depressed		Total Sample	
Percentage of meories rated as positive "then"	44.1	(12.3)	40.7	(14.9)	42.4	(13.6)
Percentage of memories rated as negative "then"	27.6	(14.2)	32.0	(18.3)	29.8	(16.4)
Percentage of memories rated as positive "now"	39.8	(17.6)	31.3	(14.2)	35.6	(16.4)
Percentage of memories rated as negative "now"	12.2	(13.5)	22.6	(14.4)	17.4	(14.8)

between depression group, time of rating, and affect ($F(1,52) = 4.12, p = .047$). Simple main effects tested within the manova were used to investigate the nature of these interactions. Because the contrasts indicated by the *a priori* hypotheses were not all orthogonal, different sets of contrasts were specified. Table 2 presents the group means for the percentage of memories rated as positive and negative "now" and "then."

The hypothesis that depressed people would retrieve more negative memories than nondepressed people was tested by investigating the nature of the interaction between depression group and affect, using simple main effect tests, holding time of rating constant. A significant difference was found in the percentage of negative memories between depressed and nondepressed groups for the "now" ratings ($F(1,52) = 7.45, p = .009$) only, and no significant differences between groups on negative memories then, or positive memories then or now. The difference between groups on positive memories "now" was nearly significant ($F(1,52) = 3.84, p = .055$). Depressed people retrieved more negative memories than nondepressed people when comparing their ratings for how they feel "now" looking back on their memories, but not when comparing their ratings for how they felt "then," at the time of the event. The Pearson correlations found similar results, such that depression correlated significantly with more negative and fewer positive memories "now," but not "then." The correlation between depression score and percentage of negative memories was $r = .20, p = .071$ for "then" and it was $r = .39, p = .002$ for "now." The correlations between GDS score and percent of memories rated as positive "then" was $r = -.15, p = .144$, and for memories rated as positive "now" was $r = -.27, p = .024$.

The hypothesis that nondepressed people would retrieve more positive than negative memories and depressed people might retrieve more negative than positive memories was tested by following the significant main effect of affect with a second set of simple effects, holding participant group and time of rating constant. The difference between the percentage of positive and negative memories for nondepressed people was significant both "then" ($F(1,52) = 11.29, p = .001$) and "now" ($F(1,52) = 38.25, p < .001$). The affect difference was not significant in the depressed group, and in fact the means are in the contrary direction. All participants gave more positive rated memories in both "then" and "now" ratings. The differences were significant for the nondepressed but not for the depressed participants.

Tests of simple interactions and main effects were used to investigate the nature of the hypothesized differences across time ratings. The time by affect by depression group interaction was due to a significant time by affect interaction in the nondepressed group ($F(1,52) = 8.25, p = .006$), but not in the depressed group ($F(1,52) = 0, p = 1.0$). In the depressed group, the percentage of both negative and positive memories changed from "then" to "now" approximately the same amount, whereas in the nondepressed group, there was a significant difference between "then" and "now" in the percentage of negative memories ($F(1,52) = 32.01, p < .001$) and not of positive memories ($F(1,52) = 3.29, p = .076$). In the depressed group, the percentage of both positive and negative memories decreased, so that more memories became neutral. In the nondepressed group, the percentage of negative memories decreased more dramatically and became neutral, while the percentage of positive memories remained fairly stable. These effects are depicted in Figure 1.

Mean Affect Ratings

Because the variables of percentage of memories rated as negative and percentage of memories rated as positive are so highly correlated, the above hypotheses were investigated using a variable which utilized the full range of information gained from the seven point affect rating scale. Instead of categorizing each memory into one rated as either positive, negative, or neutral, a mean affect rating was calculated over all memories, for both the "then" and "now" ratings. For the purposes of these analyses, the rating scale used by the participants (from -3 to +3) was transposed into a scale with positive numbers (1 to 7). See Table 3 for the mean affect ratings over all memories, "now" and "then."

A manova comparing the mean affect ratings of memories between depressed and nondepressed groups yielded significant results for the main effect of group differences ($F(1,52) = 6.34, p = .015$) and the interaction between group and time ($F(1,52) = 5.24, p = .026$). The main effect of time rating was not significant ($F(1,52) = 3.47, p = .068$). The interaction is depicted in Figure 2. Tests of the simple main effects of this interaction found no difference between time ratings for the depressed people ($F(1,52) = .09, p = .764$) but did find a significant difference between "then" and "now" in the nondepressed people ($F(1,52) = 8.62, p = .005$). Thus, while depressed people's mean affective rating did not change

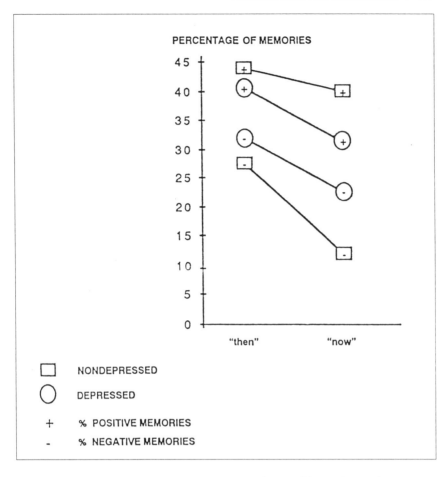

PERCENTAGE OF MEMORIES

NONDEPRESSED

DEPRESSED

+ % POSITIVE MEMORIES

- % NEGATIVE MEMORIES

Figure 1. Percentage of memories rated as positive and negative,
"then" and "now."

between "then" and "now," on the average, nondepressed people's ratings became
more positive.

Importance Ratings

It had been proposed that depressed people would rate negative events as more
important to the self than nondepressed people. A manova comparing the importance of events rated as negative "then," positive "then," negative "now," and
positive "now," between depressed and nondepressed groups, was not significant
for the main effects or interactions.

Table 3. Mean Affect Ratings "Then" and "Now"

	Nondepressed		Depressed		Total Sample	
Mean affect of memories in the unspecified condition						
"then"	4.48	(0.62)	4.22	(0.83)	4.35	(0.73)
"now"	4.77	(0.59)	4.19	(0.59)	4.48	(0.65)

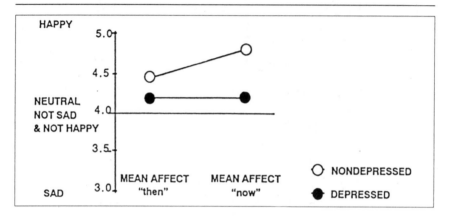

Figure 2. Mean affect ratings, "then" and "now."

DISCUSSION

Hypothesized differences in the probability of retrieving positive versus negative memories were partly supported. Depressed people retrieved more negative memories than nondepressed people, comparing their ratings for how they feel "now" looking back on their memories, but not when comparing their ratings for how they felt "then," at the time of the event. All people were found to retrieve more memories rated as positive than negative both "then" and "now," but these differences were significant only for nondepressed people. The difference in affect was greater for nondepressed than for depressed people. On the average, nondepressed people rated their memories as more positive "now" than when they occurred, whereas depressed people's ratings did not change significantly. Depressed people's percentage of negative and positive memories decreased equally, whereas nondepressed people's percentage of negative memories decreased more significantly, and their percentage of positive memories decreased less. Hypothesized differences between depressed and nondepressed participants in accessibility of memories as measured by latency to retrieve positive and negative memories, were not substantiated.

The present finding that depressed people retrieved more memories currently felt to be negative than nondepressed people is consistent with the findings of Fogarty and Hemsley [31], Teasdale, Taylor, and Fogarty [4], Natale and Hantas [32], and Snyder and White [33]. Similar to Bower's findings that in an elated mood more happy than sad events were recalled [6], this study found that non-depressed people recalled more happy than sad memories. However, contrary to Bower, this study did not find that when depressed, more sad events than happy were recalled. Bower had participants rerate events when in induced moods, and found that their evaluations were more consistent with current mood than original mood as recorded in a diary. This is consistent with this study's findings that current mood was more consistent with current evaluations of past events than with evaluations of the affect at the time of the events.

The one study which also had participants rate their affect for how they felt then and now compared depressed patients at two different times of more and less depression [2]. The present study did not support Clark and Teasdale's finding that when more depressed, depressed patients rated memories as more unhappy "now" and "then," in that there as no significant difference between the "now" and "then" ratings of this study's depressed people. The difference between the findings may be due to the fact that the depressed participants in this study were community dwelling elderly individuals, many of whom were only mildly depressed, whereas Clark and Teasdale studied clinically depressed patients. Age differences may also impact these findings. The elderly participants in this study have had more intervening time between the event and recall of the memory than Clark and Teasdale's participants, and may have done more recoding of their memories than younger people.

When latency to retrieve memories was used as the measure of accessibility, this study did not support the hypothesis that depression increases access to negative memories, as was found by Lloyd and Lishman [8] and Teasdale and Fogarty [3]. Other studies have also failed to replicate mood differences on retrieval latency [2, 4]. Difficulty achieving an accurate measure of latency in this sample reduces the interpretability of these lack of findings. The participants did not consistently indicate retrieval of their memories nor initially provide specific memories, and thus latency was difficult to measure accurately. The overall quicker latency to retrieve positive memories may be related to the use of a mildly depressed group rather than a clinically depressed sample.

The results of this study can be seen as consistent with mood congruent retrieval, because participants recalled more memories which were currently evaluated as affectively congruent with current mood. It is the affect of the reorganized memories which is more strongly associated with current mood. This is consistent with Teasdale's proposition that depressed people are more likely to direct their attention to negative current experiences. This study does not provide support for mood-state dependent retrieval effects, i.e., that events encoded in one state are most easily retrieved later when the person is in the same state [1, 6]. Participants' mood was not found to be strongly associated with the reported affective tone of the memory at the time of occurrence, and the affective tone of the event at the time is likely to be similar to the person's mood at the time the event was experienced [34]. Although this study is not longitudinal and therefore cannot make conclusions about changes over time, some hypotheses can be drawn which deserve further exploration. It may be that experiences are organized in memory tagged by current effective tone rather than original tone, and the current tone may have been recoded. The word "recoded" is intended to suggest that the original memory trace is elaborated by altering and reorganizing the affective links to the memory, not to suggest change in the original memory trace itself. When experiences have been recoded, memory may be searched by affect nodes, starting with the current affective tone of memories. The affective tone at the time the event occurred may be less salient once a memory has been recoded. Rehm and Naus suggest that repeated activation of memories would strengthen schema [7]. Perhaps memories which have been thought about more often, including those which have been recoded, have become more accessible because of repeated activation. It may not be that a person's mood increases access to memories of affectively similar events, but that mood increases access to memories of events which are currently evaluated in a way which is affectively similar to current mood, whether this is recoded affect or original affect if the experience has not been recoded. This suggests that it is the current evaluation of the past which differentiates depressed and nondepressed individuals.

The present findings are consistent with some of the previous findings of an adaptive function of reminiscence. The finding that less depression was associated with recalling more events currently felt to be happy, is consistent with those of Havighurst and Glasser [20] and Bortner and Hultsch [19]. Hyland and Ackerman's lack of correlation between mood and the percentage of pleasant versus unpleasant memories retrieved may have been due to less variation in mood than found in this sample, and/or lack of specification as to whether the participants were to evaluate the events for their affect at the time of the event or for how they felt currently looking back on the event.

This pattern of findings is consistent with the reminiscence theory of Molinari and Reichlin [13] and Romaniuk and Romaniuk [17]. Molinari and Reichlin suggest that the experiences of aging produce a negative impact on the current self, and that recall of past positive experiences can help an elderly person cope with aging. Reminiscence can help create a sense of continuity with the past and redefine the current self in light of the past, thus maintaining self-esteem. Romaniuk and Romaniuk proposed that reminiscing can perform a self-enhancement function, in that a greater connection with the past may be related to greater self-esteem. The data of the present study are consistent with the association between memory for events evaluated as positive and current lack of depression. Molinari and Reichlin's proposed use of reminiscence may not be occurring among depressed people. It may be that depression decreases the energy available to effortfully direct attention to past positive memories.

Erikson and Butler proposed life review as a natural developmental process wherein older people review and integrate past conflicts. Although clear conclusions about changes over time cannot be made, the finding that nondepressed people's memories were more positive for current than past evaluations lends support to a process of life review recoding in the nondepressed group. The finding that the nondepressed participants recalled more memories which were presently evaluated as positive, and they perceived that over time, their events were more positive than at the time of encoding the event, may be relevant to psychotherapy with elderly individuals. It is possible that increasing a person's focus on events evaluated as being happy and encouraging reworking of memories has a positive effect on mood.

REFERENCES

1. J. D. Teasdale, Negative Thinking in Depression: Cause, Effect or Reciprocal Relationship?, *Advances in Behavioral Research and Therapy, 5*, pp. 3-25, 1983.
2. D. M. Clark and J. D. Teasdale, Diurnal Variation in Clinical Depression and Accessibility of Positive and Negative Experiences, *Journal of Abnormal Psychology, 91*, pp. 87-95, 1982.
3. J. D. Teasdale and S. J. Fogarty, Differential Effects of Induced Mood on Retrieval of Pleasant and Unpleasant Events from Episodic Memory, *Journal of Abnormal Psychology, 88*, pp. 248-257, 1979.
4. J. D. Teasdale, R. Taylor, and S. J. Fogarty, Effects of Induced Elation-Depression on the Accessibility of Memories of Happy and Unhappy Experiences, *Behavior Research and Therapy, 18*, pp. 339-346, 1980.
5. J. D. Teasdale and R. Taylor, Induced Mood and Accessibility of Memories: An Effect of Mood State or of Induction Procedure?, *British Journal of Clinical Psychology, 20*, pp. 39-48, 1981.
6. G. H. Bower, Mood and Memory, *American Psychologist, 36*, pp. 129-148, 1981.
7. L. P. Rehm and M. J. Naus, A Memory Model of Depression: An Analysis of Cognition, Development, and Emotion, in *Attempts to Unify the Psychology of Depression*, C. M. Franks (chair), Symposium presented at the meeting of the American Psychological Association, New York, 1987.
8. G. G. Lloyd and W. A. Lishman, Effect of Depression on the Speed of Recall of Pleasant and Unpleasant Experiences, *Psychological Medicine, 5*, pp. 173-180, 1975.
9. D. T. Hyland and A. M. Ackerman, Reminiscence and Autobiographical Memory in the Study of the Personal Past, *Journal of Gerontology, 43*:2, pp. 35-39, 1988.
10. E. Erikson, *Childhood and Society*, W. W. Norton and Company, New York, 1950.
11. E. Erikson, *The Life Cycle Completed*, W. W. Norton and Company, New York, 1982.
12. R. Butler, The Life Review: An Interpretation of Reminiscence in the Aged, *Psychiatry, 26*, pp. 65-75, 1963.

13. V. Molinari and R. E. Reichlin, Life Review Reminiscence in the Elderly: A Review of the Literature, *International Journal of Aging and Human Development,* 20:2, pp. 81-92, 1984-85.
14. A. W. McMahon and P. J. Rhudick, Reminiscing: Adaptational Significance in the Aged, *Archives of Geriatric Psychiatry, 10,* pp. 191-198, 1964.
15. C. N. Lewis, Reminiscing and Self-Concept, *Journal of Gerontology, 26,* pp. 240-243, 1971.
16. R. Fallot, The Impact on Mood of Verbal Reminiscing in Later Adulthood, *International Journal of Aging and Human Development, 10:4,* pp. 385-400, 1979-80.
17. M. Romaniuk and J. G. Romaniuk, Reminiscence and the Second Half of Life, *Experimental Aging Research, 7:3,* pp. 315-336, 1981.
18. P. Coleman, *Aging and Reminiscence Processes,* J. Wiley & Sons, Chichester, 1986.
19. R. W. Bortner and D. F. Hultsch, Personal Time Perspective in Adulthood, *Developmental Psychology, 7:2,* pp. 98-103, 1972.
20. R. J. Havighurst and R. Glasser, An Exploratory Study of Reminiscence, *Journal of Gerontology, 27:2,* pp. 245-253, 1972.
21. W. Boylin, S. L. Gordon, and M. F. Nehrke, Reminiscing and Ego Integrity in Institutionalized Elderly Males, *The Gerontologist, 16,* pp. 118-124, 1976.
22. P. G. Coleman, Measuring Reminiscence Characteristics from Conversation as Adaptive Features of Old Age, *International Journal of Aging and Human Development, 5,* pp. 281-294, 1974.
23. D. Blazer, D. C. Hughes, and L. K. George, The Epidemiology of Depression in an Elderly Community Population, *The Gerontologist, 27:3,* pp. 281-287, 1987.
24. J. Myers, M. Weissman, G. Tischler, D. Holzer, P. Leaf, H. Orvaschel, J. Anthony, J. Boyd, J. Burke, M. Kramer, and R. Stoltzman, Six Month Prevalence of Psychiatric Disorder in Three Communities, *Archives of General Psychiatry, 41,* pp. 959-967, 1984.
25. M. F. Folstein, The Mini-Mental State Exam, in *Assessment in Geriatric Psychopharmacology,* T. Crook, S. Ferris, and R. Bartus (eds.), Mark Powley Assoc., Inc., New Canaan, Connecticut, 1983.
26. J. A. Yesavage, T. L. Brink, T. Rose, and M. Adry, The Geriatric Depression Rating Scale: Comparison with Other Self-Report and Psychiatric Rating Scales, in *Assessment in Geriatric Psychopharmacology,* T. Crook, S. Ferris, and R. Bartus (eds.), Mark Powley Assoc., Inc., New Canaan, Connecticut, 1983.
27. J. Yesavage, The Use of Self-Rating Depression Scales in the Elderly, in *Handbook for Clinical Memory Assessment of Older Adults,* L. W. Poon (ed.), American Psychological Association, Washington, D.C., 1985.
28. M. Romaniuk, W. McAuley, and G. Arling, An Examination of the Prevalence of Mental Disorders among the Elderly in the Community, *Journal of Abnormal Psychology, 92:4,* pp. 458-467, 1983.
29. D. Blazer and C. Williams, Epidemiology of Dysphoria and Depression in an Elderly Population, *American Journal of Psychiatry, 137:4,* pp. 439-444, 1980.
30. M. P. Toglia and W. F. Battig, *Handbook of Semantic Word Norms,* Lawrence Erlbaum Associates, Publishers, Hillsdale, New Jersey, 1978.
31. S. F. Fogarty and D. R. Hemsley, Depression and the Accessibility of Memories: A Longitudinal Study, *British Journal of Psychiatry, 142,* pp. 232-237, 1983.

32. M. Natale and M. Hantas, Effect of Temporary Mood States on Selective Memory about the Self, *Journal of Personality and Social Psychology, 42*:5, pp. 927-934, 1982.
33. M. Snyder and P. White, Moods and Memories: Elation, Depression, and the Remembering of the Events of One's Life, *Journal of Personality, 50*:2, pp. 149-167, 1982.
34. P. Blaney, Affect and Memory: A Review, *Psychological Bulletin, 99*:2, pp. 229-246, 1986.

Chapter 8

INCLUDING SOCIAL FACTORS IN THE ANALYSIS OF REMINISCENCE IN ELDERLY INDIVIDUALS

Simone Lamme
and
Jan Baars

By definition, elderly people have left the greater portion of their lives already behind them. It is generally assumed that they must therefore often like to think and speak about their past lives and are greatly attached to the past. This assumption is evident both in the positive stereotype of elderly individuals as wise, tempered by life, and graced with a rich tapestry of experience, as well as in the negative stereotype of elderly people as stagnant, living only in the past and unwilling or unable to adjust to modern circumstances.

Studies have been conducted by diverse researchers on the nature and degree of interest shown by elderly people in their own personal histories [1-6]. The results indicate that elderly people are indeed more preoccupied with the past than young people, or at least deal with it in a very different way. Elderly people are more likely to mythologize their past than young people [3]. Also, they use their memories mainly as a source of entertainment, whereas young people use their memories mainly as problem-solving tools [2]. An analysis of discussions between elderly people and discussions between young people demonstrated that, in their conversations, elderly people tend to refer to events in the past much more frequently than young people do [4].

However, studies of reminiscence during old age have not resulted in unambiguous conclusions concerning the origin, function, or importance of this behavior for elderly individuals.

One explanation for this may be the fact that there appear to be considerable differences between individual elderly people regarding their reminiscent behavior. Lo Gerfo determined three separate kinds of reminiscence that were very different as to origin, function, and meaning [7]. In a longitudinal study, Coleman also found that there were major variations in the measure and manner in which elderly people deal with their past. In addition, Coleman observed that neither the presence nor the absence of reminiscing corresponded to factors of well-being or adjustment to old age [6].

A second reason for the lack of clarity about the precise function and meaning of reminiscence for elderly people may be the fact that there appears to be little consensus as to how reminiscence should be conceptualized, operationalized, and interpreted [8].

By means of this article, we hope to aid the effort to clarify thoughts concerning the phenomenon of reminiscence in the elderly. We use the term "reminiscence" in its broadest possible sense: the silent or oral, purposive or spontaneous recalling of past events, and experiences in the personal life [9].

In order to provide a clear understanding, some important ideas on reminiscence in elderly individuals will be dealt with in this chapter. These ideas will be juxtaposed with the diverse theories on development from which they emerged. We will investigate whether these theories and concepts form a suitable framework for the interpretation of the varying results concerning reminiscence in elderly people. The definitions of reminiscence current in two different streams of developmental psychology will be examined in turn: Butler and Erikson's determinist theories and the dialectical theories of Riegel, Kvale, and Meacham.

We will argue that neither approach is sufficient to achieve clarity regarding the origin, function, and meaning of reminiscent behavior in elderly individuals. We will then defend the view that insights originating in the field of sociology, specifically in life course sociology, can make an important contribution to the interpretation of reminiscent behavior in the elderly individuals as well as the analysis of the situations in which elderly individuals tell others about their lives. The phenomenon of reminiscence in elderly individuals must therefore be regarded as a function of the (changed and changing) social context of aging. This means that it is imperative that social factors be considered in the analysis of this phenomenon.

BUTLER: THE LIFE REVIEW

The psychiatrist R. N. Butler used the term "life review" to arrive at a description and an explanation of the specific way in which elderly individuals were supposed to deal with their personal history [10, 11].

> I conceive of the life review as a naturally occurring, universal mental process characterized by the progressive return to consciousness of past experiences,

and, particularly the resurgence of unresolved conflicts; simultaneously, and normally, these reviewed experiences and conflicts can be surveyed and integrated [10, p. 66].

In the life review, events and actions in the past are therefore not only contemplated but also worked through. According to Butler, the latter must be considered to be the most important function of the life review; by means of dealing with the past in dream and thought, a summation of one's life is made and one is preparing for death.

Butler contends that this process is initiated once the individual knows, whether consciously or unconsciously, that death is nigh. Therefore life review behavior would also be observable in terminal patients and prisoners sentenced to death.

The explicit hypothesis intended here is that the biological fact of approaching death, independent of—although possibly reinforced by—personal and environmental circumstances, prompts the life review [10, p. 67].

In Butler's view, becoming preoccupied with memories is therefore the normal, automatic, and inexorable reaction of an elderly human being to old age and imminent death. However, this does not mean that all elderly people are equally successful in completing their life review. Some are unable to make peace with their past. Butler attributes the relatively common occurrence of depression and suicide in elderly people to failed life reviews.

ERIKSON: INTEGRITY VERSUS DESPAIR/DISGUST

Erikson's work also reflects the idea that elderly people are naturally and therefore inevitably preoccupied with their past lives, and that this is related to the closing of their lives. In his famous theory of psycho-social development, Erikson distinguished eight phases of development. In each of these phases, the individual is faced with a specific and fundamental life problem. All eight problems have been defined by Erikson by means of their two possible and conflicting resolutions. In normal development, the positive resolution is achieved and the positive quality is obtained, whereupon a new phase begins.

In the old age phase, the conflict of integrity versus despair or disgust is the central issue. Looking back on one's life is of crucial importance in this phase. As in Butler's approach, this review takes place in the context of life's closure and is evaluative in nature. The difference between the positive and the negative resolution consists of the acceptance or non-acceptance of the way in which one's life was led and the end of that life. Those who are able to accept their past lives as well as the people who have played important roles therein are also able to accept the fact that life is ending and thus they reach integrity. Those who are filled with resentment, guilt, and regret when reviewing their lives, realizing that not much time remains for change, are unable to accept their own mortality.

Despair and disgust are thus characterized by a strong conscious or unconscious fear of death [12].

COMMENTS ON BUTLER AND ERIKSON

Butler's and Erikson's ideas more or less coincide with our intuitions and for that reason they are rather attractive. When we consider the fact that many elderly people are confronted with the death of contemporaries, be they friends or relatives, it is obvious that elderly people will be preoccupied with their own lives and deaths. It is also very reasonable to assume that a realization of approaching death raises the issue of the value of life [13]. The contemplative nature attributed to the review also tallies with traditional association of old people with wisdom and a highly developed capacity for seeing the relativity of things [14]. But however appealing or plausible the idea that elderly people sum up their lives may be, and however many elderly people may indeed do so, the presupposed automatic nature and universality of life review behavior in elderly people must be doubted.

To begin with, results from empirical studies show that not all elderly people are intensely preoccupied with their past and that if they are, this behavior hardly ever matches the structure of the life review as described by Butler [6]. Generally speaking, it is not the need to resolve the past that seems to be primary in elderly people, but the need to receive attention and approval. It also seems that the elderly maintain a positive self-image by means of their often greatly mythologized and idealized life story [1-3]. Moreover, Revere and Tobin [3] found that elderly people did not demonstrate more conciliation with their past than any other age category and Lieberman and Falk [2] could not conclusively prove the connection between imminent death and a particular way of dealing with memories. In a survey article, Molinari and Reichlin therefore concluded that "[. . .] life review is neither peculiar to the aged, nor universal among the elderly" [5, p. 90]. The claim to universality for life reviewing in elderly individuals appears to be unjustified in view of the evidence of empirical research.

We may also question the validity of the underlying developmental theories, that are more explicitly detailed by Erikson than by Butler. Erikson's theory is based on the assumption of a congenital developmental plan. Therefore, psychosocial development would occur in accordance with certain laws, analogous to a biological ripening process. Social and cultural circumstances would thus have little influence on the developmental plan and therefore they would be of no importance in the structure of development. The individual himself/herself is also unable to influence this structure. S/he can only obey developmental laws. In the same way, Butler almost completely dismisses the influence of environmental factors on the initiation and progress of the life review. He lists "nature" as his source for the regularities he has observed.

Just as empirical findings have refuted the presupposed universality of life reviewing in old age, this underlying "ordered change" model has also become problematic for adult development [15]. A flood of research findings has already demonstrated the cultural and historical relativity of adult development [15-17]. Moreover, diverse theoretists have fundamentally criticized the presuppositions of the developmental model of ordered change. Especially the normative and deterministic aspects of the model have been subject to criticism. Novak has criticized Erikson's conception of culture as a non-problematic backdrop for development on two counts. First, the presupposed congruence and harmony between environment and individual is in truth not always present. Second, the development of people who do not unquestioningly conform to their environment would by definition be abnormal according to Erikson's conception.

> Nowhere in Erikson's work does doubt in the culture arise as a path to growth. [. . .] the healthy personality remains oblivious to his or her environment. He or she passively grows within it, but plays no role in shaping, changing or even thinking about it [18, pp. 198; 19].

Dannefer points out that the assumption of universality in development results in discovered regularities being enthroned as norms. Consequently, deviations are regarded as abnormalities or exceptions that may be ignored with impunity. Not only does this combination of assumptions and method result in the impossibility of empirical proof, but by presupposing and emphasizing homogeneity, something as variable as "environment" cannot be considered to play a part in the creation of either the observed phases or regularities [20].

INCLUDING SOCIAL FACTORS IN THE ANALYSIS OF REMINISCENCE

A. From Determinism to Contextualism

Since Erikson and Butler have published these theories, great changes have taken place in developmental psychology, in both content and theory. The rapid development of both psychology and sociology of old age during past decades has coincided with the rise of a lifespan perspective in which the actual functioning of elderly people has taken center stage instead of presupposed biological laws of development. The model of ordered change has increasingly given way to contextualist models of development [17, 21].

The point of departure for the contextualist theory is that the interaction between the individual and his/her historical, social, and cultural environment is the driving force behind both the individual's personal development and changes in society. The individual is therefore an active participant in his/her own growth and development [15].

These premises result in the conclusion that no such thing as normal development exists without a preconceived notion of how "normal" is to be defined, including perceptions and valuations of developmental possibilities and limitations. For developmental psychology, this means that it must now proceed in a differential and historical manner and must stop searching for the blueprints of universal human development [16].

The contextualist paradigm has resulted in a change in our understanding of development. As a consequence of this, new light has been shed on the phenomenon of reminiscence in old age.

Meacham and Kvale: A Contextualist View of Reminiscence

Following Riegel, Meacham states that the individual and his/her environment constantly interact. Processes of individual development and social-historical change are therefore interdependent and may only be understood in relation to one another.

Memories play a role in the interaction between the individual and his/her environment. Previously acquired knowledge and experience is used to anticipate and react to the environment. This leads to the conclusion that memories and the context in which they are evoked are interrelated. This means that memories are also subject to constant change. The past is constantly being reconstructed in new and different ways, depending on current (social) circumstances and needs [22, 23]. Old interpretations of personal experience and development are continuously being replaced by new ones. Reviewing the past is thus a part of the process of development. "As much as the acquisition of advanced historical awareness begins to change history itself, so does an awareness of development change the course of this development" [24, p. 33].

Kvale also describes memories as constructions of the moment; ideas that simultaneously reflect both past and present. Using the work of Skinner and Husserl, he theorized that in human behavior and consciousness, there is interaction between the early and later past. Selectivity of memory takes place on the basis of the later past. There it is determined what knowledge is functional and meaningful for any particular moment. Moreover, views of the early past are always filtered through the later past, that is to say, they include the knowledge and experience which have been gained during the intervening period. Conversely, the early past is always a part of the later past, as later events are the result of (reactions to) early events [25].

The contextualist model of remembrance leads to the conclusion that reminiscent behavior does not result in producing stable permanent images and stories. The evocation, interpretation, and integration of memories on the one hand, and the accruition of new experiences on the other are dialectically connected [26]. Reminiscence originates in the confrontation between the individual and his/her environment. In order to understand the function and the significance of this behavior in the individual, the role of the environment must also be recognized.

According to Meacham, the functions of reminiscence are personality construction, identity, and a view of life that makes integrity, continuity, and efficacy possible [22]. The strength of reminiscence is therefore not to be sought in "memory correspondence" (i.e., the similarity between the actual occurrence and the memory of that occurrence) but in "memory coherence:" the similarity between the memory and present cognitions and motivations.

Many other theorists hold similar opinions. Starr uses the term "biographical work" and states that arranging and rearranging experiences serves to create an acceptable reality, a coherent and understandable development as well as a credible and continuous "self" [27].

Diverse theorists have pointed out that the need for a coherent life story results in the past being reinterpreted toward the present: the present is not only the point of departure for memory and interpretation, it is also the target [25, 28-30]. By means of reminiscing, people define and understand themselves through their histories, whereas they understand and interpret their past from their present.

Comment on the Contextualist Paradigm

The contextualist view recognizes the fact that social environment plays an important role in individual development. Thus, it acknowledges the social, cultural, and historical variability and heterogeneity of human adult development. Moreover, the contextualist model of remembrance provides an interesting view of the nature and function of the phenomenon of reminiscence. Through relating reminiscence to the gathering and integration of new experience, and by supposing that people need a life story "(. . .) whose pieces fit and which in our retrospection can be made to seem causal" [30, p. 336], the seemingly random nature of human memory can be understood.

The fact that old people in particular are preoccupied with reorganizing, integrating, and mythologizing their past is not explained, however. Meacham states that investigating, evaluating, and reinterpreting experience can take place at any age, but that these activities are especially important in late adulthood and old age. Reviewing one's life and reorganizing one's personality would primarily be useful in adjusting to old age [22].

This statement is remarkable, because one of the premises of the contextualist paradigm is that the paths of development are not laid out once and for all, but are created in the interaction between the individual and his/her social environment [31]. This implies that great inter-individual differences in development are possible. However, this thought is hard to reconcile with the idea that there is such a thing as "old age" to which one must adjust in a particular way.

The contextualist theory of course does not rule out the possibility that elderly people evince similar behavior, but this similarity in itself then needs to be explained. One of the more obvious venues for an explanation would be a similarity of historical, social, and cultural circumstances that can account for the observed similarity in behavior.

An analysis of the social-structural and cultural circumstances in which people grow old is thus necessary to explain both similarity and variation in behavior.

Using research on the specific experiences people accumulate while aging could clarify reminiscent behavior in the elderly.

The contextualist theory itself does not provide many clues to accomplish this. It is so abstract and general that without further definition of its main clauses, it is barely applicable. The attention given to the influence of social factors on development is therefore ultimately rather disappointing. Contrary to what one might expect of an approach in which the context of development is central, most theorists use the term "social context" in a very unspecified and undifferentiated manner. As a result, it remains unclear what the role of the social environment is in establishing development or reminiscence in adulthood. Neither can concrete social situations in which elderly people remember and tell stories about their lives be analyzed in this framework [32].

In order to understand the phenomenon of reminiscence in elderly individuals, the contextualist theory should be expanded to include sociological theory, especially concerning the life course.

B. The Social and Cultural Constitution of the Life Course

The social environment plays a highly influential and complex role in the phenomenon of reminiscence in elderly individuals. Its influence is due to the fact that many of the experiences and changes over the life course that can lead to reminiscence are organized by society. The complexity is primarily the result of the fact that the social environment has a differential impact on elderly individuals. Elderly individuals should therefore be approached differentially [33-34]. Within the scope of this chapter we can only point to some topics from life course sociology relevant for a further analysis of the interaction between reminiscence and social context. Subsequently we will discuss 1) age stratification, 2) social change, 3) social inequality, 4) the organization of care for elderly individuals, and 5) the significance of cultural images of aging.

1. Sociological research on *age stratification* has produced a wealth of information concerning the way in which the life course is structured according to age categories in different societies [35]. Following Kohli [36] and Meyer [37], we might even regard the modern life course with all its chronological and categorical definitions as an institution. Most societies evince regularities in the life course that apply to all members of those societies, such as age-related rights and duties. This is why people of all ages can be faced with socially organized changes and events that greatly affect their lives and this can lead to reflection and reinterpretation of earlier experiences. However, this appears to occur more often in old age. To some extent, such changes are not socially organized, e.g., losing friends or partners. But the fact that such a majority of widowed persons aged sixty-five and older are women [38] has—apart from female longevity—something to do with the social habit of women marrying older men.

The official transition to old age, for instance, is organized by society. For many people this transition is directly related to the socially organized exit from the labor force. This is usually one of the first indications that society is removing an individual from its most central systems. Although this exit can take many forms nowadays and is often no longer regulated by the pension system, the personal wishes of the individuals involved often play only a minor role [39]. The instant that one has left the work force, one may be considered to be "old." Apart from this, the exit from the labor force is an important transition because of the diverse functions that participation in the labor process fulfills for the individual. Not only does work generate income, social status, and contacts, it is also of major significance to identity and self-esteem because it is considered to be pre-eminently a meaningful activity. The awareness of being definitively excluded from the opportunity to manifest oneself socially through work, is likely to lead to a reflection on past employed life and on personal identity as a retiree [40].

This is true for men and women, but it has rightly been observed that in many countries this transition is still predominantly—for social reasons—a male experience, especially in the older cohorts. Most of the women in these cohorts have devoted their adult lives to fulfilling the roles of wife, mother, and housekeeper. But although these roles may be continued, the moment their husbands retire, daily life will also undergo important changes for the wives. Many married women who have no work outside the house will experience this moment as a transition to old age. Another major change in their roles occurs when the children leave home. This transition is also considered to be very consequential and it is to an important degree socially regulated [41]. All these socially organized age-related transitions may inspire reminiscent behavior.

2. This often emphasizes differences between birth cohorts in both the psychology and sociology of aging have made it clear that *social change* can be an important factor [42]. It is almost a cliché to reiterate that the tempo of social change in present Western societies is rather high. That this could stimulate reminiscent behavior in elderly individuals is obvious, especially when changes are forced on elderly people in such a way that what was formerly taken for granted, has suddenly become outmoded. This applies to both cultural orientations and practical circumstances. Elderly women, for example, may be faced with change concerning the education of girls or with drastic changes in sexual or marital mores. This confrontation can result in thoughts of how different their lives might have been had they been young now [43].

Generally speaking, as social and cultural changes become more widespread, far-reaching, and faster paced, the need to reorient and reinterpret personal ideas and experiences can be supposed to grow. This may even be true in case elderly people lead a relatively isolated life. They may be confronted with innovations rather abruptly, because they are excluded from the social domains where these changes are initiated. Processes such as the introduction of new technology and computerization take place much more gradually for those who are employed than for those who are suddenly faced with a new technological restructuring of public services. What may be considered a welcome improvement in efficiency by those working in this field, may be experienced as a threat by elderly people. Even seemingly trivial changes can be important in this context. The local library might have switched to a new, computerized information retrieval system, for instance. Because things that were trusted and familiar now suddenly appear to be hopelessly passé, people can begin to feel passé themselves and start reflecting on their own lives.

3. The way in which the life course turns out for concrete individuals depends to a certain extent on the position that they occupy in society from birth. The significance that a specific society attaches to factors such as ethnic background, gender, and parental social status often determines how much education children will receive. The social status they have reached in their forties will determine to a great extent what their income will ultimately be in old age. Such structures and processes of *social inequality* lead to category-specific life courses. During such life courses, aging persons will not only be confronted with different sets of events and experiences, but as a result of this, their reaction to general, for instance age-related occurrences will also differ. Thus they accumulate socially differentiated experiences and perspectives, regarding social reality as well as themselves.

The sociology of the life course therefore faces the complex task of relating differences between cohorts to differences within cohorts. Recent studies that meet these criteria have shown that certain configurations of gender, cohort, and socio-economic background result in specific life course patterns [44-45]. In different societies life course patterns can be distinguished that are typical for members of certain birth cohorts from different social classes [46]. Such correlations can be traced to historical processes and social mechanisms all of which influence individual opportunities and possibilities to obtain certain means, to attain certain roles and positions and to perform certain behavior. Both within as well as between cohorts there is socially organized differentiation of the life course. This can even have a cumulatively positive or negative effect on the viability of the elderly people concerned [47]. All these differentiations may have consequences for the content and extent of reminiscence in elderly individuals.

4. During the process of aging there is an increasing chance that health problems will arise, which may result in a limitation of mobility. When elderly people have to move to an institution, this constitutes such a major transition that it usually leads to reminiscent behavior. Lieberman and Falk compared inhabitants of homes for the elderly with elderly people on waiting lists for same and with elderly people living independently with no plans of moving [2]. They indeed found that the elderly people on the waiting lists were most intensively occupied with restructuring their past. This means that the way in which *care for the elderly* is organized may have an important influence on the nature

and extent of reminiscent behavior. If the home care system is well-developed or if housing can be adequately remodeled to suit specific needs, mobility problems will less likely result in elderly people having to move to an institution. Consequently, in such situations there will be fewer external impulses for reminiscent behavior.

5. A number of cultural factors that deal with *cultural images of aging* also contributes to reminiscent behavior in elderly people. In this regard, it is especially important that elderly people are expected to tell stories about the past. Once again, we may refer to the classic image of old people as treasurers of the past, wardens of tradition, and wise counselors. Brandon Wallace states that this image of elderly individuals leads to their being judged according to their (presupposed) quality as storytellers. By acceding to requests and expectations, elderly people do indeed develop the ability to tell stories about their past. This was demonstrated by analyses of interviews in which elderly people were asked to tell the story of their lives. Some of the elderly people appeared to have great difficulty in performing this task, but those who had been asked to tell their life story on many earlier occasions were able to do so without any trouble [48]. Holland and Rabbit report that elderly people in homes for the aged are often encouraged by the staff to tell about their former lives [49].

Research has shown that in such stories the theme of "success" plays an important role [1-2]. This is also culturally determined. Why should success (and then: what kind of success) be interesting? Probably because the unimportance to which society usually relegates elderly individuals can be somewhat compensated by personal successes in the past. But lack of success can also dominate the stories insofar as society is blamed for hindering deserved success.

Reminiscence appears to be regarded as typical behavior for elderly individuals. The unequal distribution of reminiscence among the age categories gives one the impression that those who work have no time to reflect on their lives and postpone this activity until their retirement. But the fast pace of present society leaves little room for elderly individuals as wise counselors. The hidden cultural message seems to be that both elderly persons and the remembered past are irrelevant to the current adult world of work and activity. Should reminiscence result in well-told stories, they may be pleasant to listen to, but only when one has nothing better to do. The association of the aged with reminiscence confirms their marginal social position.

CONCLUSION

Contextualist psychologists have stated that reminiscent behavior plays an important role in the continuous interaction between individuals and their environment. Reminiscence facilitates the integration of new experiences and thus adaptation to environmental changes, by constituting a sense of continuity. Therefore, reminiscent behavior constitutes a part of human development.

It follows that to understand the meaning and function of reminiscent behavior in elderly individuals, one should consider their experiences and the transitions, changes, and cultural expectations they face when aging. Since many transitions and changes are socially organized, and differ strongly for diverse social categories, sociological life course theory can contribute to the development of a framework for the analysis of both similarity and variation in reminiscent behavior in elderly people.

REFERENCES

1. A. W. McMahon and P. J. Rhudick, Reminiscing, Adaptational Significance in the Aged, *Archives of General Psychiatry, 10,* pp. 292-298, 1964.
2. M. A. Lieberman and J. M. Falk, The Remembered Past as a Source of Data for Research on the Life Cycle, *Human Development, 14,* pp. 132-141, 1971.
3. V. Revere and S. S. Tobin, Myth and Reality: The Older Person's Relationship to His Past, *International Journal of Aging and Human Development, 12*:1, pp. 15-25, 1980-1981.
4. D. Boden and D. D. V. Bielby, The Past as Resource: A Conversational Analysis of Elderly Talk, *Human Development, 26,* pp. 308-819, 1983.
5. V. Molinari and R. E. Reichlin, Life Review Reminiscence in the Elderly: A Review of the Literature, *International Journal of Aging and Human Development, 20*:2, pp. 81-92, 1984-1985.
6. P. G. Coleman, *Ageing and Reminiscence Processes: Social and Clinical Implications,* John Wiley & Sons Ltd., Chichester, New York, 1986.
7. M. Lo Gerfo, Three Ways of Reminiscence in Theory and Practice, *International Journal of Aging and Human Development, 12*:1, pp. 39-48, 1980.
8. S. Merriam, The Concept and Function of Reminiscence: A Review of the Research, *The Gerontologist, 20*:5, pp. 604-609, 1980.
9. R. J. Havighurst and R. Glasser, An Exploratory Study of Reminiscence, *Journal of Gerontology, 27*:2, pp. 245-253, 1972.
10. R. Butler, The Life Review: An Interpretation of Reminiscence in the Aged, *Psychiatry, 26*:1, pp. 65-76, 1963.
11. R. Butler, The Life Review: An Unrecognized Bonanza, *International Journal of Aging and Human Development, 12*:1, pp. 35-38, 1980-1981.
12. E. H. Erikson, Growth and Crises of the Healthy Personality, in *Identity and the Life Cycle. Selected Papers by Erik H. Erikson,* International Universities Press Inc., New York pp. 50-101, 1959.
13. N. Feil, Resolution: The Final Task, *Journal of Humanistic Psychology, 25*:2, pp. 91-105, 1985.
14. J. C. P. A. van Laarhoven, Hoe oud en wijs is "de wijze oude"? Een historische verkenning, in *Ouder worden nu '90,* C. P. M. Knipscheer, J. J. M. Michels, en M. W. Ribbe (red.), Versluys Uitgeverij, Almere, pp. 39-44, 1990.
15. K. J. Gergen, The Emerging Crisis in Life-Span Developmental Theory, in *Life-Span Development and Behaviour, 3,* P. B. Baltes and O. G. Brim, Jr. (eds.), Academic Press, New York/London, pp. 31-63, 1980.

16. E. Olbrich, De levensloop in de moderne tijd: Historische perspectieven en levensloop-psychologie, in *De menselijke levensloop in historisch perspecstief,* H. F. M. Peeters en F. J. Mönks (red.), Van Gorcum, Assen/Maastricht, pp. 84-99, 1986.

17. M. de Winter, Naar een historisch-contextualistische benadering van de menselijke levensloop, in *De menselijke levensloop in historisch perspectief,* H. F. M. Peeters en F. J. Mönks (red.), Van Gorcum, Assen/Maastricht, pp. 19-38, 1986.

18. M. Novak, Biography After the End of Metaphysics: A Critique of Epigenetic Evolution, *International Journal of Aging and Human Development, 22*:3, pp. 189-195, 1985-1986.

19. P. B. Baltes and M. M. Baltes, Psychological Perspectives on Successful Aging: The Model of Selective Optimization with Compensation, in *Successful Aging: Perspectives From the Behavioral Sciences,* P. Baltes and M. M. Baltes (eds.), Cambridge University Press, New York pp. 1-34, 1990.

20. D. Dannefer, Adult Development and Social Theory: A Paradigmatic Reappraisal, *American Sociological Review, 49,* pp. 100-116, 1984.

21. J. J. Dowd, Ever Since Durkheim: The Socialization of Human Development, *Human Development, 33,* pp. 138-159, 1990.

22. J. A. Meacham, A Transactional Model of Remembering, in *Life-Span Developmental Psychology: Dialectical Perspectives on Experimental Research,* N. Datan and H. W. Reese (eds.), Academic Press, New York, pp. 261-283, 1977.

23. J. A. Meacham, The Individual As Consumer and Producer of Historical Change, in *Life-Span Developmental Psychology: Historical and Generational Effects,* H. A. Mc-Cluskey and H. W. Reese (eds.), Academic Press, New York, pp. 47-71, 1984.

24. K. F. Riegel, The Dialectics of Time, in *Life-Span Developmental Psychology: Dialectical Perspectives on Experimental Research,* N. Datan and H. W. Reese (eds.), Academic Press, New York, pp. 3-27, 1977.

25. S. Kvale, Dialectics and Research on Remembering, in *Life-Span Developmental Psychology: Dialectical Perspectives on Experimental Research,* N. Datan and H. W. Reese (eds.), Academic Press, New York, pp. 165-189, 1977.

26. J. D. Webster and R. A. Young, Process Variables of the Life Review: Counseling Implications, *International Journal of Aging and Human Development, 26*:40, pp. 315-323, 1988.

27. J. M. Starr, Towards a Social Phenomenology of Aging: Studying the Self-Process in Biographical Work, *International Journal of Aging and Human Development, 16*:4, pp. 255-270, 1982-1983.

28. A. Hankiss, Ontologies of the Self: On the Mythological Rearranging of One's Life History, in *Biography and Society; The Life-History Approach in the Social Sciences,* D. Bertaux (ed.), Sage Publications, Beverly Hills, pp. 203-209, 1981.

29. E. M. Hoerning, Lebensereignisse: Übergänge im Lebenslauf, in *Methoden der Biographie- und Lebenslaufforschung. Biographie und Gesellschaft: Bd. 1,* W. Voges (Hrsg.), Leske und Budrich, Leverkusen, pp. 231-259, 1987.

30. M. Lewis, Development, Time and Catastrophe: An Alternative View of Discontinuity, in *Life-Span Development and Behavior, 10,* P. B. Baltes, D. L. Featherman, and R. M. Lerner (eds.), pp. 325-351, 1990.

31. K. F. Riegel, *Foundations of Dialectical Psychology,* Academic Press, New York, 1979.

32. V. I. Tarman, Autobiography: The Negotiation of a Lifetime, *International Journal of Aging and Human Development, 27*:3, pp. 171-191, 1988.
33. G. L. Maddox and P. L. Lawton, Varieties of Aging, in *Annual Review of Gerontology and Geriatrics, 8,* G. L. Maddox and P. L. Lawton (eds.), Springer, New York, 1988.
34. J. Baars, The Challenge of Critical Gerontology: The Problem of Social Constitution, *Journal of Aging Studies, 5*:3, pp. 219-243, 1991.
35. D. I. Kertzer and K. W. Schaie (eds.), *Age Structuring in Comparative Perspective,* Lawrence Erlbaum, Hillsdale, 1989.
36. M. Kohli, The World We Forgot: A Historical Review of the Life Course, in *Later Life. The Social Psychology of Aging,* V. Marshall (ed.), Sage, Beverly Hills/London/New Delhi, 1986.
37. J. Meyer, The Self and the Life Course, in *Human Development and the Life Course: Multidisciplinary Perspectives,* A. Sorensen, F. E. Weinert, and L. R. Sherrod (eds.), Lawrence Erlbaum, London, 1986.
38. S. J. Crystal, *America's Old Age Crisis,* Basic Books, New York, 1982.
39. M. Kohli, M. Rein, A. M. Guillemard, and H. Van Vunsteren, *Time for Retirement. Comparative Studies of Early Exit from the Labor Force,* Cambridge University Press, New York, 1991.
40. M. Kohli, Social Organization and Subjective Construction of the Life Course, in *Human Development and the Life Course: Multidisciplinary Perspectives*, A. Sorensen, F. E. Weinert, and L. R. Sherrod (eds.), Lawrence Erlbaum, London, 1986.
41. M. M. Marini, Age and Sequencing Norms in the Transition to Adulthood, *Social Forces, 63,* pp. 229-244, 1984.
42. K. U. Mayer, Lebensverläufe und sozialer Wandel. *Kölner Zeitschrift für Soziologie und Sozialpsychologie* (Special issue), Westdeutscher Verlag, Opladen, 1991.
43. C. P. M. Knipscheer, Temporal Embeddedness and Aging Within the Multi-Generational Family: The Case of Grandparenting, in *Emergent Theories of Aging: Psychosocial and Social Perspectives on Time, Self and Society,* J. E. Birren and V. L. Bengtson (eds.), Springer Publishing Company, New York, 1988.
44. R. Bendix, Labor Market Entry and the Sexual Segregation of Careers in the Federal Republic of Germany, *American Journal of Sociology, 93*:1, pp. 89-118, 1987.
45. S. Arber and J. Ginn, *Gender and Later Life. A Sociological Analysis of Resources and Constraints,* Sage Publications, London/Newbury Park/New Delhi, 1991.
46. D. L. Featherman, L. K. Selbee, and K. U. Mayer, Social Class and the Structuring of the Life Course in Norway and West Germany, in *Age Structuring in Comparative Perspective,* D. I. Kertzer and K. W. Schaie (eds.), Lawrence Erlbaum, Hillsdale, pp. 55-93, 1989.
47. D. Dannefer, Aging as Intracohort Differentiation: Accentuation, the Matthew Effect and the Life Course, *Sociological Forum, 2,* pp. 211-236, 1987.
48. J. Brandon Wallace, Reconsidering the Life Review: The Social Construction of Talk about the Past, *The Gerontologist, 32*:1, pp. 120-125, 1992.
49. C. A. Holland and R. M. A. Rabbitt, Ageing Memory: Use Versus Impairment, *British Journal of Psychology, 82,* pp. 29-38, 1991.

Section III

Reminiscence and Life Review as Intervention

Chapter 9

THE AUTOBIOGRAPHICAL GROUP: A TOOL FOR THE RECONSTRUCTION OF PAST LIFE EXPERIENCE WITH THE AGED

Luis Botella
and
Guillem Feixas

From a personal construct point of view, writing autobiographical texts becomes a relevant therapeutic ingredient for elderly individuals.[1] If conducted in a context of a group, as Birren proposes [1, 2]; it promotes self-awareness, self-disclosure, and the capacity of generating alternative views of life's experiences. In a group of elderly volunteers from a recreational society of Barcelona (Spain), the guided autobiography method was used to foster the reconstruction of the participant's past life experiences. The degree of reconstruction was assessed through a design that included the administration of a repertory grid at the initial and tenth (last) session. A parallel assessment was applied to a control group of participants with similar demographic characteristics. An adaptation of the method proposed by Feixas for the analysis of autobiographical texts was used to

---

[1]Personal construct psychologists have pioneered an interesting line of research on the area of death anxiety [F. Epting and R. A. Neimeyer, *Personal Meanings of Death,* Hemisphere, Washington, D.C., 1984.] [R. A. Neimeyer, Death Anxiety, in *Dying: Facing the Facts,* H. Wass, F. Berardo, and R. A. Neimeyer (eds.), Hemisphere, Washington, D.C., 1988.] The Threat Index [R. A. Neimeyer and M. K. Moore, Assessing Personal Meanings of Death: Empirical Refinements in the Threat Index, *Death Studies, 13,* pp. 227-245, 1989.], a constructivist tool for the assessment of personal meanings of death, constitutes perhaps, one of the best known products of this research studies.

assess the assigned writings of the participants for each session [3]. Results show a significant and gradual change in the construing system of those participants in the autobiographical group. Thus, the distance of the elements self-ideal/self and self-ideal/others significantly decreased in comparison to the control group. It is suggested that the guided autobiography is an adequate therapeutic tool to promote the reconstruction of experience in aged individuals.

The Western psychological view of the elderly individual is shaped according to the "deficiency" model. This model assumes that, beginning in the thirties, a person's cognitive capacities (intelligence and learning abilities) progressively decrease with age while personality traits tend to become more and more rigid. In the psychotherapy field, this view has promoted the assumption that "one cannot cure aging" [4]. Perhaps as a consequence of this perspective, one can find few works addressing the issue of psychotherapy with elderly individuals in spite of the fact that the demographic figures for people over sixty years of age are continuously increasing. Those works that do exist point out the lack of experience and the scarcity of research in this area.

> Because not many therapists are trained to work with the elderly, it is also likely that the client will encounter a therapist who becomes anxious in dealing with an older client—who will be wondering, without knowing how to find it out, whether the client is "senile," and who may feel that depression and even suicide are understandable responses to being old [5, p. 14].

As Butler notes, most of the research conducted with elderly individuals is based on the experience of the institutionalized [6]. This only accounts for approximately 5 percent of the elderly population. One of the factors that could possibly explain this lack of attention to elderly individuals and the processes underlying their psychological health, is the high inter-individual variability which, according to Lehr [7], clearly exceeds intergroup variability. Despite the wide commonalities of needs and difficulties, aged people mostly differ in the interpretation they give to their lives and to aging.

This chapter presents the *Guided Autobiography Group* (GAG) [1, 2, 8] as a tool for preventive psychological interventions with elderly individuals. Our approach is devised within the framework of Kelly's [9] personal construct psychology, whose methods for assessing personal meanings are used to evaluate these group processes.

AGING OR DEVELOPMENT?

Adopting the term "aging" usually involved a set of pejorative implications. The idea of "old age" entails the activation of a social stereotype related to the myths of lack of productivity, engagement, and flexibility, as well as senility [10]. However, this view only reflects the values of Western culture as applied to elderly people. Certainly, if we measure human worth in the stereotyped terms of productivity and control, then old people are bound to be seen (by themselves and by others) as failing with age. In contrast, Eastern philosophy places the individual self, his/her lifespan and his/her death within the process of human experience.

> Life and death are familiar and equally acceptable parts of what self means. In the West, on the other hand, death is considered outside the self. To be a self or a person one must be alive, in control and aware of what is happening. The greater and more self-centered or narcissistic Western emphasis on individuality and control makes death an outrage, a tremendous affront to man, rather than the logical and necessary process of old life making way for new [10, p. 530].

The alternative of the "aging" view, seems to be the idea of considering old age as a continuation of human development. According to Butler [10], the "major developmental task in old age is to clarify, deepen and find use of what one has already obtained in a lifetime of learning and adapting" [10, p. 531]. However, this developmental view can easily end up considering old age as merely another lifestage. Problems about the chronological boundaries of what is meant by "old age" then arise. Therefore, considering old age as part of a developmental process involves the consideration of an appropriate model of development.

A CONSTRUCTIVIST MODEL OF
HUMAN DEVELOPMENT

Although Personal Construct Theory (PCT) does not deal specifically with developmental issues it can be seen, in itself, as a theory of development.

> Because human beings are conceived from the outset as inhabiting the dimension of time, that is to say, conceived as alive and in motion, one does not need to conjure up motivating forces to push them around. We are then left with the task of explaining only the directions his motion will take [11, p. 265].

This basic philosophy leads Kelly to explain the direction of motion in terms of his fundamental postulate: "A person's processes are psychologically channelized by the ways in which he anticipates events" [9, p. 46]. In this postulate the word "anticipation" is especially relevant since it is the motivational core of the theory [12]. Human functioning is oriented toward the anticipation of events, and thus, toward the reduction of uncertainty. This feature makes PCT a theory of constancy as well as change.

In his experience corollary, Kelly asserts that "a person's construction system varies as he successively construes the replications of events" [9, p. 72]. Here, the changing nature of the construing system is acknowledged. This process evolves through what Kelly termed the experience cycle (see Figure 1). To describe it,

Kelly compared our everyday activity with that of the scientist. Anticipations (constructs) or hypotheses are hierarchically organized in a system which serves both for understanding events and for predicting the future. As scientific hypotheses, anticipations are linked to a whole theory, the personal construct system. The first stage of this cycle, which emerges from previous cycles, refers to the anticipatory nature of human existence as well as the predictive aspiration of science. According to various degrees of investment, the person encounters events. The outcome of this encounter provides confirmation or disconfirmation of such hypotheses which in turn leads to constructive revision of the system. In case of validation of the hypothesis, the distinction which made possible that choice is consolidated in the system. In case of invalidation, new distinctions (constructs) should evolve to guide the subsequent behavior.

Feixas and Villegas consider this cycle as the fundamental core of a constructivist theory of human change [13]. Though intuitively simple, the experience cycle applies to all our thoughts and acts, and accounts for the continuous changing nature of human activity. At the same time, experience is not seen as simply the passage of time but as a (pro)active construction of events. Consequently, chronological age, by itself, does not tell us anything about experience nor about the state of the person's system of construing. Human disorders can be seen from the standpoint of Kelly's corollaries and experience cycle [14]. Thus, difficulties in different stages of the experience cycle can lead to differential disorders.

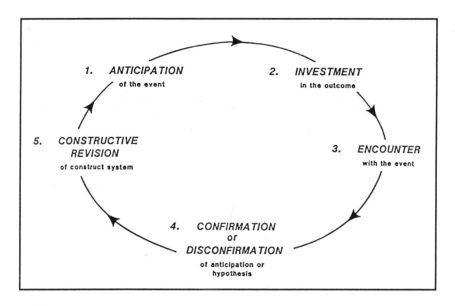

Figure 1. The Experience Cycle (reprinted from Neimeyer, 1985 [16]).

According to this view of experience, PCT does not conceive that human beings develop in definite stages. Instead, people interpret (and reinterpret) themselves and their situations in a variety of forms. In a previous study it was shown how developmental stages were seen in very different ways by group participants [8]. In that study, following Kelly's credulous approach (a principle that suggests that one should ask the client directly instead of getting indirect information on which to base clinical conclusions), we asked participants to state the turning points of their lives. Those points were related to personal meaningful events instead of chronological, conceptual, or psychosexual criteria. Salmon [15], in her research with children and adolescents, and Neimeyer [16], with his BioRep grid technique, also reached similar conclusions about the idiosyncrasy of people's perceived "developmental stages."

Actually, it is thought that if a developmental theory would embrace any stages, these should be derived from the experience cycle. If one considers experience as an overlapping series of experience cycles at different levels, then the lifecycle may be viewed as a macroscopic experience cycle in which the person's core constructs are tested and revised. This thesis is akin to that of the existential-phenomenological approach [17] which considers the person as dialectically developing his or her existential project throughout life. The relation between this project and constructive activity has been elaborated by Feixas and Villegas:

> Any constructive activity entails, necessarily, the possibility of alternative constructions. Therefore, empirical descriptions are not sufficient to determine the meaning of a given behavior. Instead, actions should be interpreted in the light of the person's original project. This is, precisely, the aim of existential analysis [13, p. 23].

From this viewpoint, old age might become a time to elaborate both the validational and the invalidational evidence received throughout the whole lifecycle in order to balance one's own achievements and losses; a time for constructive revision of one's own entire life project (or to become ready to begin a new cycle, for those who believe in life after death). Many authors have pointed to the need for acquiring a harmonic integration of past life experiences as the central issue of senescence [18-20].

Some of the autobiographical accounts produced by members of our groups reflect this sense of integration. Along with being a validation of very central and superordinate life hypothesis, this sense entails many of the positive feelings described by McCoy [21] as a result of validation: love ("awareness of validation of one's core structure"), happiness ("awareness of validation of a portion of one's structure"), self-confidence ("awareness of the goodness of fit of the self in one's core role structure"), and satisfaction ("awareness of validation of a non-core structure"). In Viney's words, this is a sensation of self-transcendence acquired through the validation of core constructs [20].

Viney has developed a socio-phenomenological developmental model for the elderly based in PCT which holds three basic principles:

1. Developmental psychology is psychology of changing experience.
2. Development occurs when people interpret and reinterpret their experiences of events, as in the process of serial reconstruction.
3. Integration of these reinterpretations is the primary task of development, integration of core constructs about self especially, with more peripheral constructs about others also being of importance [22, p. 155].

This model considers those triggering events for a developmental transition which, according to Viney [23], results from invalidation. In the elderly, two possible sources of invalidation are biological changes (illness and deterioration) as well as interpersonal changes [24]. A way to cope with these invalidating changes would be serial reconstruction]25]. When the person's constructs are able to predict events without a great deal of invalidation, psychological problems do not arise and contact with reality remains meaningful. Conversely, serial invalidation leads the elder to adopt a series of defensive strategies to cope with threat (defined by Kelly, as "the awareness of an imminent comprehensive change in one's core structures," [9, p. 533]. These strategies can be equated with what Thomae [26, p. 366] termed "defensive existential" and "evasion" techniques which include.

> . . . any effort made by an individual to exclude from consciousness those representations which are unpleasant and painful; to "repress" them and to "ignore" them. Here a defense mechanism comes into play: the individual does not seek to solve the conflict by acting upon the environment, nor by modifying his or her own behavior. He or she simply tries to ignore or even deny the situation. These attempts may bring immediate relief but are not real solutions to the problem [7, p. 17].

On the other hand, evasion techniques would correspond with what Lewin defined as "leaving the field" either by trying to physically "escape" from the situation (moving to another house or position) or through a "mental" separation [7].

Both courses are examples of what Kelly defined as hostility, that is, the distortion of evidence in favor of a prediction which has been shown to be inaccurate [9].

As a result of the serial invalidation that some elderly individuals receive regarding their expectations of physical and interpersonal abilities, they may 1) become extremely preoccupied with physical (and mental) health, 2) withdraw from social relationships, 3) develop anxiety regarding their new social role [27],

4) become more dependent on others, and 5) develop feelings of resentfulness, loneliness, and lack of social power. Conversely, those who continue to receive validation of their core constructs develop feelings of independence, integration, individuation, emotional balance, and satisfactory social relationships [22].

In this process, occurring in the later years of people's lives as a constructive revision of their system of construing, reminiscence plays an essential role. It becomes a crucial pathway to acquire the sense of transcendence characteristic of constructive revision of an entire life's experience.

THE GAG IN A PERSONAL CONSTRUCT CONTEXT

Within the theoretical model provided by PCT, the aims of reminiscence and life review as implemented in the GAG are:

(1) Promotion of self-awareness: Revision and integration of experience becomes an impossible task unless its contents can be made conscious (in Kellian terms, unless pre-verbal constructs can be verbalized). In terms of Thomas' "self-consciousness corollary":

> To the extent that a person construes his own construction of experience, he or she acquires consciousness. To the extent that a person construes his or her own process of construction he or she acquires more complete awareness of themselves as a person [28, p. 53].

In the context of the GAG this goal can be achieved in different ways. On the one hand, the task itself entails a careful reconsideration of past life experiences. Actually, writing an autobiography may be seen in terms of Kelly's creativity cycle [9]. The person's loose constructions about his or her past experiences must be tightened down to be specified in a textual form. This passage provided by Herminia, a seventy-year-old member of the GAG, constitutes a good example of how reminiscence writing may promote self-awareness:

> My memories are good, but a deeper look reveals that I was a quiet child who was missing something important. I have discovered it now, and I have the solution, but I realize I committed the same mistake in raising my children. To analyze a life story means to encounter deficiencies and errors.

On the other hand, the in-the-session comments of the leader and members of the GAG may also facilitate self-awareness. One of the controversial procedures provided by PCT, Hinkle's [29] laddering technique (see [30]) implies asking the person "why" he or she prefers to be described by one pole of a construct instead of the other. This leads to a "laddering up" of the person's construct system, which can powerfully enhance self-awareness. For example, when discussing Pedro's hobby of traveling, the following dialogue took place (Pedro was the only male member of the GAG, aged 72):

GROUP LEADER (GL): So you prefer to be considered as a person fond of traveling than as one who is not, don't you?

PEDRO (P): Quite so.

GL: Why is it so?

P: Humm . . . I'm not certain . . . Maybe because people not fond of traveling are so closed to new experiences.

GL: What's the contrary of being "closed to new experiences" for you?

P: I guess something like "being engaged in living."

GL: And why do you prefer being "engaged in living" rather than "closed to new experiences"?

P: Oh, well, if you are engaged in living you always remain young (young of spirit at least).

GL: What would you say is opposed to being "young of spirit"?

P: Being senile . . . It's curious, I think I see where this is driving me to . . . and I've never thought of my love for traveling as a way of escaping from senility . . . but it makes a lot of sense to me . . . quite a lot.

This kind of procedure allows the person to elaborate his or her construct system at different hierarchical levels. Thus, the conversation not only provides information to the group leader, but becomes, in itself, a change-promoting activity.

(2) **Promotion of self-disclosure**: Sharing life experiences in a group context is a genuine way of meaningful self-disclosure. Birren and Hedlund [2] term this process "developmental exchange" and define it as "the mutual exchange between individuals of personally important historical and emotional events" [2, p. 410]. These authors consider this process one of the more active ingredients of the positive group effects. However, one of the pitfalls that is likely to be encountered in the process of group self-disclosure with elderly individuals is that the pre-eminent values of this particular cohort we are working with seem to include the idea that one should solve one's own problems without sharing it with others [5]. This value might have affected the elderly person (a) by preventing them from establishing the habit of self-disclosing and/or (b) by incorporating the not-self-disclosing value itself. Thus, some elderly individuals may think that self-disclosing is not a good idea and, therefore, may not attempt it. A particularly striking example of this in our GAG is the case of Dorotea (the younger group member, aged 60). In almost every assigned topic she wrote about a series of sexual concerns.

"I was so in love that he changed by life, and I never had sexual intercourse with him (. . .) I used to make "things" with him that I told to my confessor, but not "copulation," I didn't know about sex" (Writing about her first boyfriend). "I got married when I was twenty-eight and my husband thirty-nine. I never experienced an orgasm, our marriage was without sex. I was frigid" (Writing about her deceased husband).

" . . . and nowadays we are a couple who's had a lot of sex on his side and a lot of curiosity about orgasm (that I've never experienced) on mine" (Writing about her present mate).

Although Dorotea's concern about sexual satisfaction among women was outstanding to the group leader (who kept a copy of the assigned writings), whenever she read out loud such passages in the group sessions. The leader was then confronted with the dilemma of respecting her reluctance or forcing her to participate in what seems to be an essential task of the GAG. The solution to this came from a "game" that the leader proposed to the group: writing a "personal important secret" on a piece of paper and, gathering them all and keeping them anonymous, submit them to group discussion. Dorotea wrote "I have never had an orgasm in my life." When discussing it in the session, she discovered that many of the other women members had not had continuous orgasms in their sexual intercourses, but they regarded it as superficial when compared with the amount of tenderness, love, genuine affection, and intimate communication they had obtained from sex.

Another interesting solution to this kind of problem is provided by the Interpersonal Transaction Group format [31, 32]. It consists of a group format in which individuals self-disclose an assigned topic (the autobiographical writing in the case of the GAG) in the context of multiple rotating dyads. It promotes a stronger feeling of group cohesion, one of the most important factors in group processes according to Yalom [33]. Besides, it is paramount to reassure the group members about the confidentiality of all the session contents and to foster a non-judgmental attitude among them, encouraging instead a strong empathic feeling towards each other's problems.

(3) Promotion of an alternative view of personal biography: PCT, along with many other approaches, considers the generation of alternatives as a core process in revising a person's system of construing. This issue is directly related to Kelly's epistemological position, *constructive alternativism.*

> We assume that all our present interpretations of the universe are subject to revision or replacement (. . .) we take the stand that there are always some alternative constructions available to choose among in dealing with the world. No one needs to paint himself into a corner; no one needs to be completely hemmed by circumstances; no one needs to be the victim of his biography [9, p. 15].

Although anything might be subject to reconstruction, one cannot be too optimistic about the plasticity of human beings. As Neimeyer and Harter [34] point out, the self should be considered an ecosystem that entails systemic relationships among one's identity constructs; therefore, a given reconstruction can only occur if it is consistent with the self ecology, that is, with the rest of the person's construct system. One implication of this principle is that even though the GAG leader provides and supports alternative views of participant's life experiences, he or she should be very sensitive to the implications that these alternative views might entail for the participants' "ecological selves." Otherwise, alternative views that are inconsistent with the existing system will be rejected, probably undermining the leader's credibility. Even though the group leader acts carefully, it is not unusual that, when discussing the autobiographical excerpts, some of the group members propose alternative constructions that might threaten the whole system of a given member. In these cases a reframing intervention is needed to prevent an open conflict between group members. For example, when discussing the topic "History of my loves," Maria (a GAG member, age 68) read the following passage:

> It's curious but, thinking about it, I have come to the conclusion that I was in love with my teacher (a young lady) for some time. I was about 13-years-old and I saw her so beautiful and elegant . . . she was quite like a fairy tale princess. I wanted so badly to be like her.

When Rosa (the oldest GAG member, age 79) heard this, she irreflexively asserted to the group that "it is normal to have homosexual tendencies when one is a teenager." Maria strongly rejected the idea of having ever had "homosexual tendencies." The leader then, pointed to the possibility that they were talking about different issues; Maria was describing a sort of "teenager fascination" towards her young lady teacher (without sexual implications) and Rosa was interpreting it as an "adult love" with full sexual meaning. They both agreed and realized they had misunderstood each other, proceeding to discuss (without resentment) the difference between "love" and "infatuation."

Many approaches use this kind of reframing procedures for the purpose of generating alternatives [35, 36]. This technique is termed "reassurance" in PCT, and it is defined as "a simplified superordinate construction placed upon a situation in order to render it meaningful and predictable" [9, p. 649]. Another way of promoting alternatives is role playing—putting the person in different roles in a given situation—which may help him/her to understand different points of view.

CASE STUDY

Adopting the premises outlined above, a GAG was organized in Barcelona (Spain). Its context was not clinical but recreational and self-discovery enhancing. It was addressed to the members of a "Golden Age Club" as an optative activity. Applicants were all given detailed information about the group task and its goals. This particular GAG was scheduled as one weekly group session (lasting about 90 minutes) during a three-month period (October-December, 1988).

Method

Participants

The GAG was formed by twelve volunteers of a recreational society for the elderly in Barcelona, Spain. The option to participate in this group was given within a set of activities regularly offered by that society. Even though twelve members participated in the group experience, only eight completed all the assessment instruments. The age of these eight participants ranged from sixty to sixty-eight years (mean = 68). The control group was formed by ten individuals, members of the same society, with similar demographic characteristics.

Instruments

Repertory grid—A repertory grid [9, 30, 37] was administered to both the control and the GAG at the time of the latter's first session. The elements consisted of a list of significant people in the participant's life; ranging from five to ten elements. The constructs were elicited using the dyadic method which involves asking the participant to provide a similarity for two given elements (e.g., "In which way your daughter and your husband are alike?"). Once this characteristic (e.g., "caring") is obtained the interviewer asks for its opposite (e.g., "callous"). This procedure is repeated with various element pairs. The number of constructs (i.e., pairs of opposites such as "caring—callous") derived from this method ranged from five to ten. A further task involved the rating of every element on each elicited construct in a five point Likert-type scale. This grid, using the same elements and constructs, was also presented at the termination of the ten-session group process and participants were asked to rate again the elements in the construct dimensions.

Guided autobiography—This method, as proposed by Birren [1, 2, 38], consists of assigning a composition to group members on a topic selected by the group leader. The sessions were divided into a small lecture (30 minutes) about the proposed topic and a group discussion (60 minutes) of the autobiographical texts produced by group members. The topics chosen for this particular GAG were "My family of origin," "The family I created," "History of my friendships," "History of my loves," "History of my hobbies," "History of my positive experiences," and "History of the persons whom most influenced me." Group sessions were conducted by one of the authors of this paper following a personal construct approach.

Hypotheses

1. Reconstruction as an outcome. This hypothesis assumes that significant change, in terms of either consolidation or loosening will occur in the construing systems of the GAG participants after the ten weekly sessions. This would be measured by changes in the ratings in the grids administered at the end of the last group session.

2. Reconstruction as a process. This hypothesis assumes that change is a gradual process. Therefore, it includes the analysis of autobiographical texts as a mid-point assessment between the first and the second grid. This implicitly entails a sub-hypothesis that assumes that measures derived from grids and measures derived from the analysis of autobiographical texts are comparable.

3. Direction of reconstruction. This hypothesis postulates the direction taken by the changes in the GAG assumed in the first hypothesis in terms of three measures of construing partially derived from Norris and Makhlouf-Norris [39]: (1) Self-Ideal distance, (2) Self-Others distance, and (3) Ideal-Others.

Procedures

The consistency coefficient [30] was used to test the first hypothesis. It consists on a rank ordered correlation among Pearson's coefficients for each pair of constructs of the first and the second grid. In a few words, consistency is a global efficient ranging from −1 to +1 that indicates the amount of change among construct inter-correlations occurring from one grid to another either in the direction of loosening or tightening. The CIRCUMGRIDS program [40] for repertory grid analysis was used for this calculation. The analysis of autobiographical texts, performed to test the second hypothesis was done using Feixas' [3] method[2] which elicits elements and constructs from free-format autobiographical texts. A binary grid matrix is also derived for co-occurrence of constructs in different elements. This matrix shows the constructs applied to different elements in a way that mathematical measures of association can be derived. For example, if the author describes different elements applying the same set of constructs (say "caring" and "sufferer"), a certain degree of association is inferred between these two constructs. Cluster analysis is then performed on this matrix using the CLUSTAN program [42], thus yielding some comparable to those obtained from repertory grid analysis. The content of the constructs was coded according to Landfield's system of categories [43]. Distances among grid elements were obtained through Bell's G-PACK program [44].

Results

Reconstruction as a Result

The mean of the consistency scores for the control group was 0.82 while the mean for the GAG was 0.52 (see Table 1 for an individualized account). There is a significant difference between them ($p < 0.05$). Therefore, his hypothesis is validated because grids administered at the end of the GAG differ significantly from those administered at the beginning.

Reconstruction as a Process

The validation of this hypothesis involves the comparison of repertory grid analysis with textual analysis. The content similarity of the constructs used in both methods was tested comparing the two most frequently used categories [43] in each method for every participant. In five out of eight cases the same

---

[2](An English version of this method [41].)

Table 1. Consistency Scores Among Pre- and Post-Treatment Repertory Grids for Control and Autobiographical Groups

Control Group		Autobiographical Group	
Member	Consistency	Member	Consistency
A	0.96	K	0.59
B	0.85	L	0.73
C	0.95	M	0.71
D	0.80	N	0.59
E	0.83	O	0.64
F	0.83	P	0.62
G	0.82	Q	0.27
H	0.85	R	0.10
I	0.74		
J	0.54		
Mean = 0.82		Mean = 0.52	

two categories appear to be the most used in both methods. This result suggests that the content of the constructs elicited in grids and autobiographical texts tend to be somewhat similar. Then, though comparative results can only be considered tentative, they can be considered indicators of some common construing processes.

Global Intensity (GL) scores were computed for both grid and textually elicited constructs. This score is the result of averaging Construct Intensity scores for a given individual. Construct Intensity measures the global relationship of one construct with the rest of the constructs. Thus, GI measures the tightness or looseness of the system of construing. To validate this hypothesis, GI scores derived from the autobiographical texts should fall somewhere in the middle, between pre- and post-grid GI scores, as below:

Pre-grid GI > Textual GI > Post-grid GI or
Pre-grid GI < Textual GI < Post-grid GI

Table 2 shows how this gradual reconstruction occurs in five out of eight cases.

Direction of Reconstruction

The mean for the value of the difference between grid 1 and grid 2 concerning euclidian distances between the grid elements "Self"—"Ideal self" for the control group was 0.42 while for the GAG was 1.32. Thus, Self-Ideal distances changed significantly in the GAG ($p < 0.05$). It can be concluded, then, that participation in

Table 2. Global Intensity (GI) Scores for Pre-Treatment Grids (G-PRE),
Textual Grids (TEXT), and Post-Treatment Grids in Rank Order.

Subj.	G-PRE	(Rank)		TEXT	(Rank)		G-POST	(Rank)
K	2.62	8	>	1.48	7	=	3.25	7
L	6.76	1	=	1.75	1	=	6.45	1
M	3.67	5	>	1.63	3	<	4.16	4
N	2.82	7	>	1.49	6	>	3.82	5
O	6.65	2	=	1.73	2	=	6.28	2
P	4.78	3	<	1.46	8	>	3.72	6
Q	3.55	6	>	1.61	5	<	2.78	8
R	3.93	4	=	1.62	4	>	4.19	3

the GAG promoted a significant reduction (for all the cases) in the perceived distance between individuals' ideal and actual self.

Similar positive findings were found for the reduction of Ideal-Others distances (Mean for the Exp. group = 0.79, for the control = 0.30, $p < 0.05$). This indicates that the GAG was successful in either accommodating Ideal image with people represented as grid elements or constructing a more positive (ideal) view of those people. The distance Self-Others (Mean for the Exp. group = 0.68, for the control = 0.52) was not statistically significant, though the direction of the difference tends to a reduction of the perceived distance between the self and the other grid elements.

Despite its small sample size, this study indicates that substantial reconstruction processes may occur during a GAG. However, it would be desirable for future research to include some methodological improvements such as including more participants, independent assessment measures, follow up testing, and a comparison of the GAG outcome with the one from other kind of groups conducted from different theoretical perspectives.

CONCLUSIONS

In taking a PCP viewpoint, this chapter tries to contribute to the existing GAG literature by providing 1) a wide theoretical rationale about the aging developmental process; 2) a conceptual understanding of the change mechanisms involved in the GAG process; 3) some guidelines for leading the particular group processes involved in the GAG with aged persons; 4) and a methodological body for assessing the impact of the GAG in the construct systems of its members. Additionally, the development of GAG experiences outside its original area, evidence the cross-cultural interest of the method.

Considering the results of our case study it can be suggested that participation in the AG produced a significant, gradual, and positive change in the construing processes of the participants. This finding provides some support to previous literature suggesting the efficacy of reminiscence, in the form of autobiographical writing, for the process of reconstruction of previous life experiences. This reconstruction involves an improvement on self-esteem and in the evaluation of important others. The relevance of these findings for the mental and physical health of elderly individuals cannot be taken for granted. This research design would benefit from the inclusion of additional assessment devices. Certainly, the replication of this study using more participants and follow-up measures would enrich these preliminary, though promising, findings.

In summary, the GAG is becoming a tool of increasing interest for the life enrichment of aged individuals. By providing within the same theoretical and gerontological framework both guidelines for conducting group sessions and a method for evaluating the group processes, the GAG constitutes a promising development in this area.

REFERENCES

1. J. E. Birren and D. E. Deutchman, *Guiding Autobiography Groups for Older Adults: Exploring the Fabric of Life*, Johns Hopkins University Press, Baltimore, 1991.
2. J. E. Birren and B. Hedlund, Contributions of Autobiography to Developmental Psychology, in *Contemporary Topics in Developmental Psychology*, N. Einsenberg (ed.), Wiley, New York, 1987.
3. G. Feixas, *L'Analisi de Construccions Personals en Textos de Significació Psicològica* [Personal construct analysis of autobiographical texts]. Microfilmed doctoral dissertation (n. 328). Publicacions Universitat de Barcelona, Barcelona, 1988.
4. C. Eisdorfer and B. A. Stotski, Intervention, Treatment and Rehabilitation of Psychiatric Disorders, in *Handbook of the Psychology of Aging*, J. E. Birren and K. W. Schaie (eds.), Van Nostrand Reinhold, New York, 1977.
5. B. Knight, *Psychotherapy with Older Adults*, Sage, Beverly Hills, California, 1986.
6. R. N. Butler, The Life Review: An Interpretation of Reminiscence in the Aged, *Psychiatry, 26*, pp. 65-76, 1963.
7. U. Lehr, *Psychologie des Alterns*, Quelle and Meyer, Heidelberg, Germany, 1977.
8. L. Botella and G. Feixas, *La Reconstruccio Autobiogràfica: Un Enfocament Construc-tivista de Treball Grupal en Gerontologia* [Autobiographical reconstruction: A constructivist approach to the group work in gerontology]. Llar del llibre, Barcelona, 1991.
9. G. A. Kelly, *The Psychology of Personal Constructs* (2 vols), Norton, New York, 1955.
10. R. N. Butler, Successful Aging and the Role of the Life Review, *American Geriatrics Society, 22*, pp. 529–535, 1974.
11. G. A. Kelly, Suicide: The Personal Construct Point of View, in *The Cry for Help*, N. L. Farebow and E. S. Shneidman (eds.), McGraw-Hill, New York, 1961.
12. J. S. Bruner, You Are Your Constructs, *Contemporary Psychology, 1*, pp. 355-357, 1965.
13. G. Feixas and M. Villegas, *Constructivismo y Psicoterapia* [Constructivism and psychotherapy], Promociones y Publicaciones Universitarias, Barcelona, 1990.

14. R. A. Neimeyer and G. Feixas, I Disturbi di Costruzione [disorders of construction], in *Le Teorie Cognitive Dei Disturbi Emotivi*, F. Mancini and A. Semerari (eds.), Nuova Italia Scientifica, Rome, 1990.

15. P. Salmon, Children as Social Beings: A Kellian View, in *Constructs of Sociality and Individuality*, P. Stringer and D. Bannister (eds.), Academic, London, 1979.

16. R. A. Neimeyer, Personal Constructs in Clinical Practice, in *Advances in Cognitive-Behavioral Research and Therapy (Vol. 4)*, P. C. Kendall (ed.), Academic, New York, 1985.

17. M. Villegas, *La Psicoteràpia Existencial* [Existential psychotherapy], unpublished doctoral dissertation, Universitat de Barcelona, Spain, 1981.

18. G. Allport, The Use of Personal Documents in Psychological Science, *Social Science Research Council, Bull. 49*, 1942.

19. G. S. Hall, *Senescence: The Last Half of Life*, Appleton, New York, 1922.

20. E. Erickson, Identity and the Life Cycle, *Psychological Issues Monograph, 1*, International Universities Press, New York, 1959.

21. M. McCoy, A Reconstruction of Emotion, in *New Perspectives in Personal Construct Theory*, D. Bannister (ed.), Academic, London, 1977.

22. L. Viney, *The Development and Evaluation of Short-term Psychotherapy Programmes for the Elderly: Report to the Australian Institute of Health*, University of Wollongong, Wollongong, Australia, 1986.

23. L. Viney, *Transitions*, Cassell, Sidney, 1981.

24. L. W. Poon (ed.) *Aging in the 80's: Psychological Issues*, APA, Washington, D.C., 1980.

25. D. Bannister and F. Fransella, *Inquiring Man: The Psychology of Personal Constructs*, (3rd Edition), Croom Helm, London, 1986.

26. H. Thomae, *Das Individuen und Seine Welt; Eine Persoinlichkeitstheorie*, Hogrefe, Gotinga, Germany, 1968.

27. R. Peck, Psychological Developments in the Second Half of Life, in *Human Life Cycle*, N. C. Sze (ed.), Clarendon, New York, 1977.

28. L. F. Thomas, Construct, Reflect and Converse: The Conventional Reconstruction of Social Realities, in *Constructs of Sociality and Individuality*, P. Stringer and D. Bannister (eds.), Academic, London, 1979.

29. D. N. Hinkle, *The Change of Personal Constructs from the Viewpoint of a Theory of Implications*, Unpublished doctoral dissertation, Ohio University, 1965.

30. F. Fransella and D. Bannister, *A Manual for Repertory Grid Technique*, Academic Press, London, 1977.

31. A. Landfield and P. C. Rivers, Interpersonal Transaction and Rotating Dyads, *Psychotherapy: Theory, Research and Practice, 12*, pp. 366-437, 1975.

32. R. A. Neimeyer, Clinical Guidelines for Conducting Interpersonal Transaction Groups, *International Journal of Personal Construct Psychology, 1*, pp. 181-190, 1988.

33. I. Yalom, *The Theory and Practice of Group Psychotherapy*, Basic Books, New York, 1975.

34. R. A. Neimeyer and S. Harter, Facilitating Individual Change, in *Working with People: Clinical Uses of Personal Construct Psychology*, G. Dunnett (ed.), Routledge and Kegan Paul, London, 1988.

35. S. Minuchin and H. C. Fishman, *Family Therapy Techniques*, Harvard University Press, Cambridge, Massachusetts, 1981.
36. P. Watzlawick, J. Weakland, and R. Fisch, *Change: Principles of Problem Formation and Problem Resolution*, Norton, New York, 1974.
37. N, Beail (ed.), *Repertory Grid Technique and Personal Constructs*, Croom Helm, London, 1985.
38. J. E. Birren, The Best of All Stories, *Psychology Today*, pp. 91-92, May 1987.
39. H. Norris and F. Makhlouf-Norris, The Measurement of Self-Identity, in *The Measurement of Intrapersonal Space by Grid Technique. Vol. 1: Explorations of Intrapersonal Space*, P. Slater (ed.), Wiley, Chichester, 1976.
40. W. Chambers and J. Grice, Circumgrids: A Repertory Grid Package for Personal Computers, *Behavior Research Methods, Instruments and Computers, 18*, p. 468, 1986.
41. G. Feixas and M. Villegas, Personal Construct Analysis of Autobiographical Texts: A Method Presentation and Case Illustration, *International Journal of Personal Construct Psychology, 4*, pp. 51-83, 1991.
42. D. Wishart, *CLUSTAN User's Manual (Release 3.2)*, Program Library Unit: University of Edinburgh, 1986.
43. A. Landfield, *Personal Construct Systems in Psychotherapy*, Rand McNally, Chicago, 1971.
44. R. C. Bell, *G-PACK: A Computer Program for the Elicitation and Analysis of Repertory Grids*, Program presented at the Seventh International Congress on Personal Construct Psychology, Memphis, Tennessee, 1987.

Chapter 10

THEMES IN REMINISCENCE GROUPS WITH OLDER WOMEN

Irene Burnside

It is predicted that by the year 2000, one person out of every fourteen in the United States will be a woman over the age of sixty-five [1]. Furthermore, many older women in 1989 lived alone (6.9 million representing 41% of older women) [2]. Although women are living longer today than they once did, they may not enjoy an increased quality of life [3]. This chapter is about the use of themes in reminiscence groups comprised of women not living in institutions and expands current knowledge about themes in reminiscence group work, a little discussed facet of group work with older persons.

LITERATURE REVIEW

No article described the process for selection of themes to be used in the reminiscence groups. An exhaustive handsearch of articles on reminiscence groups was conducted. Information was found in: 1) journals, 2) book chapters, 3) handouts from classes or conferences, 4) teaching modules, 5) unpublished masters' theses, and 6) unpublished doctoral dissertations. The data indicated that group leaders chose a wide array of themes, but rarely identified rationale for selection. The survey revealed that over three-fourths mentioned the use of themes in reminiscence groups; however, there was little information about efficacy of any of the themes, or the implementation.

Much of the research on reminiscence group therapy (RGT) has used nursing home residents as participants [4-6]. Less information is available on RGT pertaining to non-institutionalized older people [7].

Themes were rarely presented in an organized method; instead, themes were embedded in the body of the paper and had to be ferreted out. However, protocols for the themes used were found in one doctoral dissertation [4] and two masters' theses [5, 7].

In a study involving forty-one community dwelling elders in reminiscence groups, Bramlett found substantial variance in the way groups reminisced [8]. Groups differed from each other both in members willingness to adhere to the theme selected by the researcher as well as their willingness to reminisce at all. Another researcher entitled her research as life review therapy, however, it appears to have been a reminiscence group using a protocol of "structured topics" [9, p. 79]. This article is the only one that described the problems of group members straying from the specified topic and "at such times, it was necessary for the author to take a more directive role and steer the discussion back to the original topic" [9, p. 81]. It is not clear from the literature review whether one theme was the focus for the entire meeting and the members were kept on track by the leader, or whether group members were permitted to wander off onto other topics. Nor does there appear to be alternative themes that the leader used if the original topic was ineffective.

Sometimes theme selection was based on choosing non-threatening topics to evoke memories to serve as catalysts for discussion. One researcher specifically stated the importance of selecting themes that would elicit happy memories [4]. Lovelady stated, "The weekly topics were discussed by the participants with the researcher placing emphasis on pleasant memories" [6, p. 38]; another researcher in reminiscence on a one-to-one basis noted that "most people's reminiscences are quite positive" [10, p. 17]. These recommendations gleaned from the literature suggest that the modality being implemented was reminiscence therapy rather than life review therapy, because the leader tried *not* to evoke sad memories. Nor did the articles cited mention that the group leaders dealt with guilt, conflict, and despair of members that may occur during life review. Elsewhere life review and reminiscence group therapy have been differentiated [11, 12].

Themes were generally chosen by the group leader. However, among the articles reviewed, only three articles indicated that group members chose the themes [2, 6, 13, 14]. Examples of themes selected by participants in one group were old cars and neighborhoods where they have grown up [14].

THEME SELECTION

Themes did not reveal any particular method of selection; it appeared that leaders often used a "shotgun approach." When a method was employed, the most common approach was lifespan selection, "or chronological pattern" [14, p. 55]. The rationale for the theme or stage of life mentioned was lacking in numerous studies [4, 7, 14].

Few authors mentioned gender-appropriate themes; yet these are important considerations in theme selection. Two authors recommended that "thing" topics be selected for men and listed specific topics that evoked favorable responses in men [15]. No themes were specified in any article that were gender-appropriate for all-women groups. No ethnic-appropriate themes were indicated and only Wilkinson alluded to a geographic-appropriate theme (the Mardi Gras) [16]. Geographical considerations must be taken into account as well as cohort factors because all of these are crucial for effective group reminiscences.

Themes are also used in guided autobiography groups for older adults and Birren and Deutchman list salient memories [17]. However, one quickly notes that the themes selected for such groups are quite different from themes selected for a reminiscence therapy group. Both types of themes have been listed in Table 1.

DEFINITION

Themes were not defined in the articles reviewed. The most common term besides themes was "topics." The word theme, as used in this chapter, is defined as "a leader-chosen or member-chosen subject of discourse and discussion which is a unifying dominant idea for a reminiscence group meeting."

EARLIEST DATA

The earliest data on themes comes from the Gray Panthers pioneer, and although her list of "firsts" was not designed specifically for reminiscence groups, this source appears to be one of the roots of themes [18]. It is the most complete

Table 1. A Contrast of Group, Guided Autobiography Themes
and Reminiscence Group Themes

Autobiography Group Themes [17]	Reminiscence Group Themes [20]
1. The major branching points in your life	1. First memory
2. Your family	2. First toy
3. Your major life work or career	3. First pet
4. The role of money in your life	4. First day of school
5. Your health and body image	5. First playmate
6. Your sexual identity, sex roles, and sexual experiences	6. First date
7. Your experience with death	7. First job
8. Your loves and hates	8. Favorite person
9. The meaning of your life, your aspirations, and life goals	
10. The role of music, art, or literature in your life	
11. Your experiences with stress	

list of themes located even if it was not presented specifically for reminiscence group therapy.

However, an exercise Kuhn calls "life line" could well be used by leaders of reminiscence therapy groups because it is a protocol of sorts [18]. The list of earliest memories include: 1) first Christmas, 2) first day of school, 3) first love, 4) first kiss, 5) first illness, 6) first time hungry, 7) first demonstration or protest, 8) first petition, 9) first job, 10) first failure, 11) first and most recent experience with death.

The data described here is from one [19] of three studies [20, 21].

SAMPLE

The convenience sample consisted of sixty-seven ambulatory or semi-ambulatory females, age sixty-five or older, who lived independently in their own apartments. The age range of the reminiscence treatment group was sixty-six to eighty-five years of age, a range of nineteen years, and the mean age was 74.2; the standard deviation was 6.0. There were three reminiscence groups and three groups that discussed "Dear Abby" columns, plus a control group. The control group participated in pre and posttesting for the quantitative components of the study.

The participants had to be able to ambulate with assistive devices to the meetings, and hear and see well enough to participate in meetings. The participants lived independently in apartment complexes in the suburb of a mid-southern metropolitan city. All participants lived in apartments that were approximately in the same range in rental costs and services, although two apartment complexes offered more services to residents than the third site. All the apartments were located within a fifteen-mile radius.

Residents who indicated they were unable or unwilling to respond to the questionnaires were excluded. Participation in the study was voluntary, and participants were free to withdraw at any time. Each participant received $5.00 for each meeting attended in hopes of reducing the common problem of attrition.

METHODOLOGY

Qualitative data were obtained by tape recordings of each meeting that were analyzed for the amount of reminiscence each theme elicited, and the deviations from the theme protocol.

The following research question was asked to obtain qualitative data: "What themes elicit the most discussion of memories in a reminiscence group of older women?"

Follow-up questionnaires were sent one month after the study as a precautionary measure to give the researcher a chance to assess participants for any sad or untoward feelings engendered by the group experience. Wartime themes were excluded from the protocols designed for these studies because Cook observed that her participants felt sadness when wartime memories were discussed [4].

(The literature did not indicate any other themes that evoked sadness or depression in respondents who reminisced in group settings.)

A total of twenty-four tape recordings yielded data for the qualitative analysis. The coding process involved gathering and analyzing all data that had bearing on the selected themes. Coding is a "systematic way of developing and refining interpretations of data" [22].

Data from Tapes of the Meetings

The data from each of the meetings were first deductively analyzed for the use of the pre-selected themes from the protocol. Then the data were reanalyzed using the inductive process of content analysis to learn more about 1) the deviations from the protocol, 2) the affect, and 3) the characteristics of memories.

Protection of Human Rights

Before implementation, this study was approved by the Committee for Protection of Human Subjects. All apartment house managers were informed of the purpose and procedures of the study. All participants signed a consent form.

THEME SELECTION FOR THE PROTOCOL

The eight themes were based on an exhaustive search of the literature. The themes were chosen to elicit simple reminiscence and to call forth non-threatening memories easy to share in a group setting [23]. The rationale was that reminiscence as an intervention, is not nearly as likely to be a life review type intervention as it is simple reminiscence [23]. Themes were selected in a concerted effort to avoid a life review type group session. All theses were deemed appropriate for an all-female group.

ANALYSIS OF THEMES

Each of the eight themes was analyzed in-depth. The analysis was done to determine which themes might be viewed as: 1) potentially difficult to implement, 2) potentially capable of producing negative memories, or 3) ineffective in eliciting memories, that is members strayed off the chosen themes or resisted discussion. Each reminiscence group and each leader is unique; however, basic guidelines could help the reminiscence group leader. It must be noted that this was an all-women's group and these data do reflect the selection of gender-specified themes (for example dolls) as well as the emergence of geographic-specific themes (the tobacco fields and cotton gin mills of the South).

The word "first" was purposely combined with seven of the eight themes to push the memories as far back in time as possible and also to achieve greater specificity. The researcher wanted to focus on early childhood memories and adolescence, but the strategy was not always successful because on occasion a member apologized for being unable to recall whether the memory shared was the first or not. The first memory of a theme was also specified as a means to skip the initial component or "selection" in simple reminiscence [23].

RESULTS

The data interpretation which follows is related to one of the research questions: What themes elicit the most discussion of memories in a reminiscence group of older women?

Amount of Discussion

The first step of analysis was to determine the themes that elicited the most discussion of memories in the study; a line-by-line count of the typed recordings was done. It was not possible to ascertain the effect of absences or lateness of members on the amount of time each theme was discussed. That is, an absentee might have contributed a substantial amount to the reminiscence theme on that particular day. The factor is acknowledged because absenteeism is a pervasive problem in group work with elders. However, because the participants were being paid, they made a real effort to be on time. All absences were due to the participant's illness or a sick spouse. (A detailed list was kept by the researcher of the reasons for all absences.)

The number of lines of discussions were added and then rank ordered. The rank ordering of amount of discussion for each theme in the study according to a line-by-line count of the taped data can be seen in Table 2.

Favorite Holiday

"Favorite holiday" was chosen instead of first "holiday" to give a wider range of choice to the participants. Regarding the amount of discussion elicited for the first theme, the "favorite holiday" was by far and away Christmas. This is easily explained because the theme lends itself to such a wide array of topics for discussion. For example, toys and presents received was important to the respondents. Other topics discussed were 1) the tree, 2) the tree decorations (usually handmade items), 3) food served, 4) celebrations and traditions (going to church), and 5) Santa Claus. The holiday theme elicited vivid descriptions involving the senses of smell, vision, hearing, and taste. "Favorite holiday" also meant that other holidays besides Christmas could be discussed and included Halloween, Fourth of July, Easter, Thanksgiving, and even May Day. In retrospect, because "favorite holiday" offers a wide array of interesting topics to discuss, and appears less threatening than "first memory," it would have been a more appropriate theme to use in the studies. Also, by not requesting that the holiday remembered by the

Table 2. Rank Ordering
of Group Themes Which
Elicited Most Discussion

1. Favorite holiday
2. First pet
3. First job
4. First day of school
5. First date
6. First toy
7. First playmate
8. First memory

Source: Ref. 19.

"first" may have put less pressure on respondents to share because using "first" does increase anxiety for members who are concerned about their memory.

First Pet

Although the "first pet" was ranked second in order in amount of discussion elicited, it was not the most pleasurable memory for some respondents. Those who were involved with pets shared many negative memories about the death of the pet, what parents had done with the pet "took it [duck] to the city park and left it," and the vivid memory of a neighbor's dog killing a respondent's pet rabbit. But in spite of the negative memories, some participants spent time describing in vivid detail what happened to the pet and sometimes funny moments were shared when a woman stated their dog had been named, "Didhebiteyou?" She created an outburst of laughter.

First Job

Because all but three of the total sample of sixty-seven women had worked during their lives it is not surprising that jobs elicited much discussion. Their jobs were extremely important to them. For some respondents, it was a matter of pride because they had begun earning money at a young age. One woman proudly said, "I was babysitting when I was nine years old." For others, work was a substitute for high school as stated by one respondent:

> I had failed by tenth year in school and my daddy said, well he says so I quit school when I was seventeen and still living out in the country, and town was twelve miles from where we lived and we lived . . . we had a neighbor lady that worked in the poultry mill . . . and she got me a job working in the poultry mill in town and that was 1930-1931.

The work ethic was important to the respondents; however, they did not discuss how they juggled work, a job, a family, and the work at home. Though many of them took pride in their work, there were also long discussions about how difficult it had been to get ahead—either financially or in the job situation. Some discussed sexual harassment on their jobs.

First Day of School

The theme "first day of school" did not elicit as much discussion as anticipated because many of the reminiscers could not remember the *first* day, however, the inability to remember it was not related to cognitive impairment. The discussion became more general as they discussed themes which were related to going to school. Vivid descriptions of the schoolhouse they attended were common. They especially enjoyed telling about ponies or horses they rode. Bullies who had frightened them was still another important memory in the discussion. The "first day of school" was negative for many of the women which may account for lessened discussion on the theme, and introducing other themes. Some had had little education and were self-conscious about it; they tended to say little during the discussions about schools, education in those days, or their teachers.

First Date

The theme "first date" was not an easy topic for the members to discuss and it was difficult to keep the focus on the theme in all of the groups in the study. It was apparent that very few had enjoyed the "first date" and really did not want to discuss it. The conversation quickly drifted to marriage, men they had known, and even the present day morals. Like the "first day of school," this topic was not one that elicited conversation easily.

First Toy

"First toy" and games not only elicited interesting discussions, but everyone had something to contribute on these topics. It is surprising that it was not higher in the amount of time spent on the topic because the women enjoyed the topic and especially describing the dolls they had owned. However, group interruptions (for example, members arriving late) often reduced time spent on protocol themes because the leader had to intervene in the group process at that time.

First Playmate

The "first playmate" was perhaps low on time spent discussing it because of the inability of some members to remember a "first" playmate. Some could recall the child easily and even the name of the child; others could not recall anyone. Those who lived in isolated rural areas had to play with siblings; this theme held little interest for them. This theme lent itself to games they had played with "first playmates" and animated discussions ensued.

First Memory

The "first memory" was the least discussed. The "first memory" may not be an easy memory for some older women to discuss. As stated earlier, if the memory is a painful one there might be some hesitancy in sharing it during a first group meeting. In fact, Rabbit and McInnis found that 42 percent of first memories and 35 percent of second memories were traumatic experiences [24]. "In all, 63 percent of first memories . . . were of emotionally charged or significant experiences" [24, p. 340]. That information could guide leaders about selection of "first memory" as a theme. The selection of first memory for studies described in this article was based on Tobin's statement that "the request to reconstruct the earliest memory [is not] perceived as an infantilizing or threatening test" [25, p. 253]. The first memory seemed a likely starting point for a reminiscence group; however, the results of the pilot study [20] and the research reported here [19] indicated that first memory might be a more appropriate theme for life review than for reminiscence groups. The theme of first memory was problematic for these reasons: 1) too broad in range; 2) elicited powerful (and what sometimes appeared to be painful) memories which was not the purpose of the reminiscence group; 3) required the leader to frequently refocus because of the breadth of the topic; and 4) the words of the theme lacked specificity which in the initial meeting resulted in some confusion about the purpose of the group. Anxiety is always high in the beginning of any group and a more specific theme may have been more effective to launch the group.

The theme "first memory" elicited a wide range of vivid and detailed memories. One reminiscer said, "to me that was something I could still picture today." First memories included birth of siblings and reactions to them. One described losing her mother at a young age. To avoid launching the reminiscence groups with a first memory that elicited sad memories, it might have been better to qualify the theme. That is, request "the first happy memory" that would narrow the range of memories to show selection.

Themes Described by Respondents

The second step of analysis after the line-by-line count to determine themes that elicited the most discussion was to analyze the themes described by the respondents. The task was to determine if the themes in the meetings were the same as the preselected theme or different. If they were different than the planned theme, how were they different? If the conversation remained focused on the theme in the protocol, it was considered to be the theme. When the theme was not quite the same, but had similarities to the theme and the connections and linkages were obvious it was considered to be a sub-theme. The "first playmate" brought forth one detailed description of the flapper mother of a playmate. The mother had bobbed hair and was one of the few women that the reminiscer knew at that time who smoked.

When the theme bore no relationship whatsoever to the theme listed on the protocol, it was coded a non-related theme. There was not an alternative theme planned. In one group, the proliferation of non-related themes appeared to be directly related to the number of highly anxious members in the group who had great difficulty staying focused on the theme. They could not be silent very long and found it difficult to listen to contributions of other members. In one group, members were extremely anxious because of the highly educated mental health worker member in the group who wanted to control the group and frequently probed other members.

An example of a non-related theme occurred during the meeting about "first date."

> It dawned on me suddenly that it's the date of my Sonny's first birthday, my first born and I loved him so much. He was so smart . . . he had golden curls and everything and everyone thought he was a little girl. He was so pretty and kept telling me I should cut his hair . . . (more detailed description of his hair and then leader asks what happened to him). He died when he was three of spinal meningitis.

In that instance an anniversary of the death of a child took precedence over the theme for that particular respondent. In another group a reminiscer recalled the anniversary of her sister's death and brought it up at the meeting although it was not theme-related. Regarding non-related themes, it was not possible to understand the reason for the introduction of a new topic; however, the unrelated topic was often about family, and as these two examples indicated occurred at time of anniversary of a death of a significant other.

APPLICATIONS TO PRACTICE

Because the qualitative data in this study provided ideas about themes for clinical practice, the following guidelines are offered for group leaders planning to implement an all women's reminiscence therapy group.

Implications for Clinical Practice

1. The leader should *not* select themes based on her/his own curiosity about that particular topic.
2. Themes should not be selected for problem-solving reasons during reminiscence [26].
3. Unless the group is involved in a research study, and it is necessary to adhere to a protocol, the leader should be flexible about themes.
4. The wording for the intended theme should be very precise and easily understood by members.

5. Themes (props also) should be carefully organized and with sound rationale based on the literature prior to group implementation [27].
6. Themes selected should take into account: 1) gender, 2) geographical location, 3) cohort group(s), and 4) cultural aspects of the targeted group members.
7. Group leaders may wish to have a list of alternate themes to implement when the group is not moving.
8. The group leader should be sensitive to the needs of the group and quickly perceive any resistance to discuss a particular theme because the goal of reminiscence therapy is not psychotherapy.
9. The group leader should be aware that anniversary dates may have effects on group process and contributions of members.

SUMMARY

The selection of themes, and rationale for their choice is inadequately described in current literature on reminiscence groups. Leaders of all-female reminiscence groups need to be selective because themes for all-female groups are different than those for all-male groups or groups of both older males and females. Little attention has been paid to gender-specific, geographic-specific, cohort-specific, and ethnic-specific themes. The three most discussed themes in the study described in this article were: 1) favorite holiday, 2) first pet, and 3) first job. These were themes that elicited reminiscence, but of course these themes, as any theme, could also evoke sad memories for some members.

Many factors contribute to the effectiveness of reminiscence group therapy. The sophistication of the leader, the site of the meetings, the blend of members, seating arrangements all contribute to the success of a group. However, relevant themes for the particular group being conducted must also be considered as a major factor in the success of any reminiscence therapy group.

Research about the effectiveness of themes in reminiscence group therapy would be especially useful to neophyte group leaders, and could help practitioners streamline their day-to-day work. Merriam reminds us that "the potential for enhancing the lives of older persons through reminiscing is certainly worthy of further attention by researchers and practitioners" [28, p. 51].

REFERENCES

1. P. Uhlenberg, Older Women: The Growing Challenge to Design Constructive Roles, *Gerontologist, 19,* pp. 232-241, 1979.
2. AARP, *A Profile of Older Americans,* American Association of Retired Persons, Washington, D.C., 1990.
3. I. Burnside, Group Work with Older Women: A Modality to Improve the Quality of Life, *Journal of Women and Aging, 1,* pp. 265-290, 1989.

4. E. Cook, The Effect of Reminiscence Group Therapy on Depressed Institutionalized Elders, unpublished doctoral dissertation, School of Nursing, The University of Texas at Austin, 1988.

5. M. S. Lovelady, The Effects of Reminiscence Therapy on Self-esteem in Institutionalized Elderly, unpublished master's thesis, Troy State University, New York, 1987.

6. A. Tourangeau, Group Reminiscence Therapy as a Nursing Intervention: An Experimental Study, *AARN Newsletter, 44,* Part I, pp. 17-18, Part II, pp. 29-30, 1988.

7. K. King, Reminiscing Group Experiences with Aging People, unpublished master's thesis, College of Nursing, University of Utah, Salt Lake City, 1979.

8. M. H. Bramlett, Power, Creativity and Reminiscence in the Elderly, unpublished doctoral dissertation, Medical College of Georgia, Augusta, Georgia, 1990.

9. J. M. Giltinan, Using Life Review to Facilitate Self-actualization in Elderly Women, *Gerontology & Geriatrics Education, 10:*4, pp. 75-83, 1990.

10. C. R. Kovach, Reminiscence: Exploring the Origins, Processes and Consequences, *Nursing Forum, 26:*3, pp. 14-20, 1991.

11. B. Haight and I. Burnside, Reminiscence and Life Review: Conducting the Processes, *Journal of Gerontological Nursing, 16:*2, pp. 39-42, 1992.

12. I. Burnside and B. Haight, Reminiscence and Life Review: Analyzing Each Concept, *Journal of Advanced Nursing, 17,* pp. 855-862, 1992.

13. R. Tappen and T. Touhy, *The Effectiveness of Reminiscence Group Work on Mood Levels of Institutionalized Older Adults,* paper presented at the Gerontological Society of America meeting, Chicago, Illinois, November 23, 1986.

14. F. A. Youssef, The Impact of Group Reminiscence Counseling on a Depressed Elderly Population, *Nurse Practitioner, 15:*4, pp. 32-38, 1990.

15. D. M. Reed and H. R. Cobble, Tools for Reminiscence with Veterans, *Clinical Gerontologist, 4:*4, pp. 53-57, 1986.

16. C. S. Wilkinson, A Descriptive Study of Increased Social Intervention through Group Reminiscing in Institutionalized Elderly, unpublished master's thesis, Community Health Nursing, Tulane University, New Orleans, Louisiana, 1978.

17. J. E. Birren and D. E. Deutchman, *Guiding Autobiography Groups for Older Adults,* The John Hopkins University Press, Baltimore, pp. 67-79, 1991

18. M. Kuhn, quoted in D. Hessel, Life Review in *Maggie Kuhn on Aging,* The Westminster Press, Philadelphia, pp. 30-40, 1977.

19. I. Burnside, The Effect of Reminiscence Groups on Fatigue, Affect, and Life Satisfaction in Elderly Women, unpublished doctoral dissertation, School of Nursing, The University of Texas at Austin, 1990.

20. I. Burnside, The Effects of Reminiscence Group Therapy on Anxiety and Depression in Elderly Women: A Pilot Study, unpublished manuscript, 1989.

21. I. Burnside, The Effect of Reminiscence Group, Affect, and Life Satisfaction in Elderly Women, A Cross-cultural Study, unpublished manuscript, 1992.

22. S. J. Taylor and R. Bodgan, *Introduction to Qualitative Research Methods,* John Wiley & Sons, New York, 1984.

23. S. B. Merriam, The Structure of Simple Reminiscence, *The Gerontologist, 29:*6, pp. 761-767, 1989.

24. P. Rabbit and L. McInnis, Do Clever Old People Have Earlier and Richer Memories?, *Psychology and Aging, 3*:4, pp. 338-341, 1988.

25. S. Tobin, The Earliest Memory as Data for Research in Aging, in *Researching, Planning and Action for the Elderly,* D. R. Kent, R. Kastenbaum, and S. Sherwood (eds.), Behavior Publications, New York, 1972.

26. R. Havighurst and R. Glasser, An Exploratory Study of Reminiscence, *Journal of Gerontology, 27,* pp. 243-253, 1972.

27. A. W. Rodriquez, A Descriptive Study of Selected Props used to Elicit Memories in Elders, unpublished master's thesis, School of Nursing, The University of Texas, Austin, Texas, 1990.

28. S. B. Merriam, Reminiscence and the Life Review: The Potential for Educational Intervention, in *Introduction to Educational Gerontology* (3rd Edition), R. H. Sherron and D. B. Lumsden (eds.), Hemisphere Publishing, New York, 1990.

Chapter 11

STYLES OF REMINISCENCE AND EGO DEVELOPMENT OF OLDER WOMEN RESIDING IN LONG-TERM CARE SETTINGS

Sarah Reese Beaton

Styles of reminiscence used in life stories, rather than being *outcomes* of life review undertaken in old age, may be the characteristic ways in which individuals at particular levels of ego development, think about, relate to, and recount the stories of their lives. To investigate the contention that differences in the styles of reminiscence [1] of older persons could be explained by their levels of ego development [2], seventy-five women residing in long term care facilities responded to the Washington University Sentence Completion Test and told the stories of their lives. A trend from higher to lower levels of ego development was associated with styles of reminiscence in the direction predicted. Women with Affirming styles had higher levels of ego development than women with the Negating and Despairing styles. Resilience seemed the most likely explanation for cases that did not fit predictions. Life stories are suggested for routine data gathering in long term care because they allow the essence of another person to be grasped and foster a different level of engagement than do conventional data gathering techniques.

Older individuals differ in their styles of reminiscence. Typologies of styles show correspondence suggesting an underlying structure. Some researchers believe styles of reminiscence reflect differences among individuals, but these differences have not yet been explained. Can they be explained by levels of ego development?

BACKGROUND OF THE STUDY

To investigate the question—is there a relationship between styles of reminiscence older persons use when they recount the stories of their lives and the levels of their ego development—the life story framework developed by Fallot was used to elicit style of reminiscence [1]. Fallot said that life stories involve the way individuals think about and relate to their own lives. He categorized styles of reminiscence as either Affirming, Negating, or Despairing (see Table 1).

Reminiscence in old age is related to development; reviewing one's life provides opportunities for personal growth and fulfillment [3]. Evidence for

Table 1. Criteria for Styles of Reminiscence[a]

1. Affirming style
   a. Reminiscence is characterized by a general sense of self-acceptance.
   b. Both positive and negative experiences (and their internalized aspects) are taken on as one's own.
   c. Conflicts are acknowledged yet presented in a context of possible resolution.
   d. Reminiscence conveys a sense of integration of life stages and areas.

2. Negating style
   a. One's life is presented generally as benign and pleasant.
   b. Negative parts of the self and negative life experiences are often not included in these reminiscences. When they are, their impact is minimized.
   c. Style may be either more hysterical (shifting and jumping from one topic to another) or obsessive-compulsive (systematic) lessening of the negative.
   d. Reminiscence is likely to be characterized by the inclusion of public events, rather than personal reactions, in an attempt to distance oneself from the impact of recounting one's past.

3. Despairing style
   a. The individual is painfully aware of, and likely to be preoccupied with, conflicts and negative experiences.
   b. Themes of regret and unfulfilled possibilities are prominent.
   c. Attempts to deny or repress difficult or painful areas are largely unsuccessful.
   d. The self is disowned through wishes to be other than itself.

[a]Criteria adapted from The Life Story through Reminiscence in Late Adulthood, by R. D. Fallot (1976, pp. 125-126).

developmental change in old age is found in the emergence of new and different late life creativity [4] and in the self-reports of those who write in old age [5]. The idea that reminiscence in old age is related to development, introduced by Erikson [6] and expanded by Butler in his postulate about life review [7], has received support from clinicians who work with older persons [8-12].

Reminiscence appears to vary with personality structure [13]. Reminiscence styles are significant indices of individual differences among older adults [14], and styles of reminiscence vary systematically [1]. Categories of reminiscence styles [14, 15] are congruent with the dichotomy in Erikson's final developmental crisis—ego integrity versus despair and disgust—[6, p. 104] and with Butler's "effects" following life review, either "creative, adaptive or pathological" [7, p. 523]. Differences between styles have been attributed to underlying developmental phenomena [16]. But attempts to clarify relationships between reminiscence and development have led to inconclusive results, perhaps because the developmental models used by researchers were restricted by their reliance on chronological age.

In Loevinger's model of ego development [2], the explanation and measurement of personality differences in any age cohort is based on the idea that individuals stop (not necessarily permanently) at different points in a stage sequence of self-development through which they proceed at different rates. The stages also "constitute a set of personality types" [2, p. 67]. The descriptions of these personality types allow predictions of associations with other variables. Individuals function at a core level of ego development that they project in their responses to the Washington University Sentence Completion Test for Ego Development (WUSCTED). Table 2 provides some of the characteristics of each ego development level. More details are provided in the WUSCTED scoring manuals [17, 18].

THEORETICAL RATIONALE

With the ego development framework, styles of reminiscence, rather than being viewed as an *outcome* of a life review undertaken in old age, may be seen to reflect the characteristic ways in which individuals at particular levels of ego development think about, relate to, and recount the stories of their lives.

Within this framework, respondents at various development levels are expected to fit one of the sets of reminiscence style criteria in Table 1. The major contentions are that individual differences in styles of reminiscence will be explained by ego development and that the I-3/4 Self-Aware transition in ego development will be a necessary condition for an Affirming style.

It is expected that Affirmers will have ego development levels at I-3/4 or higher because self-awareness, which emerges at I-3/4, is necessary for self-acceptance. The recognition, at I-3/4, that there are contingencies and paradoxes in life, allows a person to address conflicts so that both positive and negative experiences can be

Table 3. Washington University Sentence Completion Test—Form 81

1. When a child will not join in group activities
2. Raising a family
3. When I am criticized
4. A man's job
5. Being with other people
6. The thing I like about myself is
7. My mother and I
8. What gets me into trouble is
9. Education
10. When people are helpless
11. Women are lucky because
12. A good father
13. A girl has a right to
14. When they talked about sex, I
15. A wife should
16. I feel sorry
17. A man feels good when
18. Rules are
19. Crime and delinquency could be halted if
20. Men are lucky because
21. I just can't stand people who
22. At times she worried about
23. I am
24. A woman feels good when
25. My main problem is
26. A husband has the right to
27. The worst thing about being a woman
28. A good mother
29. When I am with a man
30. Sometimes she wished that
31. My father
32. If I can't get what I want
33. Usually she felt that sex
34. For a woman a career is
35. My conscience bothers me if
36. A woman should always

Source: Loevinger, J., Revision of the Sentence Completion Test for Ego Development, *Journal of Personality and Social Psychology*, 48:2, p. 426, 1985.

taken on as one's own. Conformists (I-3), who deny their feelings, and whose characteristic responses to WUSCTED items are vague, evasive, and non-committal will use sentimental idealization. These persons at I-3, will be Negaters, who confine themselves to recounting public events rather than personal reactions. They will tell benign and pleasant life stories. Persons at lower levels of ego development (Delta/3, Delta, and I-2), who feel like victims of circumstances and blame others, are self-rejecting, dependent, and untrusting. Their reminiscence style will reflect despair.

METHODS

Sample and Consent

Data were gathered from a convenience sample of seventy-five Caucasian women, ranging in age from 74 to 103 (mean age 85.5), who resided in six long-term care facilities. They had been judged alert, oriented, and coherent by the nurses caring for them and were able to speak clearly and hear conversational speech.

The consent process was designed to avoid coercion; there were several opportunities for the women to decline participation. At the outset of the interview, the purpose of the study was briefly explained. After the woman gave an informal approval, the data collection process was described. Both tasks—sentence completion and telling the life story—were introduced. A statement of rights was read to the resident. After another verbal approval had been obtained, a written consent form was presented for signature. If adequate vision was a problem, the entire process was tape recorded. Anonymity of participants and settings was preserved with a coding system.

Measures

To validate his categories for styles of reminiscence, Fallot [1], who focused his research on women, compared his criteria for styles of reminiscence with those developed by McMahon and Rhudick [14] and Postema [15]. Percent of interscorer agreement for styles in Fallot's study ($N = 36$) was 1.00 [1].

The WUSCTED has been shown to be valid and reliable in studies with diverse samples [19], including older people [20-23]. The measure was designed for written completions but has been used also with oral responses [24-26].

Procedures

All interviews were conducted by the investigator and tape recorded. First the WUSCTED, Form 81 [27], was administered (see Table 3). Responses were given orally. After responses to the sentence stems had been completed, the investigator put the WUSCTED papers aside and invited the woman, "Tell me the story of

Table 3. Washington University Sentence Completion Test—Form 81

1. When a child will not join in group activities
2. Raising a family
3. When I am criticized
4. A man's job
5. Being with other people
6. The thing I like about myself is
7. My mother and I
8. What gets me into trouble is
9. Education
10. When people are helpless
11. Women are lucky because
12. A good father
13. A girl has a right to
14. When they talked about sex, I
15. A wife should
16. I feel sorry
17. A man feels good when
18. Rules are
19. Crime and delinquency could be halted if
20. Men are lucky because
21. I just can't stand people who
22. At times she worried about
23. I am
24. A woman feels good when
25. My main problem is
26. A husband has the right to
27. The worst thing about being a woman
28. A good mother
29. When I am with a man
30. Sometimes she wished that
31. My father
32. If I can't get what I want
33. Usually she felt that sex
34. For a woman a career is
35. My conscience bothers me if
36. A woman should always

Source: Loevinger, J., Revision of the Sentence Completion Test for Ego Development, *Journal of Personality and Social Psychology, 48*:2, p. 426, 1985.

your life." During the story, the investigator conveyed an active interest. The pace of sessions was unhurried. Content was suggested only when a woman seemed to want a prompt.

Demographic data were gathered from the stories rather than from records. Ages of participants were known prior to sample selection. The other demographic information spontaneously available in the life stories, in almost every instance, included birthplace, education, religion, marital status, and occupation.

Reliability

Using Fallot's scoring system, all stories were rated by the investigator and independently by another rater. A third rater scored thirty-eight of the seventy-five stories selected at random. Percentage of perfect agreement between two raters for seventy-five style ratings was 76 percent, Kappa [28] .61 $p < .00$. Among three raters for thirty-eight stories, the percentage of agreement was 68.4 percent, Kappa .50, $p < .00$. In cases of disagreements, the mode was assigned when there had been three raters. Style was rated after further evaluation when there had been disagreement between two raters. None of the life story raters was aware of ego development (WUSCTED) scores.

WUSCTED items and protocols were independently scored by two raters who were unaware of life story data. Scoring guidelines for twenty-seven items on Form 81 were included in the published manual [18]; the other nine were scored using "pre-publication" manuals. For total protocol ratings (TPRs)—an ordinal rating derived from cumulative frequencies of categorical item scores using specified ogive rules, [17, p. 129]—there was agreement between raters within a half step for seventy-three of the seventy-five protocols (97.3%). There was perfect agreement for forty-eight of the seventy-five TPRs (64%). Inter-rater correlation for Item Sum Scores (I-SUMs)—calculated by adding the numerical equivalents of item ratings—(see Table 2), was .93, $p = .001$. These figures compare favorably with those reported by Loevinger and Wessler [17, p. 45]. Internal consistency for this sample (Alpha .90) was also comparable [p. 49].

FINDINGS

There were thirty-four women (45.3%) in the sample with Affirming styles of reminiscence, twenty-five (33.3%) with Negating styles, and sixteen (21.3%) with Despairing styles. Stages of ego development ranged from Delta to I-5 levels. The mode for ego development was the Self-Aware (I-3/4) transition. This has been the mode for other adult samples [29].

Three sets of hypotheses were tested. First, the style and stage-specific predictions were that Affirming styles would be associated with levels of ego development at I-4 and above, Negating styles with the I-3 level, and Despairing styles with levels at Delta/3 and below. The I-3/4 level was excluded here. With alpha at .05, the hypothesis was not supported. However, some improvement (Lambda .19) in the ability to predict style of reminiscence when ego development levels were known was demonstrated.

Second, dealing only with the Self-Aware I-3/4 transition, the hypothesized equal proportion of Affirmers and Negators at I-3/4 was supported. The mean I-SUM for I-3/4 Affirmers was not significantly higher than the mean I-SUM for I-3/4 Negaters as had been expected.

Third, a trend from higher to lower levels of ego development associated with Affirming, Negating, and Despairing styles, in that order, was predicted. The I-SUM means decreased in the direction expected (167.24, 157.00, and 153.25, respectively), and the F Ratio (3.43) was significant ($p = .03$). The strongest evidence to support the contentions for a developmental trend was found when reminiscence styles were dichotomized as Affirmers ($N = 34$) and Non-Affirmers ($N = 41$). Affirmers had higher levels of ego development than Non-Affirmers, (F ratio 6.57, $p = .012$). Mean I-SUM for Affirmers was 167.24; for Non-Affirmers it was 155.54.

Styles of reminiscence were not dependent on age, birthplace, education, marital status, religion, occupation, or setting. Ego development was related to years of education, as it has been with other samples [30] accounting for 14.07 percent (Eta squared) of the variance in ego development in this sample. Mean years of education was 10.2 with a range between three and eighteen years. Religious affiliation was also related to ego development (Eta squared 18.5%).

DISCUSSION

The findings provided some support for the idea that ego development accounts for differences in style of reminiscence. Women with Affirming styles had higher levels of ego development than women with Negating and Despairing styles. The extent to which ego development levels explain differences in styles of reminiscence remains unclear, however. How can lack of support for the stage- and style-specific hypotheses be explained?

TPRs and I-SUMs reflect different psychometric treatments of the same ego development construct, and these two distinct scores—Loevinger refers to them as scoring algorithms—require different levels of statistical analysis. The first and third set of hypotheses make the same predictions, but different levels of measurement, Chi-square and Lambda compared to the more sensitive analysis of variance, led to different levels of support for the hypotheses. It is reasonable to expect that in a study with a larger sample size, the first hypothesis would also receive support.

How can the exceptional cases, those that did not fit the prediction that I-3/4 was a necessary condition for the Affirming style, be explained? What distinguished the Affirmers ($N = 8$) with TPRs below I-3/4, and the Negators ($N = 3$), and Despairers ($N = 8$) at ego development levels above I-3/4?

None of the demographic variables distinguished non-fit cases. But the concept—resilience—to which Butler [7] referred is promising in its potential to explain these cases theoretically. Butler attributed variance in the outcomes of life review—which he termed creative, adjusted, or pathological—to factors of personality.

> Although a favorable, constructive, and positive end result may be enhanced by favorable environmental circumstances, such as comparative freedom from crisis and losses, it is more likely that successful reorganization is largely a function of the personality—in particular, such vaguely defined features of the personality as flexibility, resilience, and self-awareness [7, p. 69].

In the rationale for the present study, flexibility and self-awareness had been included within Loevinger's theory, but resilience had not been taken into account. When the life stories were reconsidered with attention to resilience— defined roughly as invincibility or striving in the face of adversity—it seemed that Affirming women, including those who scored below I-3/4, told stories characterized by resilience. On the other hand, the stories of Despairers, including those with ego development levels above I-3/4, were marked by their lack of resilience. The stories of Negaters could not be said to reflect resilience or the lack thereof. Their lives were portrayed as nice, fine and wonderful. Defending by avoidance may be an expression of resilience. Resilience, the personality feature that seemed important in this study retrospectively, warrants further study in connection with aging.

Fallot has shown that it was Affirmers who benefited most from reminiscence activities [1, p. 45]. Considering this distinction, as well as the findings in the present study that Affirmers have higher levels of ego development, Affirmers are probably the best candidates for planned life review and reminiscence when these sessions are to be guided by relatively inexperienced persons. A life story, rated for style, could be used as a method to screen for Negaters and Despairers.

The relationship between religious affiliation and ego development, for which there is an indication in data for the present sample, has not been reported for other samples. It is possible that such a relationship exists with other samples but has not been uncovered; it is also possible that this relationship is specific to the older adult population.

The life story is a useful framework with which to explore reminiscence and life review. The women in this sample, without exception, immediately grasped what was meant by "life story." Elaboration was never needed. Apparently, they had previously considered their own pasts in a story form.

In gathering the data, the investigator had the consistent and distinct impression that she had gained a different level of engagement with the persons interviewed than had previously been her experience in nursing practice. The essence of another person had been grasped; the individual's self had been conveyed; a better understanding had been gained than would have been the case with conventional data gathering techniques. Use of life stories as a routine part of clinical assessment is recommended not only because the content of stories is valuable, but also because the process of telling and listening enhances the relationship with the client.

REFERENCES

1. R. D. Fallot, *The Life Story Through Reminiscence in Late Adulthood,* unpublished Doctoral Dissertation, Yale University, 1976 or University Microfilms International, Ann Arbor, MI 48106, University Microfilms No. 77-14039. Also see R. D. Fallot, The Impact on Mood of Verbal Reminiscing in Later Adulthood, *International Journal of Aging and Human Development, 10*:(4), pp. 385-400, 1979-80.
2. J. Loevinger, *Ego Development,* Jossey-Bass, San Francisco, 1976.
3. J. E. Birren, Progress in Research on Aging in the Behavioral and Social Sciences, *Human Development, 23,* pp. 33-45, 1980.
4. K. M. Woodward, Master Songs of Meditation: The Late Poems of Eliot, Pound, Stevens, and Williams, in *Aging and the Elderly,* S. F. Spicker, K. M. Woodward and D. D. Van Tassel (eds.), Humanities Press, Atlantic Highlands, New Jersey, 1978.
5. M. Cowley, *The View from 80,* Viking Press, New York, 1980.
6. E. H. Erikson, *Identity and the Life Cycle,* W. W. Norton and Company, New York, 1980.
7. R. N. Butler, The Life Review: An Interpretation of Reminiscence in Aged, *Psychiatry, 26*:1, pp. 65-76, 1963.
8. I. M. Burnside, Psychosocial Caring: Reality Testing, Relocation, and Reminiscing, in *Psychosocial Caring Throughout the Life Span,* I. M. Burnside, P. Ebersole and H. E. Monea (eds.), McGraw-Hill, New York, 1979.
9. R. N. Butler and M. I. Lewis, *Aging and Mental Health* (3rd Edition), Mosby, St. Louis, 1982.
10. K. B. Ellison, Working with the Elderly in a Life Review Group, *Journal of Gerontological Nursing, 7*:9, pp. 537-541, 1981.
11. J. M. Grunes, Reminiscences, Regression, and Empathy: A Psychotherapeutic Approach to the Impaired Elderly, in *The Course of Life: Psychoanalytic Contributions Toward Understanding Personality Development, Vol. III: Adulthood and the Aging Process,* S. I. Greenspan and G. H. Pollock (eds.), National Institute of Mental Health, Rockville, Maryland, 1980.
12. G. Safier, Oral Life History with the Elderly, *Journal of Gerontological Nursing, 2*:5, pp. 17-22, 1976.
13. B. L. Neugarten, R. J. Havighurst, and S. S. Tobin, Personality and Patterns of Aging, in *Middle Age and Aging,* B. L. Neugarten (ed.), University of Chicago Press, Chicago, 1969.
14. A. W. McMahon and P. J. Rhudick, Reminiscing, *Archives of General Psychiatry, 10,* pp. 292-298, 1964.

15. L. J. Postema, *Reminiscing, Time Orientation, and Self Concept in Aged Men,* unpublished doctoral dissertation, Michigan State University, 1970, or University Microfilms International, Ann Arbor, MI 48106, University Microfilms No. 71-11,945.
16. J. E. Gorney, *Experiencing and Age: Patterns of Reminiscing Among the Elderly,* Unpublished Doctoral Dissertation, University of Chicago, Thesis No. T17307, 1968.
17. J. Loevinger and R. Wessler, *Measuring Ego Development I: Construction and Use of a Sentence Completion Test,* Jossey-Bass, San Francisco, 1970.
18. J. Loevinger, R. Wessler, and C. Redmore, *Measuring Ego Development II,* Jossey-Bass, San Francisco, 1970.
19. S. T. Hauser, Loevinger's Model and Measure of Ego Development: A Critical Review, *Psychological Bulletin, 83*:5, pp. 928-955, 1976.
20. R. R. McCrae and P. T. Costa, Openness to Experience and Ego Level in Loevinger's Sentence Completion Test: Dispositional Contribution to Developmental Models of Personality, *Journal of Personality and Social Psychology, 39*:6, pp. 1179-1190, 1980.
21. R. N. Shulik, *Faith Development, Moral Development, and Old Age: An Assessment of Fowler's Faith Development Paradigm,* unpublished doctoral dissertation, University of Chicago, 1979.
22. J. R. Snarey and J. R. Blasi, Ego Development among Adult Kibbutzniks: A Cross-Cultural Application of Loevinger's Theory, *Genetic Psychology Monographs, 102,* pp. 117-157, 1980.
23. N. Solomowitz, *Life Styles, Life Satisfaction and Ego Development in Late Adulthood,* unpublished doctoral dissertation, University of Kentucky, 1978 or University Microfilms International, Ann Arbor, MI 48106, University Microfilms No. 9-17719, 1978.
24. S. Frank and D. M. Quinlan, Development and Female Delinquency: A Cognitive-Developmental Approach, *Journal of Abnormal Psychology, 85*:5, pp. 505-510, 1976.
25. S. Hansell, J. Sparacino, D. Ronchi, and F. L. Strodtbeck, Ego Development Responses in Written Questionnaires and Telephone Interviews, *Journal of Personality and Social Psychology, 47*:5, pp. 1118-1128, 1985.
26. E. P. McCammon, Comparison of Oral and Written Forms of the Sentence Completion Test for Ego Development, *Developmental Psychology, 17*:2, pp. 233-235, 1981.
27. J. Loevinger, Revision of the Sentence Completion Test for Ego Development, *Journal of Personality and Social Psychology, 48*:2, pp. 420-427, 1985.
28. J. Cohen, A Coefficient of Agreement for Nominal Scales, *Educational and Psychological Measurement, 20*:1, pp. 37-46, 1960.
29. R. R. Holt, Loevinger's Measure of Ego Development: Reliability and National Norms for Male and Female Short Forms, *Journal of Personality and Social Psychology, 39*:5, pp. 909-920, 1980.
30. J. Loevinger, Construct Validity of the Sentence Completion Test of Ego Development, *Applied Psychological Measurement, 3*:3, pp. 281-311, 1979.

Chapter 12

REMINISCENCE, LIFE REVIEW, AND EGO INTEGRITY IN NURSING HOME RESIDENTS

Lois B. Taft
and
Milton F. Nehrke

Institutional care for elderly persons is often custodial rather than therapeutic. The development of interventions that are meaningful to residents who face profound physical and social losses is a formidable challenge. A number of clinicians report that using reminiscence in work with elderly, institutionalized persons resulted in positive outcomes [1-5]. For example, reminiscence has been found to be positively related to freedom from depression [6-9]; improvements in cognitive functioning [10]; psychological well-being [11, 12]; life satisfaction [6,11]; and ego integrity [13].

It is difficult to compare research findings on reminiscence because of diversity in the characteristics of the participants and substantial differences in methodology. In addition, lack of concept clarity contributes to inconsistency in research findings on reminiscence. For example, several previous studies measured the impact of the frequency of reminiscence on specific dependent variables. Variables besides overall frequency may account for the variation in the dependent variable, however. One may suggest that the benefits of reminiscing in conversations with other people may differ from the benefits of reminiscing alone; for this reason, it may be beneficial to examine the frequency of interpersonal and intrapersonal reminiscence separately. Further, it may not be how often a person reminisces but why they reminisce that's important. Based on a factor analytic study, Romaniuk and Romaniuk observed three dimensions of reminiscence that reflect the following uses:

1. teaching and entertaining;
2. problem solving; and
3. life review [14].

The purpose of this study was to explore the relationship between interpersonal and intrapersonal frequency of reminiscence and the uses of the three dimensions of reminiscence for ego integrity among persons institutionalized in nursing homes. Ego integrity was chosen as the dependent variable because the maintenance or restructuring of ego integrity has been identified as an important task of aging [15]. Ego integrity reflects a positive outcome of Erikson's eighth and final stage of development. It has been defined as: "a basic acceptance of one's life as having been inevitable, appropriate, and meaningful" [16, p. 3]. Reminiscence is a bridge between the past and the present and may be a mechanism that makes it possible for the elderly individuals to achieve ego integrity.

METHOD

Sample

The target population for this investigation was adults aged sixty-five and older residing in skilled-care nursing homes. In order to participate, it was required that the respondents be able to communicate with no serious deficits in hearing, memory, or level of orientation and that they had resided in the nursing home for more than one year. The sample was drawn from four nursing homes in West Central Wisconsin. The participants were, largely, a sample of rural, elderly individuals who reported a farming background. Two of the nursing homes were located in cities of approximately 50,000 people and the other two were located in small towns with a population under 2,000. The director of nursing at each institution provided a list of residents who met the criteria. The final sample was composed of fifteen men and fifteen women from the four nursing homes who met the study criteria. The median age of the sample was eighty-five and the mean age was 84.13 ($SD = 9.42$).

Measures

Reminiscence Questionnaire

Reminiscence was classified by use based on an instrument developed by Romaniuk and Romaniuk who defined reminiscence as "the process or practice of thinking or talking about past experiences" [14, p. 477]. They constructed and tested a reminiscence survey that includes a thirteen-item Reminiscence Scale. In this scale, they identify thirteen functions of reminiscence and then classify these functions into three subscales based on a factor analysis; each subscale identifies a distinct use or purpose of reminiscence. The uses of reminiscence and sample questions follow.

- Use Number 1: Teaching and Entertaining:
  When I have talked or thought about the past, I have done so . . .
  1. Because memories are pleasant, enjoyable, and help pass the time of day.
  2. To teach others by drawing upon my past experiences.
  3. To be amusing and entertaining.
- Use Number 2: Problem Solving:
  When I have talked or thought about the past, I have done so . .
  1. To make plans for the future.
  2. To cope with a loss in my life.
  3. To deal with some difficulty which I am experiencing.
- Use Number 3: Life Review:
  When I have talked or thought about the past, I have done so . .
  1. To solve something in my past that is troubling me.
  2. To arrive at a better understanding of my past life and myself.
  3. To determine life's meaning.

The subjects were asked to choose the response (yes, no, not sure) that described whether they used reminiscence in each way. Romaniuk and Romaniuk tested the reliability of the reminiscence uses scale by measuring its internal consistency. Kuder-Richardson coefficients of internal consistency were, respectively, .64, .69, and .57 [14].

Two questions were used to measure frequency of reminiscence: 1) When you are with others, how often do your conversations turn to past experiences?; and 2) When you are alone, how often do your thoughts turn to past experiences? Participants were asked to choose a response on a five-point Likert scale. Possible responses ranged from frequently (several times a day) to rarely (a few times a year). The values assigned to these responses were added together to determine overall frequency of reminiscence.

Ego Integrity Scale

This instrument was initially developed by Boylin, Gordon, and Nehrke for their study of reminiscence and ego integrity in institutionalized elderly males [13]. The ten-item scale is based on Erikson's descriptions of behaviors and attitudes characteristic of the two alternate solutions to the final stage of development—ego integrity or despair [15]. Five of the items represent a positive resolution and five items represent a negative resolution. The items were scored on a seven-point Likert scale with responses ranging from most typical of me to most atypical of me. Examples of the integrity items are:

1. I am able to take things as they come.
2. I am proud of what I have done.
3. I am satisfied with my life so far.

Examples of the despair items are:

1. I am pessimistic, not very hopeful.
2. I am afraid of getting old.
3. I regret the mistakes I've made.

Support for the validity and reliability of the ego integrity scale was published by Walasky, Whitbourne, and Nehrke [17] and Tesch [18]. Using a semistructured interview technique, Walasky et al. observed that elderly persons who had achieved ego integrity scored significantly more positively on the ego integrity scale than did persons classified as being in the despairing status group [17]. Thus, different methods of measuring the ego-integrity construct yielded similar results and provided a measure of concurrent as well as construct validity for the ego integrity scale. Walasky et al. reported the internal reliability for the ego integrity scale for their sample to be .76 [17]. Tesch also used this ten-item scale and found the internal consistency to be .69 (Chronbach's alpha) [18].

PROCEDURE

Once the resident provided informed consent, demographic data were collected in order to assure that the participant met the study criteria and to establish rapport. After the resident responded to demographic questions, the investigator read the twenty-five items of the reminiscence and ego integrity scales to each participant. Possible responses on the rating scales were graphically depicted in large print on laminated posterboard to facilitate administration.

RESULTS

The correlation matrix between the dimensions of reminiscence use, the frequency of reminiscence, and ego integrity are presented in Table 1. Although none of the frequency measures correlated significantly with ego integrity, the use of reminiscence as a means of life review was positively related to ego integrity ($r = .56$, $p < .001$). Neither of the other uses of reminiscence was significantly correlated with ego integrity. Of further interest, the respondent's age was positively correlated with the frequency of interpersonal reminiscence, the teaching/entertaining and life review purposes of reminiscence, and with the measure of ego integrity.

DISCUSSION

Somewhat unexpectedly, there was no significant relationship between frequency of reminiscence and ego integrity. This finding conflicts with the results of Boylin et al. who observed a significant, positive relationship between these

Table 1. Correlation Matrix of Reminiscence Variables and Ego Integrity
($N = 30$)

	Reminiscence Frequency			Use of Reminiscence			Ego Integrity
	1	2	3	1	2	3	
Age	.248	.367*	.075	.321*	.195	.313*	.337*
Reminiscence Frequency							
1. Overall		.827***	.871***	.283	0	.188	.154
2. Interpersonal			.444**	.346*	.077	.255	.211
3. Intrapersonal				.149	-.067	.077	.061
Use of Reminiscence							
1. Teach/Entertain					.315*	.392*	.276
2. Problem-Solving						.569***	.110
3. Life Review							.560***

* $p < .05$.
** $p < .01$.
*** $p < .001$.

variables [13]; their sample was larger than the current sample and included only male participants, however. Such conflicting data bring into question the value of implementing reminiscence processes in therapeutic settings simply to increase the frequency of reminiscence. It may be that the use or purpose of reminiscence is more important than the frequency of reminiscence as a mediator of ego integrity for the elderly person.

Yet, these results also indicate that there was but one use of reminiscence that correlated significantly with ego integrity. As one of the three uses or purposes of reminiscence, the life-review form is, in fact, quite similar to the type of life review proposed by Butler that he described as reminiscence for the purpose of analysis and reintegration. Given Romaniuk and Romaniuk's [14] and Butler's [19] definitions, it is not unexpected that a significant correlation was found between the life-review dimension of reminiscence and ego integrity or between age and ego integrity since the likelihood of achieving ego integrity increases as one has more time to resolve issues, distance one's self from the impact of events, and approach the reality of death [15]. As such, these results are supportive of Butler's work with life review as a form of therapy. It must also be noted, however, that life review is not a process for elderly persons alone: life review is a process that occurs at all ages, just as Erikson's stages of development are in constant flux and development [15].

As to the occurrence of life-review reminiscence, Butler's premise is that life review is a universal process [20]. Lieberman and Tobin, however, found only 49 percent of the participants in their study who reported current or resolved life reviews [21]. Romaniuk and Romaniuk, on the other hand, reported that 80 percent of the elderly persons in their study had experienced life review [14]. These discrepancies along with the present observation of 67 percent who reported using reminiscence for life review mandate further research. Recommendations would include efforts to determine whether ego integrity without life review is possible; the relative timing of life review and ego integrity across the life-span; the delineation of variables that will control or moderate the life-review process; and the individual's readiness for and ability to benefit from life review. At a more speculative level, it may be suggested that further efforts should also be directed toward the other forms of reminiscence since the teaching/education form may be related more directly to Erikson's stage of generativity/stagnation while the problem-solving form may be more characteristic of intimacy/isolation or one of the other stages of development [15] .

Although a correlational study such as this one cannot be used to imply a cause and effect relationship, and the interpretability of the study is limited by the small sample size and uncertain reliability of the research instruments [22], it does invite practitioners to conduct experimental studies to determine the effect of life-review strategies on ego integrity. In the present study, elderly individuals who reported using reminiscence for the purpose of life review scored higher on an ego-integrity measure. One could conclude that providing opportunities for life-review types of reminiscence may affect the elderly person's quality of life and attainment of ego integrity.

Lewis and Butler have discussed a variety of methods of reinforcing life-review activity—including scrapbooks, family albums, autobiographies, a summation of life work, genealogies, and pilgrimages [23]. With tape recorders and word processors, the technology currently exists to facilitate recorded memoirs, and, while it may be therapeutic to record one's memories, the recorded history carries its own intrinsic value. Butler has proposed that national archives should support a major program to acquire memoirs not only from distinguished contributors to American life but from average citizens who illuminate the events of history [20].

Another approach to increase life review at either an informal or formal level may involve the development of reminiscence groups to provide a forum for initiating the life-review process and provide feedback during the ongoing review. The opportunity for life review may also be provided in individual therapy. Professionals may reinforce life-review activity through supportive listening or by encouraging others to fill this role. Family and community members may become involved in collecting memoirs and oral histories. Myerhoff and Tufte reported on positive outcomes of community involvement when anthropology and English classes at the University of Southern California joined in a Life History Experiment in which students were trained in interviewing and recorded oral histories based on the memoirs of older adults [24]. Such intergenerational projects could also be organized to involve high school students or local historical societies. Lewis and Butler have proposed that life-review activities, aside from benefiting elderly participants, may also have unique benefits for listeners as well [23]. The reciprocal contributions of the life-review process include: "a personal sense of life's flow from birth to death, personal solutions for encountering grief and loss regarding old age and death, and models for growing older and for creating meaningful lives" [23, p. 173].

REFERENCES

1. F. J. Berghorn and D. E. Schafer, Reminiscence Intervention in Nursing Homes: What and Who Changes?, *International Journal of Aging and Human Development, 24,* pp. 113- 127, 1986-87.
2. L. Dietsche, Facilitating the Life Review through Group Reminiscence, *Journal of Gerontological Nursing, 5,* p. 43, 1979.
3. K. Huber and L. Goodman, Reminisce with the Elderly—Do It, *Geriatric Nursing, 5*:2, pp. 84-87, 1984.
4. B. Ingersoll and L. Goodman, History Comes Alive: Facilitating Reminiscence in a Group of Institutionalized Elderly, *Journal of Gerontological Social Work, 2,* pp. 305-319, 1980.
5. M. A. Matteson and E. M. Musat, Group Reminiscing Therapy with Elderly Clients, *Issues in Mental Health Nursing, 4,* pp. 177-189, 1982.
6. P. G. Coleman, Measuring Reminiscence Characteristics from Conversation as Adaptive Features of Old Age, *International Journal of Aging and Human Development, 5*:3, pp. 281-294, 1974.
7. R. D. Fallot, The Impact on Mood of Verbal Reminiscing in Later Adulthood, *International Journal of Aging and Human Development, 10*:4, pp. 385-400, 1979-80.
8. A. W. McMahon and P. J. Rhudick, Reminiscing: Adaptational Significance in the Aged, *Archives of General Psychiatry, 10,* pp. 292-298, 1964.
9. C. L. Parsons, Group Reminiscence Therapy and Levels of Depression in the Elderly, *Nurse Practitioner, 11,* pp. 68-76, 1986.
10. G. A. Hughston and S. B. Merriam, Reminiscence: A Nonformal Technique for Improving Cognitive Functioning in the Aged, *International Journal of Aging and Human Development, 14*:1, pp. 23-30, 1982.
11. B. K. Haight, The Therapeutic Role of a Structured Life Review Process in Homebound Elderly Subjects, *Journal of Gerontology, 27,* pp. 245-253, 1988.
12. R. J. Havighurst and R. Glasser, An Exploratory Study of Reminiscence, *Journal of Gerontology, 27*:2, pp. 245-253, 1972.
13. W. Boylin, S. K. Gordon, and M. F. Nehrke, Reminiscing and Ego Integrity in Institutionalized Elderly Males, *The Gerontologist, 16*:2, pp. 118-124, 1976.
14. M. Romaniuk and J. G. Romaniuk, Looking Back: An Analysis of Reminiscence Functions and Triggers, *Experimental Aging Research, 7*:4, pp. 477-489, 1981.
15. E. H. Erikson, *Childhood and Society* (2nd Edition), W. Norton Company, New York, 1963.
16. W. Gruen, Adult Personality: An Empirical Study of Erikson's Theory of Ego Development, in *Personality in Middle and Late Life*, B. Neugarten (ed.), Atherton Press, New York, 1964.

17. M. Walasky, S. K. Whitbourne, and M. F. Nehrke, Construction and Validation of an Ego Integrity Status Interview, *International Journal of Aging and Human Development, 18:*1, pp. 61-72, 1983-84.
18. S. Tesch, Psychosocial Development and Subjective Well-Being in an Age Cross-Section of Adults, *International Journal of Aging and Human Development, 21*, pp. 109-120, 1985.
19. R. N. Butler, The Life Review: An Interpretation of Reminiscence in the Aged, *Psychiatry, 26*, pp. 65-76, 1963.
20. R. N. Butler, Successful Aging and the Role of Life Review, *Journal of the American Geriatric Society, 22*, pp. 529-535, 1974.
21. M. A. Lieberman and S. S. Tobin, *The Experience of Old Age*, Basic Books, New York, 1983
22. J. Nunnaly, *Psychometric Theory*, McGraw Hill, New York, 1978.
23. M. I. Lewis and R. N. Butler, Life Review Therapy: Putting Memories to Work in Individual and Group Psychotherapy, *Geriatrics, 29:*11, pp. 165-173, 1974.
24. B. G. Myerhoff and V. Tufte, Life History as Integration, *The Gerontologist, 15*, pp. 541-543, 1975.

Chapter 13

REMINISCENTIA: CHERISHED OBJECTS AS MEMORABILIA IN LATE-LIFE REMINISCENCE

Edmund Sherman

The phenomenon of reminiscence and its potential for adaptation in old age has been studied extensively in the gerontological literature. This adaptive potential has led many gerontological practitioners to try various ways of fostering reminiscence in elderly adults. One of the more common ways has involved the use of memorabilia. If we accept one dictionary definition of memorabilia as "things that stir recollection" [1]; it is easy to see why such "things" or objects have been used in reminiscence work with elderly adults in both institutional and community settings [2], and why they have been recommended for life review therapy with individuals and groups [3].

The connection between reminiscence and objects seems self-evident, so much so that it has been taken for granted in practice. This study attempts to take a more systematic look at this connection. Additionally, it attempts to explore in even greater detail a particular kind of object that can "stir recollection," a special object or cherished possession, and its relationship to reminiscence. This study also represents an attempt to look at the nature and range of objects that serve to stir reminiscence whether or not they are special or cherished.

An apt descriptive term for the full range of objects that can stir reminiscence is "reminiscentia"; a term used by Edward Casey in his illuminating phenomenological study of memory entitled *Remembering* [4]. He used the term to refer to objects that "act as *inducers* of reminiscence," that possess the "special aptitude for arousing a reminiscent state of mind" [4, p. 110]. Such objects can include photographs, letters, souvenirs, relics, and any object or trace of an object that remains and is currently available in perception.

There has been in the gerontological literature little research on objects and very little on cherished objects. This author and another investigator studied the meaning of cherished possessions for elderly adults in a mixed sample of community-based and institutionalized elderly adults [5]. Wapner, Demick, and Redondo more recently investigated the role of cherished possessions in the adaptation of older persons to the institutionalized settings of nursing homes [6]. A more comprehensive study of the meaning of objects for individuals within their own families and domestic environments was done by Csikszentmihalyi and Rochberg-Halton [7]. They studied generational differences in meaning of objects for children, parents, and grandparents living together within the same family unit. Although their focus was not entirely on elderly adults, their findings provided valuable comparative data and analytic categories for this study.

There has been considerably more written in the gerontological literature about reminiscence than about objects, and most of the practice literature has been about its use in institutional settings. This investigator has had an interest in its use with community-based groups in senior centers and apartment dwellings [8]. This research and practice experience with such groups and the use of reminiscentia in them raised a number of questions about the relationship between objects and reminiscence that led ultimately to this study.

It was evident in these groups that some objects were selected and used by participants to evoke memories about a period in their life, such as early childhood. Some were used to remember specific events or persons or to reconstruct whole eras, and some were selected because they were special or cherished. Others were used because they could stimulate recollection of the past in *general* rather than any specifics within it. Regardless of the reasons for selecting the object, there was an evident connection between the object, the person, and the act of remembering that emerged in the group reminiscence. This has been referred to as the triad of meaning (person, object, action) by Denzin [9] and is consistent with symbolic interactionist thinking, which guided the development of object-meaning categories in earlier work on the "meaning of things" [7]. This approach to the meaning of objects also guided much of the collection, classification, and analysis of data in this study.

METHOD

Participants

The participants in this study consisted of 100 volunteers, ranging in age from sixty to 102, and recruited from four senior service centers—three in urban settings and one in a suburban area. The mean age was 72.7 years, and there were seventy-five women and twenty-five men in the final sample of volunteers. Their marital status was: thirty-seven married, forty-eight widowed, five separated, and eight single (never married). Identification of religious affiliation and ethnicity was optional, but forty-five participants identified themselves as Protestant, thirty-seven as Catholics, five as Jewish, seven as None, and ten as Other. A total of eighty-four identified themselves as Caucasian, fifteen as African American and one Other (Asian). These distributions are roughly similar to those in the Albany, New York, sampling area, which has few Hispanics. The educational levels of the participants were reported as follows: four had zero to sixth grade; fifteen had seventh to ninth grade; twelve had tenth to eleventh grade; thirty were high school graduates; twenty-two had one to three years of college; eight were college graduates; and eight had graduate degrees. Their social-class status was determined by Hollingshead's [10] Two-Factor Index of Social Class position based upon education and occupation. The results were as follows: five were Class I (highest), seventeen were II, twenty-six were III, thirty-two were IV, and twenty were V (lowest). This distribution appears to be more weighted at the middle and lower ends of the social-class continuum and seems consistent with this age group in such settings.

Measures

The basic instrument for data collection was a questionnaire designed to elicit responses about the kinds of objects that serve as memorabilia, and those that represent special or cherished possessions, as well as responses about the frequency, uses, and types of reminiscence in which the participants engaged. The questions about the objects followed those about reminiscence:

1. What kinds of objects or memorabilia (books, photos, jewelry, etc.) tend to set you to reminiscing more than others? (please list):
2. Please list and describe any personal possession(s) or object(s) that is particularly special to you or that you cherish more than any others:
3. Why does the object(s) have such special meaning to you? (just briefly explain):

Classification of objects by type and by meaning from the written responses was based on the categories developed by Csikszentmihalyi and Rochberg-Halton [7]. Those categories are given in Tables 1 and 2.

Structured questionnaire items on uses of reminiscence consisting of thirteen, possible responses to the statement, "When I have talked or thought about the past, I have done so," were developed by Romaniuk and Romaniuk [11]. Additionally, these thirteen reported uses were classified into three types of reminiscence identified by the Romaniuks in their factor analysis: 1) Pleasure/Image Enhancement, 2) Problem-Solving, and 3) Life Review. Examples of uses within the pleasure/image enhancement type were: "because memories are pleasant enjoyable, and help to pass the time of day"; "to be amusing and entertaining"; and "to inform people about the successes and accomplishments in my life."

Table 1. Frequency of Items Identified as Memorabilia
and Cherished Objects

Item	Memorabilia		Cherished Objects	
	f	%	f	%
Photos	77	41.6	33	23.2
Books	22	11.9	8	5.6
Kitchen, food	3	1.6	0	0
Letters, documents	10	5.4	4	2.8
Garden, nature	3	1.6	3	2.1
Gifts	3	1.6	8	5.6
Souvenirs	3	1.6	1	.7
Old movies	5	2.7	0	0
Furniture	4	2.2	4	2.8
Children's toys	1	.5	3	2.1
Jewelry	20	10.8	31	21.8
Music, dancing	12	6.5	7	4.9
Clothing, hats	5	2.7	2	1.4
Stamps, coins	2	1.1	3	2.1
Trophies, plaques	0	0	3	2.1
Collectibles	4	2.2	11	7.7
Entire home	0	0	2	1.4
Military	2	1.1	2	1.4
Tools	3	1.6	2	1.4
Religious objects	5	2.7	8	5.6

Note: Item categories used only once: wallet, oriental rug, map, clock, sewing machine, old cars/trucks.

The three uses within the problem-solving type were: "to make plans for the future"; "to cope with a loss in my family"; and "to deal with some difficulty I am experiencing." The three uses within the life review type were: "to solve something in my past which is troubling me"; "to arrive at a better understanding of my past life and myself"; and "to determine life's meaning."

Frequency of reminiscence was measured by responses on a five-point scale: 1 = always, 2 = usually, 3 = fairly often, 4 = seldom, and 5 = never. The frequency was measured for both public (interpersonal) and private (intrapersonal) reminiscing. Public reminiscing was measured by responses to the question, "When you are with others, how often does your conversation turn to past experiences?" Private reminiscing was measured by responses to the question, "When you are alone, how often do your responses turn to past experiences?"

Table 2. Frequency of Cherished Object Meanings

Cherished Object Meanings	Frequency	
	N	%
I. Memories momentos, recollections, heirlooms, souvenirs, had it long time	28	48.3
II. Associational contexts gifts, religion	7	12.1
III. Experiences enjoyment	4	6.9
IV. Intrinsic qualities unique, special quality	4	6.9
V. Utilitarian	4	6.9
VI. Personal values accomplishment, personification	11	18.9
Totals	58	100%

Brennan and Steinberg, on the basis of their empirical findings, make a strong case for saying that "reminiscence may have more of an impact on *mood* than on *morale*" [12]. They questioned whether an intermittent behavior or process such as reminiscence could powerfully affect global psychological well-being or morale as measured by life satisfaction indices, based on the fact that they did not find a significant relationship between reminiscence and life satisfaction. However, they thought that reminiscence might affect more transient states of well-being or mood. Consequently, for this study, the *Affect-Balance Scale* was selected [13]. It is a ten-item scale based upon self-reported feelings about daily life experience "during the past few weeks" and is therefore a good indicator of mood or current sense of well-being [14].

Procedure

The purpose and nature of the study was explained to potential volunteers by this investigator in open meetings at each of the four senior centers. The volunteer respondents were paid $10.00 each for filling out the six-page questionnaire. Each of the respondents was also, briefly, interviewed by this investigator or a research assistant to check for completeness and comprehension of the questionnaire items as well as to clarify responses concerning the types, meanings, and associations of the identified objects. Although 112 questionnaires were filled out, only 100 were used in the analysis because we had some doubts about comprehension of questionnaire items or adequacy of responses by the other twelve participants.

RESULTS

All but four people could identify at least one object or piece of memorabilia that tended to encourage reminiscing more than others. A majority of respondents (60) readily identified at least two pieces of memorabilia ranging to a high of seven. On the other hand, twelve people out of 100 could not identify a most cherished object. This 12 percent compares to the 9 percent who could not identify at least one cherished possession in the earlier study of such possessions in a mixed sample of community and institutional elderly adults [5] and the 25 percent who could not name at least one cherished possession found by Wapner, Demick, and Redondo [6] in their nursing home sample of elderly adults.

Of the eighty-eight respondents in this study with cherished possessions, forty-eight had only one such object, while the remaining forty identified two or more, with a high of five ($\overline{X} = 1.48$, $SD = 0.98$). This compares to the high of seven in the memorabilia category in which thirty-six identified only one object, while the remaining sixty identified two or more ($\overline{X} = 2.10$, $SD = 1.32$). In an overwhelming number of cases, the most cherished object identified was *not* the first piece of memorabilia identified. Only fourteen objects out of a total of 127 identified as most cherished possessions were the same objects as the first piece of memorabilia identified. It became evident that the majority of cherished objects had different primary functions and meanings than as simple memorabilia in the lives of these older persons.

It is interesting to see frequency of different types of memorabilia identified by the respondents as compared to objects identified as cherished possessions. Table 1 gives these comparative figures.

Although the most frequently identified objects in both the memorabilia and cherished objects categories were photographs, photos amounted to less than one-quarter of the cherished objects identified but over two-fifths of all memorabilia identified. Clearly, photographs are the predominant type of memorabilia. Jewelry was almost as commonly identified as a cherished object as were photographs.

The meanings of the different kinds of cherished objects were an important element of this analysis because of the possible occurrence or association of these meanings in the reminiscing of the participants. Table 2 gives the breakdown of the meanings of the cherished objects. It is important to note that cherished objects actually exist in a context of multiple meanings, so any one object may appear in several of these meaning categories. For the purposes of correlational analysis, the *first* meaning identified with the object by the respondent is represented in Table 2. Although these categories do not exhaust the full range of meanings or specific personal significance for individual respondents, they do give some sense of general patterns of meaning.

One of these patterns is that the largest frequency of meanings in Table 2 falls in the "Memories" category, which includes objects of recollection, long possession, or which are identified as a memento, heirloom, or souvenir. The large frequency in the "Memories" category is consistent with the findings of Wapner, Demick, and Redondo, who found that the most frequent meanings attributed to cherished possessions fell in this category [6]. This was not so, however, in the findings of Csikszentmihalyi and Rochberg-Halton, who developed these meaning categories [7]. "Memories" was second to "Experiences," particularly current experiences of enjoyment. This difference is probably explained by the larger proportion of younger people in their sample, particularly grandchildren in their teens; a group in which objects are more valued for utilitarian reasons as well as for current experiences.

A noteworthy point in this analysis is that *all* of the fourteen cherished objects that were first identified as memorabilia fell into the category of memories. In short, these objects were cherished for their ability to evoke recollections about the past.

Turning now to the uses of reminiscence in this sample, it is of interest to note in Table 3 that numbers 1, 3, 5, 7, 9, 11, and 13 were the most frequently identified uses of reminiscence, and all seven of them compose the Pleasure/Image-Enhancement type of reminiscence identified by the Romaniuk's in their factor analysis [10]. In fact, the distribution of frequencies of uses in Table 3 is essentially the same as that found by the Romaniuks in their sample of community-based elderly adults.

All of the uses in the "Pleasure/Image-Enhancement," type of reminiscence were identified by over half of the participants in this study. This was not true of the other two types of reminiscence. Type II, "Problem-Solving," had only #4, "To cope with a loss," identified by half of the respondents. Much less than half of the respondents identified #2, "To make future plans," (36%) and #8, "To deal with a problem," (29%) within the problem-solving type. Type III, "Life Review," did contain use of #10, "To better understand my past life and self," in which over half the respondents (54%) reported they engaged. However, use of #6, "To solve past problems" (27%), and use of #12, "To determine life's meaning," (38%) were identified by considerably less than half the respondents with respect to the life-review type of reminiscence.

While these figures on the uses and types of reminiscence are of interest in their own right, of more concern in this study is their interrelationship with objects and mood as well as age and gender. Table 4 presents the correlations among most of these variables.

Beginning with the variable of age, several relationships are worthy of note. First, there is a significant negative relationship between age and the frequency of memorabilia and cherished objects. Respondents eighty and older identified

Table 3. Frequency of Different Uses of Reminiscence by Participants

Uses of Reminiscence	Frequency (N = 100)
1. Recall of pleasant events is enjoyable	83
2. To make future plans	36
3. To teach others	72
4. To cope with a loss	50
5. To entertain	68
6. To solve past troubles	27
7. To identify what was better in past	70
8. To deal with current problems	29
9. To inform others of accomplishments	54
10. To achieve better understanding of self	54
11. To describe self to others	64
12. To determine life's meaning	38
13. Recalling memories lifts spirits	71

Table 4. Correlation Matrix of Objects, Reminiscence Variables, and Mood

	Objects		Reminiscence Variables					
	1	2	1	2	3	Pub	Prv	Mood
Age	−.260**	−.222*	.048	.032	−.168*	.029	−.057	−.126
Objects								
1. memorabilia		.384***	.170*	.040	.065	.079	−.011	.299***
2. cherished objects			.122	.185*	.037	−.024	−.098	.059
Reminiscence variables								
1. Type 1				.079	.150	.098	.140	.316***
2. Type 2					.508***	.095	.182*	−.044
3. Type 3						.172*	.181*	.072
Public/ (interpersonal)							.460***	.147
Private (intrapersonal)								.007

*p < .05
**p < .01
***p < .001
Reminiscence Type 1: Pleasure/Image-Enhancement
Reminiscence Type 2: Problem-Solving
Reminiscence Type 3: Life Review

significantly fewer objects either as memorabilia or as cherished possessions. On the other hand, their cherished objects tended to be associated more with memories than with other meaning categories. Finally, older respondents engaged in significantly less life-review reminiscing than did younger participants.

Turning next to the object variables, it is perhaps no surprise that there is a significant positive relationship between the numbers of memorabilia and the numbers of cherished possessions identified. It is also no surprise that there is a significant positive relationship between the numbers of memorabilia identified and the Type I, Pleasure/Image-Enhancement, form of reminiscence. For the most part, memorabilia were associated with positive memories. This is also reflected in the significant relationship between memorabilia and mood. The more memorabilia identified, the higher the Affect-Balance Scale score tended to be. It is worth noting that, although only four people did not identify a piece of memorabilia, three of those were among the lowest in mood scores.

Cherished objects showed a different pattern of relationships with the reminiscence and mood variables. The significant positive relationship between frequency of cherished objects and problem-solving reminiscence appears to be related to another finding. Respondents engaging in problem-solving reminiscence show significantly more cherished objects with meanings associated with current experiences rather than memories or the other meaning categories ($r = .20$, $p < .05$). Based on our post-questionnaire interviews, it appears that these individuals are associating the objects with their current efforts to cope with losses and to prepare for the future. Statements like "It [object] reminds me that I've been through this before and that I can make it," or "It gives me courage." are examples of such associations.

Somewhat unexpected was the lack of a significant Pierson correlation between cherished objects and mood, since there had been a significant relationship between memorabilia and mood. It was also unexpected because the earlier study of cherished objects showed a significant positive relationship between possession of a cherished object and life satisfaction [5]. It should be noted, however, in that study it was *lack* of a cherished object that was most clearly associated with low life satisfaction. Therefore, that association was tested in this analysis, which showed that ten of the twelve respondents who could not identify a most cherished possession fell below the median on the Affect-Balance Scale ($X^2 = 4.64$, $df = 1$, $p < .05$). As a result, total *lack* of a most cherished possession is significantly associated with low mood scores. It should also be noted that the post-questionnaire interviews gave the impression that there was more often a bittersweet quality associated with cherished objects, as opposed to the more generally enjoyable quality associated with memorabilia. This might partially explain the lack of a significant positive correlation between cherished objects and mood, in contrast to memorabilia and mood.

The significant positive relationship between pleasure/image-enhancement (Type I) reminiscing and mood score is not unexpected, given the enjoyable nature of Type I reminiscing. The significant relationship between problem-solving and private reminiscing is also understandable in light of the old adage that private problems are not for public consumption. Life-review reminiscing, on the other hand, shows a significant relationship with higher frequencies of both public and private reminiscing. This speaks to the appropriateness of both group and individual life-review therapy. It should be noted that there was considerable overlap in persons engaging heavily in both problem-solving and life-review reminiscing, as evidenced by the correlation between the two ($p < .001$). Fifteen people engaged as frequently in problem-solving as in life-review reminiscing and gave every indication of going through an active life-review at the time of the survey.

There were some significant differences between men and women on a number of reminiscence and object variables. Women showed more private reminiscing and they showed lower affect-balance scores. This was particularly true among widowed women. Women also tended to attribute more person-related meanings to cherished objects in a significantly greater degree than men. Men were significantly more likely to cherish an object because it related to their personal values and embodied their ideals ($r = .294$, $p < .001$), or because it had intrinsic value ($r = .247$, $p < .01$). Women tended to identify more cherished objects overall ($\overline{X} = 1.56$, $SD = 1.00$) than men ($\overline{X} = 1.24$, $SD = 0.88$), but this was only significant at the .10 level rather than the .05 level: $t(98) = -1.42$. These findings correspond with recent findings concerning gender and cherished objects in a nursing home sample [6].

DISCUSSION

Interpretation of the significant findings of this study has to be tempered by generally low levels of correlation. This is an exploratory study and can, at best, only indicate certain general directions and patterns. Another caveat needs to be stated concerning the largely arbitrary distinction between objects identified as memorabilia and those identified as cherished objects in this analysis. There is no question that there are multiple meanings associated with cherished objects, and memories are undoubtedly part and parcel of many of these meanings. The distinction between the two object categories had to do with the initial interest in seeing whether cherished objects would be immediately identified among the reported reminiscentia (i.e., among those objects or memorabilia that readily evoke reminiscing). This did not seem to be the case, and in fact, most identified possessions were cherished more directly for reasons other than their capacity to evoke reminiscence. On the other hand, in several instances where cherished objects were immediately identified as reminiscentia and were cherished precisely because of their capacity to induce reminiscence, they seemed to serve a reconstructive function—they seemed to trigger off a process of related memories that would reconstruct whole areas of epochs of the person's life. For example, one seventy-five-year-old woman described how a photograph of the home in which she raised her children and in which she and her husband lived out their retirement until his death enabled her to recreate meaningful parts of their lives together, now that she lived alone in an apartment. Another widow said of her wedding ring, "It doesn't just remind me of him [deceased husband], it starts a whole chain of memories that help me put things about our past together." This woman, in her early 70s, appeared to be actively engaged in a life-review process on the basis of her questionnaire responses and the post-questionnaire interview.

The finding of significantly fewer memorabilia and cherished objects among the older (80+) respondents is consistent with this investigator's prior findings [5]. Also, the finding of significantly less life-review reminiscing among very old adults is consistent with the findings of Lieberman and Tobin [15]. It is also consistent with Butler's theory of the life-review, in which such reminiscing would be expected to occur developmentally in the person's sixties or seventies [16]. A number of the findings about objects, age, gender, and mood in this study appear to be consistent with prior research on both cherished objects and reminiscence. Although memorabilia were more readily identified and in larger numbers than were cherished objects by respondents, it is important to note the significant positive relationship between the two categories of objects ($p < .001$). The more readily people identify memorabilia the more likely they are to identify cherished objects, which says something about the place of objects in the lives of older persons. This is underscored by the findings of significantly lower mood and life satisfaction when there is a total *lack* of such objects in the lives of older persons.

REFERENCES

1. *Webster's Ninth New Collegiate Dictionary*, Merriam-Webster, Inc., Springfield, Massachusetts, p. 740, 1988.
2. M. B. Weiner, A. J. Brok, and A. M. Snadowsky, *Working with the Aged: Practical Approaches in the Institution and Community*, Appleton-Century-Crofts, Norwalk, Connecticut, 1987.
3. M. J. Lewis and R. N. Butler, Life Review Therapy: Putting Memories to Work in Individual and Group Psychotherapy, *Geriatrics, 29*, pp. 165-169, 172-173, 1974.
4. E. S. Casey, *Remembering: A Phenomenological Study*, Indiana University Press, Bloomington, 1987.
5. E. Sherman and E. S. Newman, The Meaning of Cherished Possessions for the Elderly, *International Journal of Aging and Human Development, 8*, pp. 181-192, 1977-1978.
6. S. Wapner, J. Demick, and J. P. Redondo, Cherished Possessions and Adaptation of Older People to Nursing Homes, *International Journal of Aging and Human Development, 31*, pp. 299-315, 1990.
7. M. Csikszentmihalyi and E. Rochberg-Halton, *The Meaning of Things: Domestic Symbols and the Self*, Cambridge University Press, New York, 1981.

8. E. Sherman, Reminiscence Groups for Community Elderly, *The Gerontologist*, *27*, pp. 569-572, 1987.

9. N. K. Denzin, *Interpretive Interactionism*, Sage Publications, Newbury Park, California, 1989.

10. A. Hollingshead and F. Redlich, *Social Class and Mental Illness*, John Wiley & Sons, New York, 1958.

11. M. Romaniuk and J. G. Romaniuk, Looking Back: An Analysis of Reminiscence Functions and Triggers, *Experimental Aging Research*, *7*, pp. 477-489, 1981.

12. P. L. Brennan and L. P. Steinberg, Is Reminiscence Adaptive? Relations among Activity Level, Reminiscence, and Morale, *International Journal of Aging and Human Development*, *18*, pp. 99-110, 1983-1984.

13. N. M. Bradburn and R. Caplovitz, *Reports on Happiness*, Aldin, Chicago, 1965.

14. N. M. Bradburn, *The Structure of Well Being*, Aldin, Chicago, 1965.

15. M. A. Lieberman and S. S. Tobin, *The Experience of Old Age*, Basic Books, New York, 1983.

16. R. N. Butler, The Life Review: An Interpretation of Reminiscence in the Aged, *Psychiatry*, *26*, pp. 65-75, 1963.

Chapter 14

MOURNING AND REMINISCENCE: PARALLEL PSYCHOTHERAPEUTIC PROCESSES FOR ELDERLY PEOPLE

Linda L. Viney
Yvonne N. Benjamin
and
Carol Preston

Mourning and reminiscence are central to the psychology of elderly people. The elderly are likely to lose so much they have loved: spouse, friends, pets, home, abilities, roles, values, health, and strength. Grieving for these losses is a constant theme in their later years. Mourning must, then, be a part of any form of psychotherapy for the elderly. Also, elderly people often verbalize their reviews of and reflections on their earlier life experiences in reminiscence. This, too, has considerable therapeutic value for them.

We have recently been funded by the Australian Institute of Health to develop and evaluate some home-based psychotherapy programs for the elderly [1-3]. Our psychotherapy, which was successful in both the short term and on follow-up, was used with a sample of forty elderly clients aged from sixty-five to eighty-seven years. They were referred to our service of three female psychologists by medical practitioners and community nurses. The reasons for their referral were anxiety, depression, passive aggression, hostility, over-dependence, family-related problems, sustained bereavement reaction, and poor adjustment to chronic illness. The average number of therapy sessions they experienced was ten, with a range from seven to twelve. Each session was about seventy-five minutes in length but varied according to the needs and abilities of each client.

As we learned to work therapeutically with elderly people, we found that they made much use of mourning and reminiscence and that the two processes seemed to be highly similar [4]. This is our theoretical account of how mourning and reminiscence function therapeutically for the elderly. It is based on personal construct theory [5], one of the sources of cognitive-behavioral psychotherapy [6]. The theory assumes elderly people make use of their personal construct systems to make sense of what is happening to them and to predict what will happen in the future. The constructs determine how elderly people act. Elderly people have developed their constructs by interpreting their own past experiences, and, because these experiences have differed, their constructs differ. Their constructs may not be flexible enough or have sufficient range for effective prediction, but they can recognize that and change them [7, 8]. Other people can relate closely to the elderly only if they understand their construct systems. Elderly people try to validate or confirm their constructs through others, but they often find this difficult to do. When they secure validation, they experience positive emotions. When they fail to secure validation, negative emotions result.

Reminiscence in the elderly serves, at least in part, to provide validation for their construct systems. As they grow older and more isolated from mainstream society, their construct systems are more rarely validated by the people around them. Mourning is grief over these sources of validation which are lost. The newly grieving widow, for example, feels as if she is standing in a strange country trying to use her old system of constructs to anticipate what it will be like. Because her customary external sources of validation fail her, she turns to her own resources and uses reminiscence as a validation source. The same lack of validation prompts reminiscence in the elderly. Mourning and reminiscence are two parallel psychological processes. In the following sections, these processes are examined, and personal construct theory accounts of them are given, together with some therapeutic case studies illustrating their close relationship.

MOURNING

Encouraging and facilitating the expression of emotions after loss has been the major emphasis of those working with the bereaved in the last decade [9, 10]. Researchers have also focused on the emotional states which are evident throughout the mourning process. These usually include shock or numbness, separation pain or longing, guilt, anger, and eventually acceptance [11-13]. Although the explanation of these emotional reactions has differed, as the literature reviewed has shown [14-16], there has been some consistency in the reported emotions and the stages of the mourning process. Possible influences on the progress of mourning are discussed as well as the personal construct theory account of the process. Then a sample of characteristic affective components of mourning (shock, guilt, and overwhelming construct invalidation) is considered.

The desired outcome of this mourning process has been described as the restoration of the bereaveds' emotional homeostasis [17]. What factors significantly affect the outcome of this process? It has been reported that widows over sixty-five years of age show less emotional disturbance after bereavement then younger widows [12]. The elderly who are bereaved also tend to replace emotional reactions with somatic complaints and to develop new illnesses and use more medications [18, 19]. Other research suggests that the following factors influence the process of mourning: the meaning of the lost relationship, the bereaveds' previous experience with death, the bereaveds' internal resources for coping, the interpersonal support available, the perceptions of the bereaved concerning the replaceability of those who have died, and the expectations others have concerning the bereaveds' mourning behavior [17, 20-24]. Very little has been reported about the effectiveness or appropriateness of therapeutic intervention in the mourning process. Therapy is often assumed to be appropriate only if the bereaved person fails to negotiate the "normal mourning process" [25].

Personal construct theory provides a framework both for understanding this phenomenon of bereavement and for developing strategies which can be employed by therapists working with the bereaved. Using this model, bereavement can be understood as a major disruption to peoples' ways of construing and living in the world. When significant and irretrievable loss confronts people, many of the constructs which they have used to interpret and predict their experiences suddenly become ineffectual or meaningless. The process of mourning is then understood, not as emotional readjustment, but as an attempt by the bereaved to reestablish some effectiveness and continuity within their construct systems [26-28]. This is a process which can be assisted and guided in therapy. The profound emotional states which are evident throughout mourning are indications of the changes that are occurring in peoples' construct systems. They give direction for the therapist and the bereaved in working through mourning. Use of this approach allows assessment of the degree to which any of the factors observed to influence mourning are relevant for a particular individual. These factors can then be specifically dealt with and used to assist the bereaved to move in the most constructive ways through the mourning process.

Protecting the Predictability of the Construct System

The numbness and shock, which are often observed after bereavement, can be understood as the bereaveds' attempts to protect and maintain the predictability of their construct systems. People refuse or fail to recognize the reality of their loss because their construct systems are unable to account for the event or because changes to their construing implied by such loss are too threatening. People who go over and over the details surrounding the death of a loved one may be seen to be searching for an explanation of their loss that they can integrate into their construct system, that is, for a validation of their constructs. When therapy began with seventy-five-year-old Mary T., this was her need. Her husband had died after a long illness and her reaction eight months after his death was still one of shock and disbelief. She continued to expect her husband to walk through the door of their house; she looked for him in her bed when she woke; she repeatedly reviewed the days leading up to his death, the words he had spoken, and her experience of nursing him. She was unable to integrate the fact of his death into her construct system which was being invalidated by her own experiences. Mary was encouraged in therapy to explore her construct system for possible interpretations of death in relation to her husband and for herself. The constructs of herself as a caring person helped her to become comfortable with construing his death as relief from his pain and suffering. Her religious beliefs enabled her to construe her husband as being with God and thus in a place where they would one day be reunited. Personal construct theory suggests that Mary developed an account of her loss which she could integrate into her construct system. This would have freed her to move on to dealings with other aspects of her mourning.

Guilt and Consolidation of the Loss

Once bereaved people have consolidated the reality of their loss, they are likely to become more aware of feelings of guilt. The bereaved may remember things in the past they now wish they hadn't said or hadn't done. They may feel guilty that they are alive while the other is dead. In personal construct terms this guilt represents the bereaveds' awareness of their constructs about themselves and the discrepancy they now see between these core constructs and how they have been in the past. People experiencing this guilt need assistance to evaluate the extent to which their self expectations can be validated. Jean W. at seventy-five was recently widowed. She had spent time with her therapist reviewing her marriage. She had experienced conflict between living out her husband's constructs of a good wife and her own constructs about herself. After his death she felt guilt about the occasions on which she had chosen to behave in accordance with the self constructs about herself which were important to her and, in so doing, had not lived up to his expectations. She was coping with this guilt by trying to behave in ways of which he would have approved and by constantly referring to things he had told her to do in the past. This reaction may have blocked Jean from being able to consider all the alternatives open to her. If this personal construct approach is valid, she needed to be able to reconstrue herself as having been a satisfactory wife in her own terms and secure validation for these constructs. She did so, and went on to make decisions about her future based on advantages and disadvantages for herself rather than on guilt from the past.

Intensity of Mourning and the Extent of Validation

The intensity and duration of the mourning process will vary from person to person depending on how much of the construct system is invalidated and needs revision. For many elderly people, mourning can involve dealing with sudden multiple loss, and the task of rebuilding and restoring meaning to their lives can seem overwhelming. Sarah V.'s husband died suddenly and unexpectedly when she was seventy-three. She was deeply shocked and numbed by the experience. She was unable to comprehend or deal with the implications of this loss for her future. Her core constructs involved her role as a wife, mother, and homemaker. Her children, made arrangements to sell her home and build her a "granny flat." However, when Sarah moved in, she found the stairs to her rooms were difficult to manage and the shops too far to walk to. Although the children arranged meals on wheels for her and her daughter-in-law did the washing and cleaning, in her own home Sarah had been within walking distance of the main shopping center, transport services, her church, and her friends. Within nine months she had experienced the loss of the central relationship in her life, of her home, her homemaker role, her independence, her church, and some of her friends. Sarah showed many of the signs reported as pathological patterns of grief—withdrawal into apathy, despair, belief that death is near, preoccupation with worthlessness, and development of physical illnesses [9, 26]. Sarah's reaction is one which can be understood in personal construct theory in terms of the enormity of the disruption to her construct system. All the important ways in which she understood herself and her world had been invalidated. In order to restore any validity and meaning to her life, Sarah needed to mourn all her losses. She needed assistance to draw out of the chaos those aspects of her life over which she might be able to gain control. Our theory suggests that she needed support to move slowly toward testing new constructs and building into her life some things to give her a sense of identity and purpose. This was accomplished through a psychotherapeutic relationship in which she could test her construing.

REMINISCENCE

Although reminiscence is not an activity limited to the elderly [29-31], it has been observed to be prevalent in and also characteristic of them [32, 33]. These observations have led to many functions being ascribed to reminiscence. Prior to Butler's work [34], predominantly negative aspects of reminiscing by the elderly had been emphasized [4, 35, 36]. Later writers have stressed the adaptational functions of reminiscence. These functions operate for the elderly in the same way that characteristic behaviors in earlier developmental stages are suitable adaptive devices for coming to grips with the problems of those stages [36-38]. Butler emphasized the life review function of reminiscence in related to the aged [34, 39, 40]. His writings have given rise to experimental studies exploring the parameters of reminiscence as well as to the use of reminiscence as a therapeutic tool. Butler defined life review reminiscence as a common mental process marked by the return to awareness of past experiences. Threat is oftcn part of these experiences. Therapeutic uses of reminiscence are considered below, as are more therapeutic case studies to illustrate them.

At least three types of reminiscence have been differentiated [36]. The first type is story telling, a social form of reminiscence providing an oral history and also enhancing the self-esteem of the storyteller. The second type is memories, which contain the data for life review. The third type of reminiscence is defensive reminiscence, used to combat the anxiety of physical and psychological decline by idealizing the past and deprecating the present. A similar set of categories has been described by another writer [41]. An evaluative component is an essential factor in the life review form of reminiscence [42]. This is in contrast to the social function of story telling for information-giving and for the pleasure of recollection. It is through the process of life review that unresolved threats from the past may arise. They can cause anxiety and feelings of depression. People who reminisce may then attempt to cope defensively with their distress by guilt, denial, selective memory, or glorifying the past. Reminiscence and nostalgia have been distinguished [43]: reminiscence is seen as an active process of recalling often specific past events, whereas nostalgia refers to an effect usually signifying a more general wish for something from long ago. Carlson's nostalgia [43] is similar to McMahon and Rhudick's defensive reminiscence [36].

A personal construct theory account of this phenomenon of reminiscence is provided as follows. Over a lifetime, the elderly have formed construct systems to interpret the meaning of their lives and the world around them. The constructs have enabled them to predict, with varying degrees of accuracy, the external results of behavior based upon these constructs and their own psychological comfort or discomfort resulting from this behavior. The elderly experience world changes in technology, culture, and values at a time of much personal change and many losses. Like other people, when overloaded with invalidating information, the elderly tend to tighten their long established constructs in order to defend against what seems incongruous to them, and they resort to reminiscence to provide some of the missing validation for their constructs.

Anger, Invalidation, and Reminiscence

We found no evidence that specific individuals used a specific type of reminiscence. Within any one individual, we heard storytelling intermingle with favorable evaluative life review, and with defensive recall. Each type provided therapist and client with insights into the elderly person's construct system and revealed blocks to the integration of the past and present self. As personal construct therapists, we found that we were able to channel unproductive and obsessive reminiscence into forms that were therapeutic and satisfying to the client. Judith P., aged sixty-six, was very active and delighted to be close to facilities for social outings. She was involved in both painting and yoga. Her husband, Peter P., aged seventy-four, had severe emphysemia. Although he talked incessantly, it was with a gasping struggle for breath. Judith whispered to the therapist: "He lives completely in the past." Attempts to interview Peter were invariably met with a monologue on the history of his district and its people over the past century. After several sessions with no change in direction, the therapist asked: "How are things different today?" His response was angry, revealing his invalidation-generated frustration about his invalidism, as well as his envy of his wife's activities. His main construct about himself proved to be "Now I am useless." These feelings of shame and anger had not been expressed to his wife or anyone else. Their communications had been politely evasive with much concealed anger. His children avoided visiting him because of his tedious monologues of oral history, so that he had lost some other important sources of validation. He and his wife then agreed to work with the therapist on learning to express to one another their feelings about their interactions. In personal construct terms, Peter may be said to have regained an important source of validation, and invalidation, of his construct system.

Developmental Transition, Invalidation, and Reminiscence

If people have not been able to resolve the midlife developmental transition, they may not deal successfully with the one which occurs during old age [44]. Integration through reminiscence and mourning may be unsuccessful. Jim D. had not resolved the young/old conflict. In his forties he had left his first wife and children, and, with no material resources, had started a new life with a twenty-five-year-old woman in much the same way as would a man in his early adult developmental period. When the therapist met him in his late sixties, she therefore explored with him his "young/old" "good/bad," "attractive/ unattractive" constructs. He had not been aware of these constructs or of their implications for his view of himself. By making visible the submerged poles of the constructs, more alternatives became available. He was eventually prepared to see "old" as "not necessarily bad" or "unattractive" and agreed, with some trepidation, to experiment with the new values by attending an Over Fifties Walking Group. He was not rejected by the other members, as he had expected, and so he was prepared to continue to attend the Club. If these personal construct theory accounts of mourning and reminiscence are valid, once Jim completed these processes his expressions of anger would become healthy and constructive rather than destructive.

THE THERAPEUTIC VALIDATION OF THE CONSTRUCT SYSTEMS OF THE ELDERLY

With the exploration of personal constructs, the bereaved can face the full implications of their own losses. For some, mourning may involve dealing with the loss of a loved one and reestablishing their identity without validation from that loved one. For others, it may involve restoring all possible meaning to their present experience by isolating their construing of loss. Bereavement may necessitate modifying old constructs and experimenting with new ones in order to secure validation in a new set of conditions. Bereavement may involve interactions with others that are new and unpredictable. It may mean reevaluating goals and future directions. It may mean all of these things. Personal construct theory has provided a way of understanding the mourning process which goes beyond or behind the emotions expressed. The techniques for psychotherapy that come from this approach assist the bereaved to understand the changes occurring in them and to work toward a positive outcome. More positive feelings and a lessening of the sadness and confusion of grief are an indication that the world of the bereaved is providing more validation, some important meanings from the past have been restored to the construct system, and new constructs have been established to rebuild the bereaveds' sense of identity using new sources of validation.

The elderly people who reminisced during our psychotherapy were sometimes storytellers gaining enjoyment in recall. Many reported our attention to their stories surprised them and they felt important, indicating their lack of sources of validation for their constructs and their enjoyment of our validation of them. At other times, the elderly people were actively reviewing their lives and evaluating events and behaviors. From these reviews, there was a range of reactions. When self-validation during reminiscence was effective, satisfaction and integration of their past and present selves occurred. When self-validation was not sufficient, dissatisfactions, anger, denial, and avoidance emerged. In talking about their past lives, all these people were telling their therapists what they had found sufficiently important to remember over a lifetime. Their avoidances and denials were equally useful to the therapists. They laid out a map of who they were and how they became who they were. With this information, as personal construct therapists, we were able to help them become aware of their constructs and the possible sources of validation of those constructs and give them the opportunity to reorganize their construct systems, if they chose.

Psychotherapy is concerned with both the lack of validation for the predictions made by clients' construct systems and with the provision of sources for that validation. Elderly clients who mourn have, according to our personal construct model, lost important sources of validation. Therapeutic mourning should help them find other sources, either within themselves or through other people. One way of achieving this is reminiscence. This personal construct view of the parallel processes of mourning and reminiscence leads to a series of predictions about the processes and outcomes of psychotherapy. Reminiscence by clients may be better understood as a means to deal with mourning. Also, clients may be helped to use reminiscence to replace lost sources of validation. However, elderly clients should also be encouraged, personal construct theory would argue, to develop other sources of validation outside the therapeutic relationship. Such external sources should reduce the drain on clients' internal sources, avoid inappropriate isolation and alienation for them, and ensure that unnecessary dependence on therapists is minimized.

REFERENCES

1. L. L. Viney, *The Development and Evaluation of Short Term Psychotherapy Programs for the Elderly: Report to the Australian Institute of Health*, University of Wollongong, Wollongong, 1986.
2. L. L. Viney, Y. N. Benjamin, and C. Preston, An Evaluation of Personal Construct Therapy for the Elderly, *British Journal of Medical Psychology*.
3. L. L. Viney, Y. N. Benjamin, and C. Preston, Promoting Independence in the Elderly, *Clinical Gerontologist*.
4 M. Kaminsky, Pictures from the Past: The Use of Reminiscence with the Elderly, *Journal of Gerontological Social Work, 1*, pp. 19-32, 1978.
5. G. A. Kelly, *The Psychology of Personal Constructs, Volumes 1 and 2*, Norton, New York, 1955.
6. A. Beck, *Cognitive Therapy and Emotional Disorders*, Meridan, New York, 1976.
7. F. R. Epting, *Personal Construct Counseling and Psychotherapy*, Wiley, New York, 1984.
8. L. L. Viney, Experimenting with Experience: A Psychotherapeutic Case Study, *Psychotherapy, 18*, pp. 271-278, 1981.
9. B. Raphael, *The Anatomy of Bereavement*, Basic Books, New York, 1983.
10. D. R. Unruh, Death and Personal History: Strategies of Identity Preservation, *Social Problems, 30*, pp. 340-351, 1983.
11. M. S. Caserta, D. A. Lund, and M. F. Dimond, Assessing Interviewer Effects in a Longitudinal Study of Bereaved Elderly Adults, *Journal of Gerontology, 40*, pp. 637-640, 1985.
12. C. M. Parkes, The First Year of Bereavement, *Psychiatry, 33*, pp. 444-467, 1970.
13. L. Pincus, *Death and the Family*, Faber & Faber, London, 1974.
14. J. Bowlby, Loss, Sadness, and Depression, in *Attachment and Loss*, Hogarth, London, Volume 3, 1980.
15. S. Freud, Mourning and Melancholia, in *Collected Papers*, Basic Books, New York, Volume 4, 1917.
16. C. M. Parkes, Psychological Transitions: A Field for Study, *Social Science and Medicine, 5*, pp. 101-115, 1971.
17. Z. Ben-Sira, Loss, Stress, and Readjustment: The Structure of Coping with Bereavement and Disability, *Social Science and Medicine, 17*, pp. 1619-1632, 1983.
18. J. M. Richter, Crisis of Mate Loss in the Elderly, *Advances in Nursing Science, 6*, pp. 45-54, 1984.
19. L. W. Thompson, J. N. Breckenridge, D. Gallagher, and J. Peterson, Effects of Bereavement on Self-Perceptions of Physical Health in Elderly Widows and Widowers, *Journal of Gerontology, 39*, pp. 309-314, 1984.
20. M. Baum and R. C. Baum, *Growing Old: A Societal Perspective*, Prentice Hall, Englewood Cliffs, New Jersey, 1980.

21. E. Brubaker, Older Parents' Reaction to the Death of Adult Children: Implications for Practices, *Journal of Gerontological Social Work, 9,* pp. 35-48, 1985.
22. H. Feifel, *New Meanings of Death,* McGraw-Hill, New York, 1977.
23. K. Ferraro, The Effect of Widowhood on the Health Status of Older Persons, *International Journal of Aging and Human Development, 21,* pp. 9-25, 1985.
24. E. H. Volkhart and S. T. Michael, Bereavement and Mental Health, in *Understanding Death and Dying,* S. G. Wilcox and M. Sutton (eds.), Alfred Publishing, New York, 1977.
25. A. J. Sholomskas, E. S. Chevron, B. A. Prusoff, and C. Berry, Short-Term Interpersonal Therapy (IPT) with the Depressed Elderly: Case Reports and Discussion, *American Journal of Psychotherapy, 37,* pp. 552-567, 1983.
26. A. Hoaglands, Bereavement and Personal Constructs: Old Theories and New Concepts, in *Personal Meanings of Death: Applications of Personal Construct Theory to Clinical Practise,* F. Epting and R. Neimeyer (eds.), Hemisphere, London, 1984.
27. L. L. Viney, Mind over Matter: The Personal Construct Approach to Death and Loss, in *Innovating Approaches to the Bereavement of the Terminally Ill,* J. Stillion (ed.), Hemisphere, New York.
28. R. L. Woodfield and L. L. Viney, A Personal Construct Approach to Bereavement, *Omega, 16,* pp. 1-13, 1985.
29. P. Cameron, The Generation Gap: Time Orientation, *The Gerontologist, 12,* pp. 117-119, 1972.
30. L. M. Giambra, Daydreaming about the Past: The Time Setting of Spontaneous Thought Intrusions, *The Gerontologist, 17,* pp. 35-38, 1977.
31. M. Romaniuk and J. Romaniuk, Life Events and Reminiscence: A Comparison of the Memories of Young and Old Adults, *Imagination, Cognition and Personality, 2:2,* pp. 125-136, 1982-83.
32. M. A. Lieberman and J. M. Falk, The Remembered Past as a Source of Data for Research on the Life Cycle, *Human Development, 14,* pp. 132-141,1971.
33. V. Revere and S. Tobin, Myth and Reality: The Older Person's Relationship to His Past, *International Journal of Aging and Human Development, 12,* pp. 15-26, 1980.
34. R. N. Butler, The Life Review: An Interpretation of Reminiscence in the Aged, *Psychiatry, 26,* pp. 65-75, 1963.
35. M. I. Lewis and R. N. Butler, Life Review Therapy: Putting Memories to Work in Individual and Group Psychotherapy, *Geriatrics, 29,* pp. 165-173, 1974.
36. A. W. McMahon and P. J. Rhudick, Reminiscing: Adaptational Significance in the Aged, *Archives of General Psychiatry, 10,* pp. 203-208, 1964.
37. S. Merriam, The Concept and Function of Reminiscence; A Review of the Research, *The Gerontologist, 20,* pp. 604-609, 1980.
38. A. Pincus, Reminiscing in Aging and Its Implications for Social Work Practice, *Social Work, 15,* pp. 47-53, 1970.
39. R. N. Butler, Successful Aging and the Role of the Life Review, *Journal of the American Geriatric Society, 22,* pp. 529-535, 1974.
40. R. N. Butler, The Life Review: An Unrecognized Bonanza, *International Journal of Aging and Human Development, 12,* pp. 35-38, 1980.
41. M. Lo Gerfo, Three Ways of Reminiscence in Theory and Practice, *International Journal of Aging and Human Development, 12,* pp. 39-48, 1980.

42. V. Molinari and R. E. Reichlan, Life Review Reminiscence in the Elderly: A Review of the Literature, *International Journal of Aging and Human Development,* 20:2, pp. 81-92, 1985.
43. C. M. Carlson, Reminiscing: Toward Achieving Ego Integrity in Old Age, Social Casework: *The Journal of Contemporary Social Work, 65*:2, pp. 81-89, 1984.
44. D. L. Evans, L. Millicovsky, and C. R. Tennison, Aging, Reminiscence, and Mourning, *Psychiatric Forum, 12,* pp. 19-32, 1984.

Contributors

JAN BAARS, PH.D. has been teaching sociological theory and social philosophy at the university level for over twenty years. During the last five years he has included "aging" in his topics of theoretical research. In this context he is especially interested in the ways aging and the study of aging are socially constituted: implicitly or explicitly regulated by social interests and cultural images.

SARAH REESE BEATON, PH.D., R.N., is Associate Professor of Nursing at Lehman College of The City University of New York. An authority on nursing research in long-term care, she specializes in gerontological nursing and psychiatric/mental health nursing. Dr. Beaton is interested in life stories as a context for nursing practice and in fiction about aging. She is co-investigator for a study about nursing diagnosis and related outcomes in long-term care funded by the National Institute for Nursing Research of the National Institutes of Health. She is also consultant for nursing education and nursing research at Coler Memorial Hospital and is on the faculty for the New York City Health and Hospital Corporation's Nursing Research Internship Program.

YVONNE N. BENJAMIN gained a B.A. with first class honors from the University of Wollongong, as well as an M.A. Hons. (Applied Psychology), also with a completely first class academic record. She pioneered Drug and Alcohol Services in the Illawara Region of New South Wales, and published her work on developing and evaluating personal construct therapy for the acutely physically ill in hospital and the chronically ill at home. She is now deceased.

LUIS BOTELLA, PH.D., is Associate Professor of Psychotherapy at Ramon LLULL University (Barcelona, Spain). He also maintains a part-time private practice in psychotherapy. He is co-author of "La Reconstruccio Autobiografica (Autobiographical Reconstruction)." He has a major research interest in constructivism and personal construct psychology, and he has published over twenty articles and chapters on this subject (in English and Spanish). In addition to his activities as a scholar and practitioner, Dr. Botella is an active participant in the Spanish Society of Psychotherapy Integration and in the European Personal Construct Association.

IRENE BURNSIDE received her Ph.D. in gerontological nursing from the University of Texas at Austin. She has been in nursing education for twenty-seven years. She developed group work for older adults as practiced by nurses and recently revised *Working with Older Adults: Group Process and Techniques,* now in its third edition. She has written prolifically and has edited nine books in the field of gerontological nursing.

She has been a visiting professor in Melbourne, Australia, as well as at the Medical University of South Carolina, University of North Carolina. She is currently an adjunct professor at San Diego State University, San Diego, California.

DEBRA DAVID, PH.D., is Director of the Gerontology Center and Professor of Health Science at San Jose State University. She is also a Core Faculty Member of the Stanford Geriatric Education Center. Her teaching and research interests focus on long-term care, health ethics, ethnogerontology, and social psychological aspects of aging. She has received major training, evaluation, and research grants from several government and private organizations, which have resulted in published articles, chapters, and training manuals. She received her doctorate in Sociology from the University of California, Berkeley, in 1981.

MARY KAY DeGENOVA, PH.D. is an Associate Professor of Family Studies at Central Michigan University in the Department of Human Environmental Studies. Her research interests include regrets and reminiscence in later life, gender differences in regrets, and AIDS and the family. She received her doctorate in Family Studies from Purdue University.

GUILLEM FEIXAS, PH.D., is Professor of Psychotherapy and Director of the postgraduate course on "Cognitive/Social Therapy" at the Universitat de Barcelona. He also directs SEPI (Spanish Society of Psychotherapy Integration, a branch of SEPI) and is Clinical Accredited Trainer of ASEPCO (Spanish Association of Cognitive Psychotherapies). He has also co-authored several books in Spanish, *Aproximaciones a la psicoterapia* (Approaches to psychotherapy) with M.T. Miró, *Constructivismo y psicoterapia* (Constructivism and Psychotherapy) with M. Villegas, and *La reconstrucció autobiografica* (Autobiographical reconstruction) with L. Botella, among others, and book chapters and articles in English, Italian and German.

PREM S. FRY, PH.D. is a counseling psychologist trained at the Pennsylvania State University and the University of Michigan. Currently, she is a visiting professor of psychology at the University of Victoria, Victoria, British Columbia, and was a professor of educational psychology at The University of Calgary, Alberta, during the years 1966 to 1993. A former Fulbright scholar, Woodrow Wilson Fellow, and Killam Scholar, she has published widely in clinical, counseling, and developmental psychology journals. She was Editor-in-Chief of *The Canadian Journal of Behavioral Science* for the period 1989-1993, and currently serves on the editorial boards of several psychology journals, including *International Journal of Aging and Human Development, Journal of Genetic Psychology,* and *Genetic Psychology Monographs.* While at The University of Calgary, she was recognized with a distinction in teaching award in 1983, and a distinguished lecture aware in 1986. She is a Fellow of the American Psychological Association, the American Psychological Society, the Canadian Psychological Association, the British Psychological Society, and the Gerontological Society of America. In 1985 she received the Presidential Award of the Psychologists Association of Alberta for distinguished contribution to the discipline of Psychology. She is a member of the Board of Directors of the Canadian Psychological Association and of the Canadian Association on Gerontology. She is author of over 100 papers published in scientific journals and also of three monographs and six books, including *Depression, Stress and Adaptations in the Elderly,* and *Psychological Perspectives of Helplessness and Control in the Elderly.* In recent years she has been the recipient of a number of grants from the *Social Sciences and Humanities Research Council of Canada* for some of her research in aging and human development. Currently she holds a research grant with the B.C. Health Research Foundation for her research on mediators of depression and health outcomes in women.

BARBARA K. HAIGHT, R.N.C., Dr.PH, F.A.A.N. received the BSN from St. Joseph College, West Hartford, Connecticut. She received a masters degree in gerontological nursing from the University of Kansas, Kansas City, Kansas, and the Doctorate of Public Health at the University of South Carolina, School of Public Health, Columbia, South Carolina.

She is a tenured Professor of Gerontological Nursing at the Medical University of South Carolina. Dr. Haight teaches in the graduate program and spends 50 percent of her time researching the therapeutic role of the life review in elderly people. Other areas of research interest include the use of nursing diagnosis, attitudes of students toward older people, research priorities in long-term care, determining the variables of successful reminiscence, and the use of life review as a preventive measure for depression and suicide.

Dr. Haight is a fellow in the American Academy of Nursing, the Gerontological Society of America, and the Florence Nightingale Society. Dr. Haight was the recipient of the Rosamande Boyd Award for Excellence in Gerontological Research and Teaching from the South Carolina Gerontological Society and the Gamma Omicron Research Recognition Award from Sigma Theta Tau. She was named the South Carolina Career Woman of the Year for 1989 by the Business and Professional Women's Club of South Carolina. In 1990, she was honored by the Health Science Foundation of the Medical University of South Carolina as one of three developing research scholars.

Dr. Haight has presented and published nationally and internationally on the subject of the life review. She is also the author of many book chapters and the editor of a book on life review. Dr. Haight is also a member of the Editorial Review Board of the *Journal of Gerontological Nursing, Holistic Nursing Practice, the Geriatric Patient Education Resource Manual,* Aspen Publishers, and *Geriatric Nursing.*

Most recently, Dr. Haight has completed an appointment as Honorary Research Fellow in the Department of Psychology, University College, London.

JON HENDRICKS, PH.D., is Professor and Chair, Department of Sociology, Oregon State University. He is President, Association for Gerontology in Higher Education and has previously served as an officer of The Gerontological Society of America and The American Sociological Association. Hendricks is Associate Editor for the *International Journal of Aging and Human Development*, Series Editor for *Perspectives on Aging and Human Development Series*, and Consulting Editor for Gerontology, Baywood Publishing Company, Inc., NY. Hendricks is a member of Worldwide Umbrella Exchange and is widely published in the field of social gerontology.

SIMONE LAMME (1962) studied pedagogics at the University of Amsterdam, followed by the study of social gerontology at the *Vrije Universiteit*, Amsterdam. In 1991 she graduated with distinction with a thesis on reminiscence. Since 1989 she has been working in different positions at the department of sociology and social geron-tology of the *Vrije Universiteit*. Currently she is working as a researcher on the program "Living arrangements and social networks of older adults," writing a disser-tation on the social networks of elderly widows and widowers.

PETER MARTIN, PH.D. is an associate professor in the Department of Human Development and Family Studies and the coordinator of the Gerontology Program at Iowa State University. His research focuses on the oldest old, personality, life events and coping, with an emphasis on adaptation and mental health. More specifically, Martin has published research on findings from the Georgia Cen-tenarian Study, as well as research on the intergenerational transmission of family stories, parenting, and family themes.

SHARAN B. MERRIAM is a professor of adult and continuing education at the University of Georgia. She received her B.A. degree from Drew University in English, her M.Ed. degree from Ohio University in English Education, and her Ed.D. degree from Rutgers University in Adult Education.

Her research and writing activities have focused on adult learning and develop-ment, and qualitative research methods. She has been coeditor of *Adult Educa-tion Quarterly*, the major journal of research and theory in adult education. Dr. Merriam has written or coauthored a number of books including *Philosophical Foundations of Adult Education, Coping with Male Mid-Life, Adult Education: Foundations of Practice*, winner of the 1985 Cyril O. Houle World Award for Literature in Adult Education, *Themes of Adulthood Through Literature, A Guide to Research for Educators and Trainers of Adults*, and *Case Study Research in Education*. Her most recent publications include a textbook titled *Learning in Adulthood: A Comprehensive Guide*, and a popular book on adult development titled *Lifelines: Patterns of Work, Love, and Learning in Adulthood*.

MILTON F. NEHRKE, after conducting research for sixteen years, has spent the last five years as a Clinical Psychologist in a 475 bed domiciliary at the V A Medical Center in Bath. He has also continued with his administrative research activities. His most recent endeavor has been to initiate a smoking cessation clinic for the veterans in the hospital, the domiciliary and the ambulatory care program. As a result of the success of the clinic, he has become part of a community agency where the emphasis is on tobacco use among teens. Thus, once again he finds himself involved with people of all ages, and circling back to the perspectives of his degree in Life-Span Developmental.

LYNN P. REHM received his Ph.D. from the University of Wisconsin—Madison in 1970 and did his internship at the VA Hospital in Milwaukee. He has been on the faculties of the UCLA-Neuropsychiatric Institute in Psychiatry, the University of Pittsburgh in Psychology and Psychiatry, and, currently, the University of Houston in the Psychology Department. He was Director of Clinical Training at Pittsburgh and Houston.

Dr. Rehm's research centers on depression theory, psychopathology, and treatment. He has made scientific presentations and given clinical workshops on Self-Management Therapy for depression nationally and internationally. He is a diplomate of the American Board of Professional Psychology in Behavioral Psychology and a Fellow of the American Psychological Association and its Clinical and Psychotherapy Divisions.

CAROL PRESTON was awarded a Bachelor of Arts majoring in Psychology in 1982 from The University of Wollongong. She completed a Ph.D. in 1987 at the same University, under the supervision of Dr. Linda Viney, with whom she worked as a research assistant. Her Ph.D. thesis was entitled "Constructing religious experience," and focussed on the subjective understanding and implications of religious experience in the everyday lives of people. The psychological approach utilized for the research was Personal Construct Psychology. This was also the approach used in the research in which Carol and Dr. Viney were involved. The research was directed at understanding the experience of people with chronic illnesses with the aim of helping those who work with the chronically ill to better understand the experience and thereby be better equipped to help them to deal with their lives. From this work numerous articles have been published in conjunction with Dr. Viney and others involved in the research.

Subsequent to this work Carol has been involved in the development of an Institute for Contemporary Church Leadership, a program designed to train leaders of the Christian church. Carol currently co-ordinates one of three centers for such training, which are located in local churches. Her work involves teaching in the areas of Personal Development and Pastoral Counselling, as well as supervision of students and overall co-ordinating of the program. Her background in Personal Construct Psychology has been most helpful in researching the needs of both churches and ministers of religion as they attempt to develop and maintain a relevant and meaningful Christian experience.

EDMUND SHERMAN is Professor of Social Welfare, State University of New York at Albany, where he teaches graduate courses in clinical practice and theory. He is also Faculty Research Associate in the Ringel Institute of Gerontology of the

University at Albany. He received his Ph.D. from the Graduate School of Social Work and Social Research of Bryn Mawr College. Dr. Sherman has published several books and numerous articles on aging and practice with the elderly. His most recent books include *Counseling the Aging; Working with Older Persons; Meaning in Mid-Life Transitions;* and *Reminiscence and the Self in Old Age.*

LOIS TAFT, M.S.N., R.N., C.S., is currently a doctoral candidate at Rush University, College of Nursing in Chicago where she is completing dissertation research on interventions in dementia care and factors influencing caregiving approaches. She is a clinical instructor at the University of Illinois, College of Nursing in Chicago. She is also a Clinical Specialist in Gerontological Nursing and is employed as a neurological/neurosurgical nurse at Evanston Hospital, Evanston, Illinois.

LINDA L. VINEY has completed a Bachelor of Arts at the University of Tasmania, and a Master's research degree at the Australian National University. She then went to the United States to do a Ph.D. in Clinical Psychology. That training was largely psychodynamic, and involved her in three years of psychotherapy as a client, that she has since found of very great value both personally and professionally.

Her research over the past two decades has focused on people's psychological responses to illness, psychotherapy process and outcome, and the psychosocial development of adolescents, adults and the elderly. She is also a teacher and psychotherapist. Of all of this work, two achievements have been particularly meaningful to her. The first has been conducting research that successfully demonstrated that psychological changes are associated with physiological changes in people recovering from physical illness. The second has been developing and gaining acceptance for the first Ph.D. degree in Clinical Psychology, in Australia, which combines professional training with research.

The personality theory that she now finds useful for all of these activities is personal construct psychology (Kelly, 1955). Its assumptions about people as active makers of meaning remind her that all of the students, clients and research participants with whom she works are also active makers of meaning. She has published books about how this psychology can be usefully applied to research (*Interpreting the interpreters,* Melbourne, Florida, Krieger, 1987) and to psychotherapy (*Life stories: Personal construct therapy with the elderly,* Chichester, Wiley, 1993), as well as over thirty book chapters and 100 journal articles in these areas.

JANET ANDERSON YANG, PH.D. is the Director of the Center for Aging Resources, a mental health clinic serving older adults and training Clinical Psychology graduate students. She is on faculty at Fuller Seminary's School of Psychology, and she works in private practice with adults of all ages.

Janet Yang majored in psychology at Yale University, after which she worked with older adults in community and nursing home settings. She received a Masters degree in counseling at the University of Pennsylvania, followed by receiving her Ph.D. in Clinical Psychology at the University of Houston. Her internship and post-doctoral work were done at the Neuropsychiatric Institute at UCLA, where she conducted psychotherapy, personality and neuropsychological assessment with younger and older adults. Her research has focused on depression, family relationships and geropsychology. Additional interests include working with victims of child abuse, elder abuse, and community psychology.